# MY GREAT SPORTING MEMORIES
## from Local Club to Olympic Games

As told by 72 Sportspersons
and Sports Journalists

Published by Lorcán O'Rourke
Droichead Nua
Contae Chill Dara

First published 2011

A CIP record for this book is available from the British Library

ISBN 978-0-9570599-0-0

Printed in Ireland by Print Procedure Ltd.

## DEDICATION

This book is dedicated to Our Lady of Russia, to the people of Belarus who have suffered so much because of the Chernobyl nuclear disaster, to Chernobyl Children International and to the many Irish volunteers and families who care for Belarusian children.

# CONTENTS

# ACKNOWLEDGMENTS

I wish to thank all the players, athletes, administrators and journalists who penned their sporting memories: their generous contributions made it possible to compile a wonderful collection of inspirational stories. Well over one hundred people have helped to bring this publication to fruition; their cooperation is greatly appreciated.

I thank all those who provided contacts for the authors, especially GAA County Secretaries, Marc Howard of the Irish Sports Council, John Foley of the Athletics Association of Ireland, Fran Whearty (FAI), Karl Richardson (IRFU) and the staffs of GAA Handball Ireland, the Camogie Association and Cumann Peil Gael na mBan.

My thanks to Ray McManus of Sportsfile and the RTÉ sports library for providing the images for the book.

I am especially grateful to Brian Carthy, RTÉ Gaelic Games Correspondent, and Liam Hayes for their advice and support in developing the project. My particular thanks to Páraic Duffy, GAA Director General, for his encouragement.

Thanks to Rossa Moore of Print Procedure who took charge of the production and printing process in a very professional way, to Mick Lynam for formatting the book and to Liam Kenny who lent his considerable expertise to the editing process.

Sincere thanks are due to the following sponsors of Great Sporting Memories: Central and Provincial GAA Councils, Martin Donnelly & Co, Newbridge Credit Union, Envirogreen Building Services, GAA Handball Ireland, Cumann Camógaíochta na nGael, Cumann Peil Gael na mBan, Michael Murphy EZ Living (Newbridge and New Ross), Kingswood Plant and Ballybrittas Motors. Without their financial support it would not have been possible to undertake such a major task.

I also appreciate the help I received from Adi Roche, Miriam Forde and Jayne Davies of Chernobyl Children International from concept stage to finished product.

Finally, my thanks to my wife, Phil, and our family Ciarán, Aoife and Enda.

Lorcán O'Rourke
November 2011

# FOREWORD

The purpose of this collection of *My Great Sporting Memories* is to raise funds for Adi Roche's Chernobyl Children International (CCI) to mark the 25th anniversary of the disaster that shocked the world and destroyed people's lives, and those of generations yet unborn. In addition, it offers the reader an opportunity to appreciate some of the emotions, the hardships, and the highs and lows experienced by sportspersons or witnessed by sports journalists.

Organised sport has played a major role in the social and cultural life of Ireland since the late nineteenth century and every year throws up new and iconic players and athletes who are 'swifter, stronger, higher'. I hope the fruits of the stories of the colour, emotion and excitement the 72 writers experienced will add threads of many colours to the tapestry of the lives of Chernobyl children and help to make them healthier, stronger and happier.

Lorcán O'Rourke

# PAUL BRADY

## I was determined to become world handball champion

**P**AUL BRADY from Mullahoran, County Cavan, is the only player in the history of handball to win the Men's World Open Singles title on three occasions – 2003, 2006 and 2009. He was the first Ulsterman to win an All-Ireland 40x20 title and achieved this in singles, and in doubles, with Michael Finnegan from Kingscourt, in 2003.

Paul holds 14 All-Ireland senior titles – eight singles and six doubles – six US Open Nationals Singles titles and US National and World Open Doubles titles. He won a Cavan senior football medal with Mullahoran in 2006 and has been on the county panel since 2002.

With astonishing power, accuracy, mental strength and fitness allied to an ability to 'kill' the ball from almost anywhere in the court, he is regarded by many as the greatest player in the history of 40x20 handball.

Growing up playing handball, it was a big deal to travel around the country to play at various venues. I had just turned 12 when it all began for me, in St. Patrick's College, Cavan, under the tutelage of Fr John Gilhooly. He brought us to numerous tournaments but the usual result was losing to more experienced opponents who had been playing the game for several years. It certainly wasn't a nice feeling in those early years of competition, but later when my fortunes turned and I began to win All-Ireland and US juvenile titles, as well as minor and intermediate All-Irelands, I was determined to go on and win at senior level.

Unfortunately, it wasn't that simple. Tony Healy from the Ballydesmond club in Cork was a couple of years older than me and he was the best player in the country at the time; he was leading the way and I was struggling to keep up with him.

In the year 2000 at the age of 20, my first year in senior ranks, I made a breakthrough and got to the All-Ireland senior final, but Tony beat me at the O'Loughlin Gaels club in Kilkenny. Two weeks later, Michael Finnegan and I lost the senior doubles final. In late April I lost the final of the Irish Nationals and with it the chance to represent Ireland at the World Handball Championships in Chicago the following October. And we lost the final of the doubles trials for the Irish team about two weeks later.

Four senior finals in as many months, four losses, and no sign of turning a corner!

So, I kept at it and worked harder than ever on my game. I went to the Worlds in Chicago that autumn at my own expense and reached the semi-finals, where I lost a close tiebreaker to John Bike, an experienced Californian who was ranked number four in the world at the time. However, I knew I was getting there, inch by inch.

In 2001, I was coasting well in training when the Foot and Mouth epidemic broke. I was due to play Tony Healy in the All-Ireland semi-final but Munster didn't travel and the game was put back to October. I spent the summer working and training in New York and came home, only for Tony to beat me narrowly. I could've won it, but 'could' was no good to me by this stage.

A couple of weeks after that match, Tony and I both qualified for the US Pro Tour at a qualifier in Atlanta, Georgia. It had been an ambition of mine growing up to play at that level, so it was a dream come true to compete on the world stage. The American game suited my style of play from the outset, and within a couple of months of regular competition in the States, I could sense a defining juncture in my adult career was imminent. I played my first tournament on the Tour in Peoira, Illinois and became the first Irish player to reach a semi-final, before losing to David Chapman. It was small consolation – I hated losing – but I could feel a breakthrough coming.

That finally arrived a year later in December 2002. Following a two-year absence from Gaelic football, I was called up to the Cavan football panel earlier that year by Mattie Kerrigan, and the extra training was beginning to stand to me. In November, Vince Munoz, a brilliant Californian, beat me in the quarter-final at a tournament in Seattle, Washington. But coming out of the court I vowed that I would beat him the next time we played. I said as much to him, which was out of character for me, but I wanted to win so badly. "Yeah, we'll see, man", he replied defensively, but the promise I made to myself materialised a month later in Milwaukee, Wisconsin. I felt really fresh coming into the tournament and beat Munoz in the final. I had just won my first Pro Stop, a first for any Irish player and, in hindsight, it was the turning point in my career.

In early 2003, I played a lot of inter-county football for Cavan and put more intensity into my training. I was fitter than ever, and the win over Munoz had given me the belief that I could take on, and beat, the best in the world. I had begun to get the better of my great rival Tony Healy in US events, and I was determined to carry that form into the domestic championships.

That March, I beat Tony in the All-Ireland senior singles final and Michael Finnegan and I added the senior doubles title a fortnight later. After three years of domestic heartache, three years of sporting hell, all the sacrifices and hard work had finally paid off. I was now the best player in Ireland. No Ulster player had ever won a senior All-Ireland and I can still remember my over-riding emotion was one of relief.

That summer, I skipped the US Nationals in Michigan and concentrated on Ulster championship football, before knuckling down to train hard for the World Championships in October. I wanted to stay fresh and focused as I attempted to achieve every player's ultimate goal; to become World Open Singles champion. If I didn't seize this opportunity, I would have to wait three more years for my next chance to come around.

I was so hungry and so determined to win, and again my opponent was Tony Healy. I was heading for victory in the final at Croke Park when I had to take a two-minute time-out due to severe cramping. I then had to take a maximum 15-minute injury time-out but did not recover in time to resume the match. Tony could have claimed the title but offered his injury time-out to me and after treatment I was able to continue and closed out the game. At 23 years of age I had achieved my ambition and was champion of the handball world by virtue of my training, determination and will to win... and, in the spirit of handball, a most generous gesture from my friend, colleague and final opponent, Tony Healy.

# MARTIN BREHENY
## Sunday, 27 September 1964
## Galway 0-15 Kerry 0-10

**M**ARTIN BREHENY is GAA Editor of the *Irish Independent*. A native of Galway, he worked with the *Tuam Herald*, *Irish Press Group*, *The Title* Sports Newspaper, *Ireland on Sunday* and the *Sunday Tribune* before joining the *Irish Independent* in 2000. He is a former Sports Journalist of the Year award winner.

A ten-year-old boy from Kilkerrin, north Co. Galway bounds out of a neighbour's house after watching the All-Ireland football final, gallops home, collects a ball and heads for the nearest field.

For the next hour, he's lost in the happiest world of his own, re-enacting what he's seen from Croke Park, only this time Galway scored six goals, all expertly finished past hapless Kerry goalkeeper, Johnny Culloty.

A variety of Galway forwards hit the target but two goals came from the boot of No.13, Christy Tyrrell. When Kerry attacked, the best efforts of Mick O'Dwyer, Tom Long and JJ Barrett were swatted away by Galway goalkeeper, Johnny Geraghty.

I was the ten year old and my devotion to Geraghty and Tyrrell was based on their being fellow parishioners from Kilkerrin. They were our local heroes, the men who gave us an identity in the bigger world as they joined the elite from the rest of Galway to generate a compelling force which had embarked on what would develop into a three-year domination of Gaelic football.

National sporting figures they may have been, but Geraghty and Tyrrell were local lads too in a very meaningful way. They regularly joined a large group, aged from around eight to forty, who gathered on Sunday afternoons to play football in a field where the cattle had to be hunted to one side before the action began.

Jackets were used as goalposts, there were no lines and no referee, the teams were chosen so that good, bad and in-between were divided evenly. Imagine your modern day inter-county footballer spending a free Sunday involved in a loosely arranged game in a field where clumps of rushes presented as big a threat to life and limb as an awkward tackle. It was different back then as Geraghty and Tyrrell regularly joined in, sometimes even the week before a big game in Croke Park.

Geraghty, possibly the most agile goalkeeper ever to play the game (any wonder Manchester United took an interest in him?) would always take time before or after the game to allow young lads like me kick a few shots at him. We'd beat him occasionally too (he let us, I'm sure), leaving us with a magical feeling after scoring a goal against the best keeper in Gaelic football.

Some years later, Geraghty taught me Irish and Latin in Coláiste Sheosaimh, Glenamaddy where, of course, he also ran the football show. He was a superb teacher but then he had the advantage of being a star name so he didn't have to work very hard to command attention!

Galway's win in the 1964 All-Ireland final was the start of a three-in-a-row run by a team that's revered in the county to this day. I can still recall vividly watching the All-Ireland semi-finals and finals on black-and-white TV (Geraghty conceded only one goal in six major championship games in Croke Park over three seasons) and I have no doubt that Galway's successes in that era shaped my life in a very direct way.

They gave me a love of Gaelic football which has never waned and, as the years passed and I went through secondary school, the thought of writing about the game grew increasingly appealing. Luckily, after spending a few years in careers as diverse as air traffic control and insurance, I got a break from the *Tuam Herald*, thanks to editor, Jarlath P Burke who took me on as a trainee journalist.

An expert in all matters journalistic (the best newspaper man I ever came across), he was a great judge of football and hurling too and while he could be a tough taskmaster, he filed off more rough edges in a month than most of the modern-day journalism courses would do in two years, if indeed at all.

I have attended every All-Ireland final, except one, in both hurling and football for the past 40 years, most of which I have written about. I missed the drawn Cork-Meath football final in 1988 because I was covering the

Olympic Games in Seoul for the Irish Press Group. I covered four Olympics in all, plus many world title fights involving Barry McGuigan, Steve Collins and Dave 'Boy' McAuley and have been lucky enough to attend many other major sporting events at home and abroad in a professional capacity.

However, none can ever compare with the feeling I experienced on that September evening back in 1964 when Galway won the All-Ireland final, just as the greatest sense of sporting desolation I ever felt (at least it seemed that way) was when the pursuit of the four-in-a-row ended against Mayo in June 1967.

I was convinced on that warm Sunday evening that the birds had stopped singing in mourning at Galway's loss of their crown. I could never have thought as I watched the 1964 All-Ireland final, through Galway eyes only, that many years later I would become very friendly with one of the Kerrymen.

His name? Mick O'Dwyer, arguably the greatest GAA man in the history of the Association. Micko, who had injury problems in 1964-65, suffered torture at the hands of Sean Meade (1964) and Noel Tierney (1965), something I kept reminding him of with as much mischief as I could muster when I worked with him on his autobiography in 2007.

As we reflected on that era it was difficult to believe just how far back it was but, for me at least, the memory of the 1964 All-Ireland final, in particular, is as fresh now as it was on that Sunday evening when I picked up the ball and kicked a few goals past Johnny Culloty.

# TREVOR BRENNAN

## Alone, all alone on Lansdowne Road pitch

**T**REVOR BRENNAN played rugby for Barnhall, Bective Rangers, St Mary's College, Leinster (1996-2001), Toulouse and Ireland. He captained St Mary's to their only AIB League title in 2000 and played in three successive European Cup finals winning in 2003 and 2005.

He made his debut for Ireland against South Africa in 1998 and had 13 Test appearances, including the 1999 Rugby World Cup. In 2007 he won the William Hill Irish Sports Book of the Year Award for his book *Heart and Soul*.

Following retirement from professional rugby in 2007 he and his family remained in Toulouse where he owns the De Danu Irish Bar. On request from Sean Boylan, manager of the Irish team, Trevor, a former Gaelic footballer, was part of the coaching staff in the International Rules series with Australia in 2008.

It's not an easy thing to choose my best sporting memory because there have been so many in my 25-year rugby career. Was it the under-14 McGowen Cup when I ran out for Barnhall in a game we won which was played in Lansdowne Road where our international team played, or was it when I captained St Mary's to victory in the AIB League in the 1999/2000 season? Or was it in '98 when I toured South Africa with the Irish team and made my debut as a second-half replacement for Victor Costello in a game we lost 37-13 which became known as 'the battle of Bloemfontein'? Playing for your international team is something that every rugby player dreams of and despite the result that day I achieved that ambition.

If I were to be honest my best sporting memory would have to be when I played in the final of the 2002/2003 Heineken Cup with Toulouse against Perpignan, which again was played in Lansdowne Road. After a hard battle we won 22-17. What made this so special was that I had left Leinster and gone to the south of France to play for Toulouse and in my first year we reached the Heineken Cup final, and it's played in Dublin, the city I had left the previous year.

The night before the game, after dinner and a long video session of the opposition lineouts in Fitzpatricks Hotel in Killiney, the captain, Fabien Pelouse and vice-captain, Emile Ntmack called me aside as they wanted to have a word. I thought it might be the usual 'penalty counts, stay focused', but I was overwhelmed when they asked me to lead out the team for the game. At first I refused – it was the captain's job, but they persuaded me; it was Dublin, Ireland and we had battled long and hard to reach this final beating a lot of great teams like Munster on the way. I had started every game that season and they wanted me to be the first player onto that sacred pitch because it was my home in front of my family, but with my team, Toulouse. I accepted.

In the tunnel the next day, both teams stood side by side. I tried not to make any eye contact with the opposition and focused purely on the stairs which led up to the pitch. It was at that moment Emile put his arm around me and said, "This is our day, this is your day, we are going to win this for you." I don't think I even replied verbally, just a nod of the head as I was totally in the zone when the referee blew his whistle for both teams to run onto the pitch. I jogged up the stairs and sprinted onto the pitch past the Heineken Cup. When I turned around to say, "Come on lads, get stuck into them", I was a bit shocked as both teams were still down in the tunnel. What was probably only 10 seconds felt like an eternity. Even Perpignan let me have that moment.

It's only when I look back on my career that I realise how special this privilege was. Running out onto the Lansdowne Road pitch in a Heineken Cup final is not something many Irish players achieve. For me this only really hit home when I got back to Toulouse bringing the cup out onto the balcony at Place Capitol in front of thousands of fans where we celebrated a famous victory with all the colour a French crowd can bring to an occasion like that. A very special memory which I savour, along with leading the team out for the European Cup final in Lansdowne Road.

# PHILIP BROWNE
# Why are they smiling?

**P**HILIP BROWNE is a native of Dublin and was educated in St Columba's College Rathfarnham, The High School Rathgar and Trinity College Dublin. He holds an honours degree in Natural Science, a PhD and an MBA.

He joined the staff of the IRFU in 1992 and was appointed Secretary of that body in 1995 at a time of great change as it was during his tenure that the game of rugby became professional. He was named as the first Chief Executive of the IRFU in 1998.

Philip is married to AnneMarie, with two children, and his pastimes include hill walking, swimming and sailing. He rowed competitively for 10 years, winning many Irish and international titles at club level and he represented Ireland at two World Rowing Championships.

Rowing is a curious sport. For an oarsman the most memorable moments are not only measured in terms of success in competition but also in terms of those rare occasions when you are part of a crew that masters the intrinsic technical variables of rowing along with the prevailing water conditions, resulting in a crew of eight, plus a coxswain, operating together in perfect unison.

The curious thing is that such perfection invariably happens whilst training, or at least one was never aware of it in the heat of racing. I was fortunate to have had many successes as a competitive oarsman along with the inevitable failures and disappointments that one experiences and learns from over a rowing career. These were all memorable in different ways, marking the different stages of my rowing career.

However, the most vivid memories I have are of the four or five occasions in a rowing career when I was part of a crew, usually an eight, where eight straining bodies suddenly stop working against each other and against the momentum of the racing shell. In an instant time seems to slow down and miraculously there appears to be more time to prepare and think about each individual stroke.

Individual effort seems to diminish, yet the paradox is that this allows each individual to make a greater effort as the boat has become a stable and predictable platform. As eight blades lever the boat past the point of water entry, the technical battle between precision, finesse and application of power seems to resolve and become seamless.

For those looking at a crew experiencing such a moment, it may not be immediately obvious that anything special is happening. The 'split times' may not reflect the change, the body movements during the stroke, and the recovery phase may not have changed in any substantial way and the movement of the shell through the water may not be noticeably different.

In fact the only noticeable evidence is probably the smiles on the faces of the oarsmen at the end of the training spin as it is almost something private to the crew, something only they can experience. You can also be sure that the moment will not be forgotten by those in the crew – I know because over 20 and more years have passed since I finished competitive rowing and I can still have a detailed conversation with my former crewmates about that 1000m piece we rowed in Blessington on the evening before the National Championships in 1987.

# JOANNE CANTWELL
## My father, my hero

JOANNE CANTWELL is a sports presenter with RTÉ and fronts the rugby magazine programme *Against the Head* on RTÉ Two. She also presents live All-Ireland League and Under-20s rugby and works as touchline/sideline reporter for rugby and with *The Sunday Game*. On Saturday afternoons, she presents *Saturday Sport* on RTÉ Radio One.

She is a former Dublin Ladies Gaelic footballer and played with her club St Brigid's for 12 years. Joanne is associated with a number of charities, most notably the Breffni Challenge for the Friends of Saint Luke's – a 20 kilometre charity run, which takes place in County Cavan every summer.

In the last couple of years, she has returned to playing junior football with her local club, Celbridge GAA. She lives in Celbridge in County Kildare with her husband, Shay and their baby daughter, Emmy.

They're one of the often unspoken-about aspects of every team, but they almost always have an effect. They come in all sorts of guises and play a variety of roles – whether they're supposed to or not. I'm talking about the parent.

There are those who are directly involved – the coach or the mentor, and they can often come in their own separate categories – most of whom just want to be there for their son/daughter, some of whom who took over simply because no one else would. Most parents, though, fall into the supporter category. There are both those who know the game inside out and those who barely know the rules, but still give it their all in terms of encouragement, supplying cheers and, let's be honest, a good slating of the referee when necessary (knowledge of the rules is never essential in this aspect).

There are those who can only see their own child on the pitch and can't understand why every strategy doesn't revolve around them. There are those who, instead of simply supplying encouragement, feel it's their place to instruct, regardless of the coach's game plan – sometimes passing on their wisdom not only to their son/daughter, but to everyone else's as well.

Quite often, you'll find the most critical of parents are the ones you only tend to see at county finals and vital matches, but are rarely spotted for the division six league game away in Ballywhatchamacallit many, many miles away. You always see the same few cars at meeting places; and the same players who have been dropped off and left for someone else to ferry off to pitches in the back of beyond. Of course, if for some reason, one or two of the regular cars aren't able to make it, problems arise. In the pre-safety belts in the backs-of-cars days, there was many a transport law broken in pursuit of match-day travel. In fact, my husband's family has a story that has become the stuff of legend. Only his father, who happened to be the coach, turned up for one of their under-10 games with Clonsilla and the entire team squeezed into his Morris Minor. We're talking fifteen-a-side Gaelic football here.

There are so many different types of parents – some of whom fall into neat and tidy categories, some of whom are once-offs. Then there's my dad.

My father, now happily retired, spent most of his life as a PE teacher, taking everything from basketball to badminton to goodness-knows-what after school hours, and setting up a gymnastics club in the local area. But he was still an ever-present when it came to every one of his five daughters and their activities – and when it came to me, that meant football.

My father could always be seen on the sidelines at my matches… could always be heard is probably more accurate. It's never been in his nature to stand quietly by. But there was never any haughty instruction given, never any shouted criticism; just good natured, very, very vocal support.

When I was 16, I got the call-up to train with the senior Dublin team. A couple of players from my club got the same call, but after a few months, I was the last one standing. Not only was I the only one from my club, but the only one from my area, practically the only one coming from north of the Liffey at the time. Making it to the Phoenix Park for training proved doable initially, but when training was switched to Thomas Davis Club on Kiltipper Road in Tallaght, making sessions became an issue for sixteen-year-old me. Or at least it should have become an issue. But it didn't. Every Tuesday and Thursday, and many Saturdays, my father would drive me across the M50. It was too far for him to drop me off and come back. So, I'd get out of the car, run off to my training session, which could often be very lengthy, and then come back to the same car, which hadn't moved an inch. Inside, the seat on the driver's side would be reclined all the way back, my father's eyes would be closed and BBC Five Live would be blaring, staticy and with a background of white noise, a sound familiar to any dedicated sports fan in this country. That was how my father spent at least two nights of his every week. And when Sundays came along, he'd drop me at the Foxhunter in Lucan, where I'd be collected by the team bus to be taken to whatever match we had that week. And when we arrived and got kitted out, warmed up and on to the field, there, on the side of the pitch up in Donegal, or over in Mayo, or down in Cork, would be my father. I may not have seen him straight away, but I always heard him. Everybody heard him. And he knew every name; not just those given by their parents, but those given by our coach, Alan Byrne, who had a way with nicknames – there was Solo and Rambo and Bangers and Roger and Shifty and Shaft and many more. My father shouted support to them all, and they all appreciated that there was always someone there, on the side of some pitch somewhere in the middle of the country, who cared whether we won or lost.

Women's football in Dublin is in a glistening state at the moment but back then it was about hard slogging and very little else. When people like my father and our captain Christina McGinty's parents made long treks all over the country, it wasn't to witness potential All-Ireland champions, and they knew that only too well. The greatest feat of my team was going from division three to division two to division one in the National League in successive years, and then winning Dublin's first ever senior Leinster championship game, before making the county's first ever provincial final (where we lost by a single point after Meath scored a fluky goal in the final minute – yes, it still hurts). But the same few faces were ever-present, regardless of success or lack of it.

I haven't played for Dublin in over 10 years; and in that time the county has made strides of such magnitude that in 2010 they were finally crowned senior All-Ireland champions. I don't often get to see the women with whom I fought side by side in torrential rain, trained with in the darkness of car parks when nobody would let us use their pitches, and giggled with for hours on long coach journeys back from National League matches in the middle of nowhere. But there are rare occasions when I do get to bump into them and reminisce about those days, and when I do, every one of them always asks the same question – how's your dad? Well, he's the same as ever – barking mad and one of a kind. My father, my hero.

# BRIAN CARTHY

## Dermot Earley – A personal memory

**B**RIAN CARTHY is best known as a leading commentator on hurling and football and has been RTÉ Gaelic Games Correspondent since the mid-1990s.

A native of Ballymore, near Strokestown, County Roscommon, Brian, who celebrated his 30th year in RTÉ in 2010, has written 18 books, including the best-selling *'Football Captains All-Ireland Winners'* and the *'A-Z of Country and Irish Stars'*.

He has compiled *'Football and Hurling The Championships'*, a complete record of all championships games since 1995. He lives in Dublin with his wife, Trish and their children, John Brian and Sarah Marie.

It is so difficult to comprehend that Dermot Earley has gone from us, all too soon for a man who always gave his very best in every facet of life.

I was privileged to know Dermot as a friend for a long time. He was a man with unique qualities. Even though Dermot was very ill for several months, we were all hoping and praying that he would make a full recovery.

One evening as I was leaving Dermot's home in Newbridge in the latter stages of his illness, I said to his wife, Mary: "We're looking for a miracle". I was hoping against hope that the 'miracle' would mean a complete recovery or, if death from the illness was as inevitable as it seemed, that he would not have to suffer too much.

I suppose we all held out hope, particularly in the early stages of his sickness that Dermot would somehow recover because of the battling qualities that were such a hallmark of his life, both as a footballer and as a leader in the Army. It was not to be.

Dermot was a special person, but he would be the first to say that he was blessed with a wonderful family. He met his future wife, Mary Egan from Moyne in County Tipperary, when he was just 20. Mary was the central part of his life for over 40 years.

Like his mother Kitty and late father Peadar, and the place of his upbringing Gorthaganny in west Roscommon and all his family and friends, Mary helped shape his life. He adored his family and they all cared for him so considerately, night, noon and morning, in the final months of his life.

His proud son, Dermot, displayed extraordinary courage when he lined out for Kildare against Antrim in the All-Ireland football qualifier first-round match in what was a highly emotional championship game in Newbridge, just hours after his Dad was laid to rest with full military honours. It was a most fitting tribute to the memory of his father who raised a family steeped in the GAA tradition. Like his father, Dermot won two All Stars and his sister Noelle also won an All Star in recognition of her prowess as a Ladies Gaelic footballer with Kildare.

Dermot senior had a special affinity with the county of Kildare where he spent most of his adult life. He also played for several years with Sarsfields in Newbridge, a club with which he won two county senior championship medals, in 1982 and 1986, and later served as chairman. Dermot also had spells as manager of Roscommon and Kildare.

I remember the overwhelming sadness I felt on the day, June 23rd, 2010 when I heard the news of Dermot's untimely death. He was just 62.

That very day, I was due to appear on the Derek Mooney Show on RTÉ Radio One to talk about Diego Maradona. I have always taken a keen interest in Maradona's career as I believe he was unrivalled as a world-class soccer player. I had visited Maradona's home place on two occasions while on trips to Buenos Aires with the GAA All Stars.

Derek recognised the significance of the death of such a legendary figure as Lieutenant General Dermot Earley, who had risen through the ranks to become Chief of Staff of the Defence Forces.

The coincidence of being on air on Derek's programme gave me the opportunity to share with listeners my own personal memories of a fellow Roscommon man, who had made us all so proud and provided us with some of the most memorable sporting moments of our youth.

Quite apart from his magnificence as a footballer, Dermot had wonderful personal qualities and had respect for everyone he came in touch with in his daily life. His trademark was that strong almost bone-crushing handshake.

I was a youngster when I met Dermot for the first time in the late sixties and some years later interviewed him at his home in Kildare for the *Roscommon Champion*. He took an interest in my career thereafter and encouraged me at every opportunity.

I spoke to Dermot's driver, Private Paddy Murray, at the month's mind Mass and he told me about his first meeting with the future Chief of Staff. Like anyone starting a new job, Paddy arrived at Dermot's house with more than a little apprehension. But that trepidation soon disappeared when he met Dermot. Paddy told me that "Dermot sat in the car, gave me a firm handshake and then said: 'Paddy Murray from Gracefield in Offaly, you and I are going to get on mighty'". And mighty is how they did get on.

Indeed, Dermot used the word 'mighty' on a regular basis because for him it was all about accentuating the positive.

He was a sportsman supreme, a superb midfielder and a leader on the field of play. He won five Connacht senior championship medals with Roscommon as well as a National Football League medal in 1979 and two All Stars, in 1974 and 1979. He was a key member of the team that won the All-Ireland under-21 football title in 1966 and also gained two Railway Cup medals with Connacht, in 1967 and 1969.

Remarkably as a 17-year-old in 1965, the year he joined the Army as a Cadet, Dermot represented Roscommon at minor, under-21, junior and senior levels. Even at that early stage, his name was on the lips of all avid Roscommon supporters as someone who was destined for greatness.

We all recall his outstanding performances, the high fielding, the free-taking, the wonderful skills and the leadership qualities. He was Roscommon through and through. He could rally a team like few others when he set off on that trademark solo run.

He reserved many of his most memorable displays for the games against Mayo and had huge respect for that county and their great players, none more so than the late John Morley.

Dermot also had enormous admiration for Galway, the most successful county in Connacht. Galway have won nine All-Ireland senior football titles, including the three-in-row of the sixties, as against Roscommon's total of two. Yet, in 2009, when Galway were honouring their All-Ireland senior medal winners from 1925 to 2001, Football Board chairman John Joe Holleran asked Dermot to be the guest of honour and deliver the keynote address. It was testimony to the esteem in which Dermot was held among the football fraternity in Galway and throughout the province.

Dermot wore the primrose and blue of Roscommon from his days as a minor in the early 1960s to the mid '80s. He was a proud Gorthaganny man and played for several years with Michael Glaveys – a club founded by his late father Peadar. Dermot lined out for Roscommon in the 1980 All-Ireland final loss to Kerry. It was a heartbreaking defeat for Roscommon, who certainly had ample opportunities to win that game.

Despite his disappointment at losing out on that elusive medal, Dermot always treasured the opportunity to have played in an All-Ireland final and to have tested his skills against some of the best players of that era on the biggest day of all in the Gaelic football calendar.

Of course, it would have been wonderful had Dermot won that senior All-Ireland in 1980 but the measure of a sportsman is not determined by victories alone. The bonds of friendships forged between players remain long after the exploits on the field of play are forgotten about.

Dermot is regarded by many as one of the greatest players never to have won an All-Ireland senior medal. That is also a compliment attributed to another Roscommon legend, the great Gerry O'Malley, who played for the county from the late 1940s to the mid-1960s. Gerry captained Roscommon in the 1962 All-Ireland final but sustained an injury early on and had to leave the field. Kerry won that day despite a brave effort from Roscommon, who missed the influence of their inspirational captain.

Gerry was a good friend of Dermot's for a long time and clearly recalls kicking football with him in Gorthaganny in the early 1960s. Gerry was visiting Dermot's father Peadar that day and he willingly had a kick-around with the up-and-coming young star. Little did Gerry realise that many years later their names would be indelibly linked as two of the greatest Roscommon people of all time.

Gerry often recounted to me stories of Dermot's kindness, including the day of Jimmy Murray's funeral. Jimmy was a wonderful gentleman and an iconic figure in Roscommon for his exploits in captaining the county to All-Ireland successes in 1943 and 1944. Dermot delivered the oration at Jimmy's graveside and afterwards he gave Gerry a lift back to his old home place in Brideswell.

Gerry travelled with me to Newbridge to visit Dermot one last time and it was a special privilege to be in their company on what was a sad but uplifting occasion. Gerry held Dermot's hand and talked to him about Roscommon football. Gerry also told him about that winter's day with snow on the ground when he kicked football with young Dermot while visiting his father in Gorthaganny. It was a privilege to be there on that poignant afternoon in the Earley household when two Roscommon legends, who had lifted our spirits, whether in victory or defeat, in places like Coman's Park, McHale Park and Croke Park, said their last goodbyes.

Gerry told me later that Dermot gripped his hand more tightly when he spoke to him about his father and Gorthaganny.

I joined in the conversation from time to time, but I could not stop my mind from wandering back to when these two great men provided such inspiration and enjoyment to our county. Both men shared something deeper than any of us could even dare comprehend. Dermot Earley and Gerry O'Malley knew what it was like to wear the Roscommon jersey and carry the expectations of a whole county on their shoulders.

Dermot played his last championship match for Roscommon in Hyde Park in 1985. Mayo won convincingly that day. But the occasion will forever be remembered for the sportsmanship of the Mayo players who carried Dermot Earley shoulder high in recognition of his greatness as a footballer.

It was easy to see why Dermot had such a distinguished military career because he possessed rare leadership qualities. He treated everyone with respect. He never lost the sense of place that defined him and made him a leader on the international stage. There was no need to change. Why should he! He was what he was – a mighty man from Gorthaganny.

There was a huge outpouring of grief at home and among the Gaelic games community across the globe when the news broke of Dermot's death. But nowhere was his passing felt more acutely than in Roscommon, the county that both shaped him and revered him and that he in turn inspired. He was family.

GAA president Christy Cooney led the tributes to a 'true legend of Gaelic football' while President of Ireland Mary McAleese and Taoiseach Brian Cowen also expressed their condolences. Mr Cowen, who had presented Dermot with a Distinguished Service Medal two months previously, said the General was "a true champion of peace, whose commitment, intelligence, leadership and charisma brought distinction to himself, his family and Ireland".

Thousands, including sporting, political and religious leaders, came from all over the country and abroad to sympathise with the Earley family at St Brigid's Church in the Curragh and later at St Conleth's Parish Church in Newbridge.

People travelled in large numbers from Roscommon and some of those sympathisers wore the county's primrose and blue jerseys in remembrance of days past when the whole world was young and their hero Dermot Earley filled their lives with joy and happiness.

Dermot's Roscommon team mates, including the captain Danny Murray, who played alongside him in the 1980 All-Ireland final, came to pay their last respects to a man that had motivated and inspired them all.

Memorial cards distributed at Dermot's funeral detailed the five points of his 'Plan for Life', which clearly personified his life as a husband, father, son, brother, soldier and Christian:

1) *Enjoy time with my family*
2) *Give the best to my work*
3) *Give back to my community*
4) *Spend my leisure time well*
5) *Make time for God in my life*

There is no doubt that his mother Kitty, his wife Mary, sons David, Dermot and Conor and daughters Paula, Anne-Marie and Noelle along with his brothers, Peter and Paul and sisters Denise and Margaret and his extended family have been consoled by the knowledge that Dermot touched the lives of so many throughout his sporting and working career.

I always came away refreshed and renewed after a conversation with Dermot. He was an inspiration and he never lost the common touch. Dermot Earley's legend will live on and will inspire young Roscommon people to play Gaelic football and dream the dream. And there would be no greater tribute to his memory than to see a young generation of Roscommon footballers rise up and bring the Sam Maguire Cup back to the county.

Roscommon would also rejoice should his son Dermot win an All-Ireland medal with Kildare. That would make his father and the people of Roscommon 'mighty' proud too.

# BRIAN CODY
## Club is the cornerstone

**B**RIAN CODY, born on 12 July 1954, is a lifelong member of James Stephens Club, 'The Village', in Kilkenny with whom he won three county senior titles, two Leinster and two All-Ireland club titles. A 'Village' man to the last, he has managed its teams at all levels.

He captained Kilkenny minors to All-Ireland success in 1972 and won two under-21 titles in 1974 and 1975. He captained the seniors to victory in 1982 and holds four Celtic crosses, one as a substitute. He has eight Leinster senior medals, two National League titles and won two All-Star awards.

Since his appointment as Kilkenny senior manager in 1998 the county has achieved unprecedented success winning 10 Leinster titles, eight All-Irelands and four National Leagues in 12 years. Brian is married to Elsie, a former Wexford camogie player, and they have two sons, Donncha and Diarmuid.

Two months after I was born Christy Ring captained Cork to All-Ireland senior hurling success against Wexford by 1-9 to 1-6 on 5 September 1954 winning his eighth Celtic cross, his third as captain. I don't recall that occasion but when I was growing up I remember Kilkenny teams winning an occasional All-Ireland – they won in 1957, 1963 and 1967. All the while Fr Tommy Maher was pioneering modern coaching methods and Eddie Keher would soon be making headlines as Ireland's top scorer. And I was dreaming of representing my club and county at the highest levels.

I was very fortunate to achieve my ambitions, and much more than I had ever dreamed of, with club and county. When I am asked to recall the most important moments, the highlights and the most rewarding days of my career as a player or manager I cannot overlook the days of glory with my club James Stephens, better known as 'the Village'. While success at inter-county level grabs the national headlines and players are feted and well known in their own county and elsewhere, the basis for all success stems from the work put in at local level, in clubs and schools, by coaches, teachers, mentors and club officials.

I have had many great days and victories with my county but nothing compares with the feelings, the emotions and the satisfaction I experienced when the Village won the county title in 2004 after a gap of 23 years, and then winning the All-Ireland club title on St Patrick's Day, 2005. I was not involved directly with the team but I had a very special interest as my son, Donncha, was right full back and my sense of pride was overwhelming.

Naturally, there is a wonderful sense of fulfilment every time Kilkenny win but involvement with club is much more special. The Village, the parish, the community, the club and the hurling mean everything to me. Our club had not won the Kilkenny title since 1981 and the longer the valley period went on the more frustrating it became. In the final we were up against Young Irelands for whom DJ Carey belted in three goals but we held on to win by a single point. The final whistle sounded; heavenly music to my ears!

County final day is special in every county and it is matched, for players, members and supporters, by an All-Ireland final appearance in Croke Park, particularly when one's team wins.

But it all begins at home in the club. I know it's a cliché to say that club success is achieved with your neighbours and friends; when you are playing for your club you are representing something very special and building on the achievements of previous generations of players, and taking care of the jersey for the next generation. You must take special care of that privilege and do your best to add to and hand on the tradition you have inherited.

Every player should have the ambition to wear the county jersey but you can only achieve that through the club because if you are not playing well at club level, you're not going to make it at county level. The club provides the opportunity to do anything you want as a player. Some players who do not make a county minor team can, with ambition, determination and drive go on to represent their county at senior level: Martin Comerford and Derek Lyng are cases in point – they were not famous college or county underage stars but they applied themselves exceptionally well and achieved success because of their dedication to improving all facets of their game.

Club culture should be a very important part of any player's make-up.

It came naturally to me through my father's involvement with James Stephens. He was so involved in the growth and development of the club, and so keen on making it successful that I could not possibly have avoided being influenced by his role in how it became a strong and vibrant unit. He was at the heart of the drive to raise standards in coaching and training and later, as club chairman, led the way in how the club was organised and administered. He was always very happy to be doing something for the club and that influenced me and helped make me the player I became and inspired the success I have enjoyed as a manager.

I am firmly convinced that if you are not passionate about your club you will not be passionate about your county. Players must always remember that: when the Kilkenny panel breaks to go back playing with their clubs I always insist that they give full commitment to their clubs. They must not be selective about how and when they perform. Clubs need their county players to perform at optimum level and to give of their very best in all games, challenge or competitive. They are the ones who inspire their colleagues and the stars of the future. After all, it is the club that has made them what they are as county players.

From my early days I have always believed in the principle of giving your best at all times, whether it is for club or county. If you follow that principle you will be happy in the knowledge that you have done your best, and have no regrets on that score. And I have no regrets.

# COLM COOPER

## My dream came true – ten years later!

**B**ORN on 3 June 1983, the youngest of seven children, Colm Cooper follows Liverpool FC and admires the skills of Lionel Messi, Barcelona FC. He is delighted to offer his contribution to this book as he feels privileged to live in Ireland without health risks from the environment.

Colm has won three Kerry senior football medals, seven All Stars, four All-Ireland senior medals, five Munster senior medals, Munster and All-Ireland under-21 medals, a Munster minor medal and three National Leagues. In his leisure time he plays golf and supports the sporting endeavours of his nieces and nephews.

Sport, especially Gaelic football, has always played an integral part in my life. Being the youngest in a family of seven, five boys and two girls, I followed in my brothers' footsteps and joined Dr Crokes GAA Club in Killarney as soon as I started school.

My first day in Croke Park was on St Patrick's Day, 1992 as a nine year old. I was chosen as Dr Crokes' team mascot for the All-Ireland club final and it is a day I will never forget. I ran onto the field wearing the club's black and amber tracksuit (my mother still has it) with the team. The atmosphere in the dressing room was electric and as a young boy I began to realise what lining out for one's home place means to so many people.

Dr Crokes won their first All-Ireland club title that day and two of my brothers were on the team. I promised myself there and then that I would do everything possible to play in Croke Park on All-Ireland final day.

The year 2000 was memorable also as Dr Crokes won the Kerry county championship and all five of us brothers played in the team. I was just 17 years of age and my brother Vincent gave a man-of-the-match performance.

My All-Ireland final dream was realised in 2002 when I lined out beside many modern-day legends of Kerry football like Séamus Moynihan, the Ó Sé brothers – Darragh, Marc and Tomás, Mike Frank Russell and Eoin Brosnan, my club mate. Unfortunately for Kerry and for me, it was Armagh's day and they won an historic first All-Ireland title, beating us by one point – 1-12 to 0-14. It would be an understatement to say I was bitterly disappointed but I resolved to get back to Croke Park again.

We were back in the 2004 final, this time against Mayo, and I lined out at right corner forward. At 21 I was physically stronger and I felt I could hold my own against most opponents. I scored my first goal in an All-Ireland that day, 26 September, a day I will remember for a long time. There are no words to describe how fantastic it felt to be part of a Kerry All-Ireland winning team and to follow in the footsteps of so many of our boyhood heroes like Dara Ó Cinnéide, Maurice Fitzgerald, Mike Frank Russell, Liam Hassett and William Kirby.

When Dara Ó Cinnéide walked up the steps of the Hogan Stand, accepted the Sam Maguire Cup from GAA President Seán Kelly and delivered his rousing acceptance speech in his native tongue felt I was half way to paradise.

There was a surreal atmosphere on arriving home in Killarney accompanied by the coveted Sam Maguire trophy. However, the best part was celebrating with my parents and family. Sadly for me, that was the only All-Ireland I had the chance to savour with my dad as he passed away suddenly in April 2006, RIP. I still miss him and I think about him every day, especially on good days when my team wins.

We did not win the Kerry title again until 2010 which is why I had the honour of captaining the Kerry team in 2011. The good luck and congratulatory emails, texts and cards we received from many parts of the world, and nearer home, emphasise the importance of the GAA and the club in Irish life, and especially what they mean to so many of our people around the world as expressed in the following messages:

*Best of luck to all the lads on Sunday! I've no doubt ye will take it down, best wishes to all involved!* Michael O'Grady, Perth, Australia...

*Best of luck today. Hope Gooch is leading Kerry out next year.* Mike Grady in Waterford...

*Every good wish to the Dr. Crokes in the county final* from all in Scoil Bhríde, Loreto National School, Killarney...

*Congrats to Dr Crokes ... it was a well-deserved victory and the best of luck for the Munster Club and All-Ireland Club.* Mike Crowley, Monaleen captain...

*Great win for Dr Crokes. Watched it live on your site.* Teddy Cronin, Glen Mills, Pennsylvania...

*Just wanted to congratulate everyone involved in the county final victory. For a club that was so good to me and left me with nothing but great memories, it was fantastic to see the great Dr Crokes GAA Club finally get the victory they so richly deserved.* Aaron Fahy...

*Congratulations on your win as county champions. It's great to have the Bishop Moynihan Cup back in Killarney.* Officers, members and players, Spa GAA...

*Congratulations to all in Dr Crokes on winning the county final and to Colm Cooper on his 6th All-Star award.* Officers of East Kerry Board...

*All the best Sunday in Munster final lads, be rooting for you down here.* Donal Kav in N.Z....

The pride and the passion, the bonds of friendship, the team ethic and the club spirit and tradition: these are the bits and pieces of GAA life which drive us on to be the very best we can be for the glory of the Black and Amber of our Dr Crokes – and the Green and Gold of the Kingdom.

# LAR CORBETT
## The Queen and I

LAR CORBETT has had a remarkable hurling career with Tipperary and is best known for his scoring feats – three goals in the 2010 All-Ireland final and a four-goal and four-point fiesta in the 2011 Munster final. He has represented his county for 11 years winning two All-Irelands, four Munster medals, two National Leagues and an interprovincial medal.

A member of the famous Thurles Sarsfields club, he won county minor (1999), under-21 (2002) and three senior county titles, the first of these in 2005, and was Tipperary captain in 2006.

Lar has won three All-Star awards, and was Texaco Hurler of the Year and GPA Player of the Year in 2010. Apart from his exploits on the field of play he will be remembered for explaining to Prince Philip during the visit of Queen Elizabeth II to Croke Park that a player must learn to play the game from a very young age.

I was only six years of age when Richard Stakelum declared: "The Famine is over" after the replayed 1987 Munster hurling final between Tipperary and Cork in Killarney. The 'famine' had lasted 16 years, an eternity in Tipperary hurling. I was lucky not to have to endure another 'famine' as the county won All-Irelands in 1989 and 1991, and I was part of the successes of 2001 and 2010.

Tradition has a huge impact on how young people view various sports and in my case this was never an issue. I heard of the glorious tales and heroic feats of the great Thurles Sarsfields and Tipperary teams of the golden years from the late 1950s to the early 1970s. When my club, Thurles Sarsfields, was on top in the county, Tipperary dominated the charts wining six of the nine All-Irelands they contested in that period.

The names of Jimmy and John Doyle, Donie Nealon, Liam Devaney, and the full back line of Mick Maher, Kieran Carey and Mick Burns were revered in the Premier County, and feared in every other hurling stronghold. It is always nice to be asked if I know Jimmy Doyle from

Thurles Sarsfields, and to realise that people from all parts of the country remember him as a wonderful hurler.

My own heroes were of a later era; Nicky English, Pat Fox, Declan Ryan, Michael Cleary and the Bonnar brothers were among those who inspired me as they graced the Croke Park arena with the All-Ireland victories of 1989 and 1991. I also admired Joe Deane of Cork, a left-handed hurler like me, and DJ Carey of Kilkenny. They brought great style and skill to the game and I always took note of their scoring ability and how they could read the game so well.

My very special memories are all associated with Thurles Sarsfields and Tipperary games. Winning a county under-12 football medal with my club was a dream come true as were minor and under-21 hurling victories. And winning our first Tipperary senior hurling title in 2005 was a really memorable occasion, the first of three such achievements.

Tipperary's All-Ireland victories in 2001 and 2010 are stand-out memories which brought pride to my club and county: it was then that I appreciated fully the time, dedication and effort put in by my coaches and mentors, too many to mention, from juvenile to adult level in Thurles Sarsfields. I know they shared that satisfaction and were proud of the historic achievements of those teams, happy in the knowledge that some of their own protégés played a part in bringing the Liam MacCarthy Cup home again.

I was lucky enough to be part of another historic occasion at Croke Park when Queen Elizabeth II of England and Prince Philip visited the famous stadium. That was a fantastic day and I was privileged, along with Pádraig Maher from my own club, Kevin Nolan of Dublin and Joe Sheridan from Meath, to be part of it and to be asked by the royal couple about the rules of hurling, at what age players take up the game and how hurleys are made. Pádraig and I said it was one visit to Croke Park where we couldn't lose because when we're there, we're usually playing in matches where it's win or lose.

I love playing in Semple Stadium and Croke Park: there is nothing better in sport than to be on the field of play in a Munster or All-Ireland final in front of a packed stadium of 55,000 or 82,300 people, especially when victory is our lot.

The privilege and honour of representing the people of Thurles and Tipperary gives me immense pleasure and it is very satisfying and humbling to realise that our team can bring so much joy and happiness to our supporters when we pull on the blue and gold jersey.

While I am playing with Thurles Sarsfields and Tipperary I will always train to the best of my ability and play as well as I possibly can and I will be happy with that. My full focus will be on playing the game while I can and I have never thought of what I might do when I retire: it is not on the radar and I hope it will not be for many a year to come.

Just as I carried a hurley in my childhood, I love to see boys and girls carrying hurleys to and from school or to the local club. That gives me a great thrill. It is an indication of a healthy sporting life in a community, it shows that parents are happy to have their children involved in hurling and it is a sign that the ancient sport of the camán and sliotar inspires people in every generation to great deeds on the playing fields of Ireland.

My best sporting memories are all tied in to hurling, the greatest game of all. Hurling has been in my veins for over 25 years and if I live to be a hundred I will be forever grateful to the people, especially my mother, Breda, who always encouraged and supported me and helped show me the way to deliver 'what it says on the tin'.

I hope the tradition and love of hurling lives on and that future generations benefit from that tradition wherever they find it. And I hope, too, that there will never be another 'famine' in the history of Tipperary hurling.

# MICHAEL CORCORAN
## Pride in the performance

**M**ICHAEL CORCORAN is a Rugby Commentator and Sports Broadcaster with RTÉ Radio since 2000. In 2011 he broadcast his fourth Rugby World Cup, he has completed three tours with the British and Irish Lions to Australia, New Zealand and South Africa and has commentated on over 115 Ireland international games.

The Cork native has broadcast over 150 Heineken Cup games, including Leinster's wins in 2009 and 2011 along with Munster's successes in 2006 and 2008.

Michael has travelled to Australia, New Zealand, South Africa, Argentina, America, Canada, Italy, England, Tonga, Samoa, Wales, France, Scotland, Spain, Switzerland and Russia to broadcast rugby for the listeners to RTÉ Radio. He was short-listed on three occasions for the PPI Sports Broadcaster of the Year Award.

Because of my job, Cardiff's Millennium Stadium will forever hold fond memories for me. Yes, it has been the scene of many heartbreaking days for Irish rugby in the past but the good days far outweigh the bad ones.

In 2005, Ireland travelled to play Wales in the final game of the RBS Six Nations Championship, both sides going for the Grand Slam. Hopes were high for an Ireland win but Wales to their credit were full value for a 32-20 win; you had a feeling from the moment Max Boyce led the singing before the game Ireland would be second best. We were.

Conor Counihan famously said, "Failure is the fuel for success" when he was speaking in the immediate aftermath of Cork's win over Down in the 2010 All-Ireland football final – more about that anon.

Ireland supporters paid a return visit to Cardiff in 2009; the objective was the same, to win a first Grand Slam since 1948. At half time, I was not very optimistic and neither was my side-kick Donal Lenihan. However two early second-half tries settled our nerves and we were back in the ball game. Those dramatic last few minutes remain with me; I still replay them in my head from time to time. But the result always remains the same; we won!

Prior to that great day, I had been to the Millennium Stadium for Heineken Cup finals and had witnessed the anguish on the faces of the Munster players after their defeat to Leicester. Worse still, I had to travel on the plane with them on their return to Limerick.

However, those dark days were long forgotten in 2006 and 2008 when they beat Biarritz and Toulouse respectively to win European Rugby's greatest prize. Who will ever forget Peter Stringer's try against Biarritz, the look on the face of Serge Betsen when he realised he was left flat-footed by the Munster scrum-half, the crucial part played by Trevor Halstaad when he blasted over for a try.

There was huge tension as the clock ticked down towards full time and when Chris White blew the whistle years of frustration, hurt and disappointment came to an end. It was a moment never to be forgotten.

And it was to be repeated in 2008 when the aristocrats of the European game, Toulouse, were the opposition. The end result was the same and when the cup was hoisted high in the sky, Munster players and fans celebrated as if it was the first time they had won it.

It's hard to believe that Cardiff would provide even more drama in the Heineken Cup final of 2011. Having won the trophy for the first time in Murrayfield in 2009, Leinster were hoping to dine at the top table for a second time.

Like Ireland in 2009, at half time it did not look great for Joe Schmidt's side. Whatever happened in the changing room during the break, it worked. Shane Jennings came on and upped the pace of the ball supply to the backs. Jonathon Sexton grabbed the game by the scruff of the neck and we witnessed one of the greatest ever comebacks. Wow, what a second half, what a win, what a day!

I love sport; nothing beats being at an event, watching the drama unfold in front of your eyes.

One of my earliest sporting memories is travelling to Limerick Racecourse in 1979 for the World Cross Country Championships. The previous year John Treacy had won the title in Bellahouston Park in Glasgow: could he repeat the feat? Not alone did he, but Ireland men's team won the silver medal: Danny McDaid was 11th, Gerry Deegan came 43rd, my club mate Donie Walsh was 47th just behind Mick O'Shea. The junior team powered by Ronnie Carroll and Paul Moloney were 4th, cruelly missing out on a medal. The women's team finished high up also.

A distant memory now, but the postal and telephone strike of 1979 caused a lot of problems for the race organisers and a commemorative stamp to honour the occasion was only issued five months after the championships.

Some of my fondest memories are from the GAA pitch however. In 2004, the Cork hurlers won the Liam MacCarthy Cup for the 29th time and for the record they beat Kilkenny by 17 points to nine. I had a personal interest in the game as my first cousin, Brian Corcoran, was playing full forward that day. I had followed his career, hurling and football, with interest, from his defending days to his scoring days.

I was high up in the Cusack Stand watching the game and late in the match he won a ball near the Kilkenny goal. He was hassled and harried by defenders and was almost on his knees as he struck a point at a crucial time. I rose to my feet with joy and shouted my head off, I never met Cúchulainn but I'm sure even he would have been impressed by the genius that was Brian Corcoran.

The Cork senior footballers put me through the emotional wringer in September 2010, All-Ireland final day against Down. I was reduced to tears after the game; I was an emotional wreck. I have always had a fondness for the footballers, even though I prefer hurling.

In 1993, I attended the All-Ireland football final between Cork and Derry with my dad. We stood at the Canal End and jumped for joy when Joe Kavanagh blasted the ball to the back of the net early in the game.

However, our joy was short-lived as Sam Maguire decided he wanted to travel up north for the third year in a row. It was the last time I attended a major game with my dad, as he sadly passed away in 1994. That was on my mind in Croke Park on All-Ireland football final day in September 2010, a game I attended with my son Conor.

We were not happy at the short whistle when it looked as if my beloved Cork were doomed. However, their never say die attitude and spirit won the day by 16 points to 15. It was an incredible second-half performance. I've never met Aidan Walsh, Daniel Goulding, Donnacha O'Connor or even Graham Canty but I was the happiest man alive that day and, boy, did we celebrate!

# EAMONN CREGAN

## JP McManus and the 1973 All-Ireland hurling final

**E**AMONN 'BLONDIE' CREGAN was a household name in GAA circles long before his 21st birthday. By then he had captained Limerick to win the Munster minor hurling title in 1963, won Harty and Croke Cups with Limerick CBS in 1964 and played under-21 and senior hurling and football with Limerick.

He holds four Munster senior hurling medals, a National League medal and won an All-Ireland title in 1973. He has three Railway Cup medals and three All-Star awards and was on the inaugural All Stars in 1971.

Eamonn was a key member of his club Claughaun's successes in winning eight county football and three county hurling titles. He managed Offaly to All-Ireland victory in 1994 – against his native county – and managed Limerick for six years. He lives in Castletroy with his wife Ann and they have five children and four grandchildren.

It is amazing what comes to mind when one sits and thinks about one's best sporting memories. Naturally, in my case hurling tops the list – and there were scores of memories – many positive, right up there on the Richter scale, and some negative which are best consigned to the 'forgotten' file.

Some of my highlights include the night Stoke City football team came to the Markets Field in Limerick. The great Stanley Matthews was playing and on three occasions Denis Linnane dispossessed him by simply keeping his eye on the ball; or when Garryowen won the Munster Cup in the mid-fifties and paraded up O'Connell Street with the cup on a donkey and cart, Gordon Wood making sure the cup did not fall onto the ground; or seeing Dick O'Connor go up the right wing and cross the ball to a well-placed team mate.

In Limerick you followed all sports; all games were played in 'the Bommen Field', or the People's Park.

Of course, successes in the Munster Colleges Harty Cup senior hurling championship which Limerick CBS won in a record-equalling four-in-a-row run from 1964 to 1967 and All-Ireland Colleges Croke Cup victories in 1964 and 1966 were the forerunner of what was to come for the county hurling team. After a regime of winter training which started in October 1969 under Down native, Joe McGrath, Limerick began to be taken seriously. We reached four National League finals and a Home National League final, an Oireachtas tournament final and the 1971 Munster final, losing that to Tipperary, which made us battle-hardened; and the fact that Clare beat us in 1972 further toughened us for the road ahead. That road widened out into a motorway which yielded four Munster titles in eight attempts between 1971 and 1981, defeating Tipperary (1973), Clare (1974 and 1981) and Cork (1980).

Our first Munster final success, against Tipperary, was a very high-scoring game by any standards, 6-7 to 2-18. My brother Michael had the Limerick team in superb physical condition throughout the season, and we were at peak fitness, mentally and physically, for the All-Ireland. On final day we were in our dressing room under the Cusack Stand gearing up to 'Go forth and fight on behalf of Tribe Limerick' in urgings of which Patrick Sarsfield would have been very, very proud.

The names of Limerick heroes of the past were rattled out, litany style, and pierced our hearts and focused our minds on winning for the Treaty County: names such as Mick and John Mackey who won All-Ireland medals in 1934, 1936 and 1940, as well as 15 county hurling medals and five county football titles each, stirred the emotions. Others legendary names to spur us on were Jackie Power, father of Ger of Kerry football fame, brothers Dave and Peter Clohessy and, of course, my father Ned, and Peter Cregan – no relation. The extraordinary feats of the heroic men of the golden era of Limerick hurling when the county contested five All-Irelands, winning in 1934, 1936 and 1940, were to be emulated.

As well as names of legendary heroes, the mention of famous clubs from city, town and village echoed and bounded from past decades... Ahane, Patrickswell, South Liberties, Claughaun, Kilmallock, Bruree... and pumped our hearts as blood coursed our veins in preparation for the siege by Limerick.

The fact that Kilkenny provided the opposition was another weapon of attack: they had beaten Limerick in 1933 and 1935 before Limerick avenged those victories in the '36 and '40 encounters. In addition, the

'Cats' were the 1972 All-Ireland champions and Limerick hadn't been in an All-Ireland final since 1940 after which Kilkenny had won six finals. When we were reminded of the obligation we had to our clubs and county to win the Liam MacCarthy Cup losing was not an option.

And this is where the tale of the unorthodox entry of a visitor to the dressing room comes into my pre All-Ireland story. Before we entered the field of combat Declan Moylan and Eamonn Grimes, our captain, were talking to a spot ten feet up the dressing-room wall when I heard a noise above my head. I saw a small window which someone opened inwards and a head came through, and with encouragement from Declan and Eamonn, the rest of the body followed and dropped to the floor. This Limerick supporter was grabbed and brought out onto Croke Park with the team on that glorious day for Limerick when we beat Kilkenny by 1-21 to 1-14 in an exhilarating contest.

The fact that JP McManus trotted out with the Limerick team which bridged a 33-year gap to win the Liam MacCarthy Cup on Sunday 2 September 1973 is still a vivid memory... and the memories that led up to and followed that historic day will last forever.

# EIMEAR CREGAN

## Italia '90 focused my mind on sport

**E**IMEAR CREGAN'S impressive international hockey career began in 2001 winning her first cap against Wales at the age of 19. She went from strength to strength and earned her 100th cap against Italy in 2007 and was Irish captain from 2008 to 2011.

Her 150th cap was against Belgium at Champions Challenge II in 2009. She amassed an outstanding Irish record of 171 Irish caps over ten years but had to retire prematurely in February 2011 due to injury. She said then: "It is with deep sadness that, in consultation with medical staff, I have considered the long-term implications of continuing to train and compete at this level and have been forced into retirement."

A forward, she scored 26 international goals and played in World and European Cups, and in Olympic Qualifier games. The Limerick native works as a PE teacher at Ursuline Convent, Thurles.

My best sporting memory was Italia '90, the soccer World Cup finals when our Irish soccer team with the likes of 'Captain Fantastic' – Mick McCarthy, Liam Brady, Paul McGrath, Ray Houghton, Ronnie Whelan and Packie Bonner got to rub shoulders with some of the greatest players in the world. Before Ireland had even kicked a ball in the tournament they were a success and everyone in the country hailed them as heroes. The reason for this was that they were the first Irish soccer team ever to compete in World Cup finals. The Irish players, however, weren't there to just make up the numbers: they were there to compete. They had a job to do. This Irish team's performance led by Mick McCarthy played a pivotal role in my sporting career and inspired me to strive for success no matter what the odds.

During the group stages of the tournament Ireland performed better than expected. They drew with the big guns, England. They also drew 1-1 with Egypt, and a Niall Quinn equaliser in the last group game against the Dutch ensured they made it into the last 16 where they were drawn against Romania. By this stage World Cup mania had swept across the entire country.

My family were all invited to my dad's sister's house to watch the game which was Ireland's biggest match of the tournament. Put simply, if Ireland won they were through to the quarter-final but if they lost, they were out. We all got dressed up for the big occasion. My brothers had t-shirts with a picture of Jack Charlton on them with him saying 'Put 'Em Under Pressure' and 'OLÉ OLÉ OLÉ OLÉ' and I was dressed from head to toe in Irish soccer/Limerick GAA gear. I was determined that if I was supporting the Irish team in their last group game I was going to do it right!

I remember the game against Romania was an enthralling affair but neither team was able to put the ball in the net during normal time or extra time and the game was forced into a penalty shootout. After eight penalties the score was 4-4. At this stage everyone was biting or had bitten off their nails. A player by the name of Daniel Timofte walked nervously from the halfway line to take Romania's last penalty. I remember thinking Packie Bonner (wearing his purple Irish jersey) looked very confident and incredibly focused. He knew along with the millions of Irish supporters back home that this penalty had to be saved.

Then came the moment, as if in slow motion: Timofte started his run up and while the whole of Ireland watched in anticipation, urging him to miss, he struck the ball with the inside of his boot and aimed for the left side of the goal. Meanwhile, Packie Bonner had other ideas and he launched himself low to his right and at full stretch he batted the ball away from the goal. The expression of absolute disbelief etched on Packie's face as his arms made contact with the ball preventing it from going into the net was a thing of beauty and a moment never to be forgotten in Irish sport. He had saved the penalty and celebrated by jumping high into the air whilst pumping his fists. Every member of my family erupted and whoops and cheers of delight could be heard all around the neighbourhood. And all the while poor Daniel Timofte was holding his head in his hands making his way back to his team with a feeling of utter dejection.

Once we got over the shock and relief of the penalty save, we all realised that in order for Ireland to win, we had to score the next penalty. But who would take it? Suddenly David O'Leary emerged from the circle of Irish players at the halfway line. Both my brother and my dad looked at each other and said: "David O'Leary . . . sure he never takes penalties, how the hell did Jack allow that to happen?" Anyway, it didn't matter what they thought, David O'Leary was taking the penalty and that was that. He picked up the ball on the edge of the box, and boy was he focused! It seemed to take him an age to place the ball on the penalty spot. Once this was done, he looked at the goals and started to walk backwards. If ever there was a time for someone to show guts it was here. There he was, David O'Leary stepping up to take the last penalty to put Ireland through to the last eight of their first ever World Cup.

The referee blew his whistle and everyone watching in my aunt's house simultaneously held their breaths. One step, two steps, three steps by David O' Leary (everyone still holding their breaths): this was the moment of truth. O'Leary struck the ball with venom . . . it flew through the air sending the keeper the wrong way and rattled the back of the net. David O'Leary had scored and sent Ireland through to the last eight, making Ireland the only team in history to ever make it that far without winning a group game. Packie Bonner was the first player to embrace David O'Leary in celebration. Within seconds the remaining Irish players and management, Maurice Setters being the first to get there, had swallowed up the heroes of the night, Packie Bonner and David O'Leary.

The Italia '90 World Cup was my first major sporting memory and one that has inspired me greatly throughout my hockey career. I have carried Jack Charlton's motto of "Put 'em under pressure" with me throughout my career and it showed me that so much can be achieved through hard work, tenacity and the right attitude. That Irish team led by 'Captain Fantastic', Mick McCarthy, showed tremendous team spirit and determination throughout the campaign and against all the odds they succeeded in qualifying for the last eight of a tournament having never competed at that level before.

Italia '90 enhanced my love of sport and inspired me to strive for success no matter what the odds. Attitude, guts and determination will go a long way in sport if you are willing to try.

# PADDY CULLEN
## The pub and the silver medal

PADDY CULLEN'S Gaelic football career with Dublin spanned 14 years from 1966 to 1979 during which he won three All-Ireland medals in 1974, 1976 and 1977. He collected an All-Star award in each of those years and a fourth in 1979.

His penalty save from from Liam Sammon of Galway in the 1974 final is ranked as number 17 in the Top 20 GAA Moments. He was at the centre of one of the great GAA controversies when Mikey Sheehy of Kerry lobbed a ball over his head in the 1978 final while Paddy was arguing with the referee; the goal is number 12 in the Top 20 GAA Moments.

Paddy managed Dublin in 1991, winning the National League and taking them through the epic four-game first-round saga against Meath which Dublin eventually lost by a point. In 1992, Dublin reached the All-Ireland final under his stewardship but lost to Donegal.

'The Friday Night Lads' (TFNL) had saved for three years to attend the Olympic Games in Los Angeles in 1984. Our plan was to be there to see (or so we hoped) Ireland's great athlete, Eamonn Coghlan, go for gold. He was right on target when we opened our 'Book' to start saving in 1981. Who are the TFNL? Jimmy Keaveney (Jem); Gerry Duffy, the most capped Irish cricketer until recently; Mick Leech of Shamrock Rovers and an Ireland striker; John Drumgoole, Drummer; Joe Holmes, MBS (master bull*****er); John Pardy, banker; Willie Corr, another banker, and yours truly, Pa.

We met every Friday to share a few jars and discuss the events of the week: SPORT. It probably filled the void that was left when we retired from packing our bags to go training. My great friend Fr Jim Toal gave us his home in Burbank, LA for our three-week stay. About three weeks before the Games Eamonn Coghlan had to pull out due to a stress fracture

– I would hate to imagine how he felt. Now 'Lads', no Eamonn, no medal. Mick Leech had to pull out of the trip so my relation John McGeer was in.

We were flying out of Shannon and drove two cars to the famous Matt The Thresher's hostelry in Birdhill, a stopover I had arranged as I had two drivers to take us to the airport from there. Time to water the horses Lads! I was interested in a public house premises in Ballsbridge, and my 'arranged' stop was to hopefully receive a phone call (landline) to say the bid was in my favour. After we had a few jars one of the staff called out: "Is there a Paddy Cullen here?" I owned up and took the call amid a barrage of abuse. "Lads, I just bought a pub." All hell broke loose: more drink, but we had drivers. LA here we come!

Track and field and boxing were our ticket purchases, and not cheap either, and no Coghlan. The renovated LA Memorial Coliseum just has to be seen: it is awesome. To see world-class athletes up close is something to behold, having shared many a dressing room! The boxing arena was so large that we questioned why we were sitting in the half way section. Ah! The track and field in the open air, with 110,000 people packed in – can you imagine that? And eight Irishmen sitting in a row with Ireland stamped across our chests, in capital letters.

We witnessed the famous Mary Decker 'trip' behind the barefoot Zola Budd and saw our own Declan Hegarty in action in the hammer event. We were so proud to hear 'Hegarty, Ireland'.

On the last day of the Games we wonder if we will catch a glimpse of John Treacy or maybe Jerry Kiernan on the big screen in the stadium. Hardly. O ye of little faith! Treacy never ran a marathon before. My God, there's Kiernan, but Treacy is on the screen again and again: is this possible? They approach the stadium to a deafening sound. Carlos Lopes of Portugal is in first, way ahead, but Treacy is next. They have to complete a lap of the stadium. God, can he stay on his feet? He looks tired, but John always runs like he's tired. Charlie Spedding from Germany is not too far behind John, and is gaining. The Lads have a short discussion and agree we will settle for bronze – just stay on your feet John. Lopes is well home in a new Olympic record, and we were there! Now John, the outsider, just get over the line. John did just that by two seconds ahead of Spedding. He had that little kick at the finish, pity he didn't tell us! Thank you, John, for a wonderful end to our first Olympic Games. Jerry Kiernan came in 9th. SUPER DAY!

The Tricolour flew in that wonderful Coliseum in LA '84, a treasured memory.

We celebrated in style at a function during our visit with the greats, Eamonn Coghlan, Ronnie Delany and the charming Pat O'Callaghan who won Ireland's first Olympic gold medal in 1928 and a second in 1932 in the hammer event.

# JOHN DELANEY

## Goals to savour

JOHN DELANEY is a past pupil of Abbey CBS in Tipperary town. A chartered accountant by profession he became the Waterford United delegate to the League of Ireland and FAI in 1997. He was elected to the FAI Board of Management in 1999 and in 2001 was elected as Honorary Treasurer of the Association.

John became the youngest ever Chief Executive of the Football Association of Ireland in 2004 and has overseen massive changes in the organisation since then in addition to being at the forefront of plans to redevelop Aviva Stadium.

He is Chairman of the Aviva Stadium Company, is a member of a UEFA Committee, and vice President of the Olympic Council of Ireland. John played hurling for Arravale Rovers and soccer for St Michael's, Dundrum United and Tralee Celtic. He is married to Emer and they have two children.

There are two sporting memories that stand out for me above all the others I have had the honour and privilege to witness.

Both involve special goals but while one was scored in front of a packed stadium, a global television audience of millions and its significance reverberated around the world, the other was in front of a much smaller crowd and its impact was only felt within the Delaney family.

The first took place on Sunday, 12 June 1988 at the Neckar Stadium in Stuttgart. For many people involved in Irish football it is a cherished moment but there were several things which happened to me personally that have ensured this day is one of my special sporting memories.

It felt absolutely fantastic to be in Stuttgart on that sunny Sunday afternoon following Ireland rather than sitting at home wondering what it would be like to qualify for a European Championships or World Cup. I think a lot of others felt the same way and they travelled in their thousands by land, sea and air to be there. Not surprisingly, there was a passionate rendition of the National Anthem and six minutes into the game Ray Houghton headed the ball into the back of the English net for the sweetest and most special goal ever scored in the history of Irish football.

Of course, that magical moment came at a price because for the next 84 or so minutes every Irish fan, whether in the stadium, watching on television or listening on radio, had to endure an emotional roller coaster.

I was sitting beside the legendary RTÉ commentator Philip Greene who had retired and was at the game as a guest of the FAI in recognition of the fantastic contribution he made to the sport as the voice of Irish soccer for so many years.

During his career, Philip had more or less seen it all and he had regaled me before the match with stories of the great games and the heartbreak moments that seemed to be forever associated with Irish soccer, like the day in 1957 when Johnny Ateyo's last-minute equaliser denied Ireland a famous win over England but allowed Philip to utter that famous sentence: "The goal was greeted with silence so deafening it could be heard at Nelson's Pillar."

Philip, probably more than anybody in the Neckar Stadium that afternoon, understood the significance of what was unfolding as we got to half time with our lead intact and then to the hour mark. He was also acutely aware that, in the past, Ireland had been on the verge of famous victories only to be heartbreakingly denied, often in controversial circumstances.

We were all on the edge of our seats as the game entered its final 20 minutes when I got a dig in the ribs from Philip. I turned round and saw that he had his head in his hands.

"I can't watch it anymore. Tell me what's happening," he asked.

I couldn't believe my ears. Here was one of the greatest soccer commentators asking me to commentate to him on the biggest game ever played by Ireland. I started in a hesitant fashion. "Packie's just saved an England shot," I said.

"Who shot? How far out was he?" came the reply.

I soon realised Philip wasn't looking for the basics and soon I was providing a highly detailed running commentary as Ireland held on for an unbelievable win. At the final whistle, I screamed: "We've done it" and Philip took his head out his hands, leapt up, punched the air and then turned around and gave me a great big hug as tears streamed down both of our faces.

The final whistle kicked off a party to remember and it was one of those days you hoped would never end. At the post-match reception I got great pleasure out of shaking hands with the Chairman of the English FA, Sir Bert Millichip, and commiserating with him. The shock on his face was a sight to behold.

While I share one of my sporting memories with many Irish people, the other is much more personal and happened a couple of years ago.

One of the most important parts of my job as Chief Executive of the FAI is to visit our clubs and leagues around the country and so one Friday night while on the way to Monaghan I promised my son Thomas that I would be back home in Waterford to take him soccer training at The Villa the next morning.

I got back to Waterford at around 4 a.m. and a few hours later I was awoken by a tap on the shoulder from a young six year old already dressed in his tracksuit and wondering if it was time to go. It was one of those moments when you feel like saying: "Would you not ask your mother?" Thankfully, I resisted the urge, got up and headed for The Villa. It proved to be a shrewd decision for during the little game at the end of training Thomas scored his first ever goal and ran a few yards to celebrate it with me.

I get photographed a lot in my job but that day there were no photographers present to capture a moment that will be forever etched in my memory as he wrapped his arms around me and smiled from ear to ear.

I often tell the story of Thomas's first goal to encourage parents to take an interest in their children's activities and to realise that nothing compares to sharing those special moments like the first goal. I told that story during our Festival of Football in Wexford in 2010 and Ray Houghton, who is now an FAI Ambassador, spoke after me and joked that his father spent 20 years following him before he saw his first goal.

Ray's goal in Stuttgart was his first for Ireland and thankfully it wasn't his last. Hopefully, Thomas will also continue to find the net on a regular basis and I want to be on the touchline to see those goals because every goal, no matter what level it is scored at, is special.

# RONNIE DELANY
# From boxing to Olympic Games history

R ONNIE DELANY graduated from Villanova University in 1958 and established a marketing consultancy in 1988 following a successful executive career in the transport / tourism sector in Ireland.

He is best known as Olympic Games 1500 metres champion in Melbourne 1956 and was voted 'Champion of Champions 1950 – 2000' by the Irish public. He recorded an unprecedented and unsurpassed 40 straight victories 'indoors' in America from 1956 to 1959 including 33 mile races and was mile world record holder from 1958 to 1962.

A Freeman of Dublin City, he was conferred with a Doctorate of Laws by University College Dublin and an Honorary Fellowship by the Royal College of Surgeons in Ireland. Ronnie is an honorary member of several sporting and social clubs, is Patron of GOAL, and President of the Irish Olympians Association. Aged 76, he has four children and 15 grandchildren and enjoys music, theatre, reading, golf, tennis and swimming.

The first champion of the modern Olympics held in Athens in 1896 was James Brendan Connolly competing for the United States in the triple jump or the hop, step, and jump as it was known then. Connolly's father was from the Aran Islands and James Brendan was one of many Irishmen who won Olympic gold for the USA. This was especially so in the hammer throw event with the names of John Flanagan, Mathew McGrath and Patrick Ryan enshrined in the history of the early Olympics. Martin Sheridan from Bohola, County Mayo won successive gold medals in the discus representing the USA.

James B Connolly, a Harvard student who quit college when refused leave to take part in the Games paid his own way to Athens. He later became an acclaimed author of sea sagas and a reporter for *The Boston Globe* and *The Boston Post*. He never did return to Harvard.

John Pius Boland, born in Dublin in 1870 was Ireland's first Olympic gold medal winner in the men's singles tennis final in Athens. He later won a second gold in the doubles, partnered by Fritz Thraun from Austria. Supposedly, John Pius was holidaying in Greece and was persuaded to take part in the Games by his young Greek host, Konstantinos Manos who coincidentally was secretary of the Athens Olympic Organising Committee.

A remarkable fact perhaps is that John and I were both educated at the Catholic University School (CUS) in Leeson Street where he first became interested in tennis. He subsequently studied at Bonn University and Oxford. I went to Villanova University to complete my education. John Pius Boland, apart from being a gold medallist, was a politician, barrister, author and orator. Elected to Westminster as an MP for South Kerry from 1900 to 1918, he had a distinguished political career and enjoyed the respect and admiration of many of the leading politicians of the time and the friendship of his peers, Maud Gonne MacBride and George Bernard Shaw.

My lifelong interest in tennis was also fostered in CUS. The height of my achievement was playing for the school team and winning two Leinster Schools championship medals. I sometimes muse if I had given up my athletic ambitions could I have gone on to even greater tennis success – say Wimbledon perhaps.

But as a child I was first enthralled by the history of the heavyweight boxing championships of the world. I learned about the John L Sullivans and Jack Johnsons, Jack Dempsey and Gene Tunney and the greatest perhaps of all Joe Louis – I used to listen to the radio commentary from Madison Square Garden of so many World Championship fights in the middle of the night bonding especially with my late father and my brothers. This was a shared experience and a poignant memory for so many of my peers of their dads.

The most exciting fight of them all was in 1941 when Irishman Billy Conn took on Joe Louis for the heavyweight crown. Billy had us on the edge of our seats for perhaps eleven rounds; he was out-boxing the champ but like many others was knocked to the canvas, out cold.

I recall the British boxer Bruce Woodcock boxing beautifully against Joe Baski in Madison Square Garden 'til struck a hammer blow that dropped him into oblivion. The shock in the British commentator's voice was perhaps more remarkable.

The wonderful thing about radio commentary I recall was that you had to visualise the action with no replays or close-ups to follow. That's why I think my Olympic victory remained so visible in the minds of Irish men and women over the decades following 1956 – you could not see the race but your imagination continued to recall the lap-by-lap sequence of the race as if you were there – or so I am told. The astonishment in the English commentator's voice was palpable.

I was to move on from boxing to become inspired by the history of the Olympic Games and the greatest athletes of all time, Paavo Nurmi, Emil Zatopek, Jesse Owens, and Fanny Blankers Koen to name but a few. When I began to aspire to taking part in the Olympics I focused more and more on the Irish diaspora and their history of success. Hence my stories about James Brendan Connolly and John Pius Boland.

But when I began to dream of winning a gold medal my heroes became Dr Pat O'Callaghan, 1928 and 1932 gold medallist in the hammer, and Bob Tisdall who won gold in the 400 metres hurdles in Los Angeles. Less than 25 years before me they had won Olympic gold for Ireland. They had shown the way. They had demonstrated the achievable – the realisable.

Good luck Team Ireland in London 2012.

# TONY DORAN

## Magical memories of Wexford hurling

**T**ONY DORAN from the Buffers Alley club represented Wexford and won three All-Ireland hurling medals, one each at minor, under-21 and senior levels. He was selected as an All Star and was Texaco Hurler of the Year in 1976.

He holds two National League titles, an Oireachtas medal, four senior and four underage Leinster medals, 11 county senior titles, two Leinster club medals and an All-Ireland club medal. He played for Leinster for over a decade winning seven Railway Cup titles.

A keen quiz enthusiast, Tony came second in the GAA 125th Anniversary question time. His occupation as a farmer often came second to hurling but he also had time to have an interest in current affairs and sport in general. He is married to Mary and they have three daughters, Therese, Noelle and Marie and two sons, Tony and Pat.

Luckily for me my sporting memories stretch over a long number of years starting with that of the Wexford hurling team of the 1950s. I was totally wrapped up in their exploits and never tired of reading about them in the local and national newspapers. In those pre-television days we had to form our own images of the various players through the magical voice of Micheál O'Hehir on Radio Éireann. The names of the Rackards – Bobby, Billy and Nicky, Art Foley, Nick O'Donnell, Ned Wheeler, Jim English, Tim Flood and many more were assuming legendary status not alone in Wexford but all over the country, and how we loved them.

Before that the feats of the county footballers kept the memory bank full to capacity: they had contested six All-Ireland finals in a row from 1913 to 1918 winning the last four, the first ever four-in-a-row for any county. But things were changing rapidly in the1950s when a gallant band of heroes, many of them huge men, took the hurling world to their hearts as they blazed a trail to three All-Ireland finals in succession.

The disappointment of Wexford's loss to Cork in the 1954 All-Ireland final was a huge blow to an eight-year-old boy who thought his team should always win. Thankfully it all changed a year later when we beat Galway in the final and then had revenge over Cork in 1956. Wexford's victories over all the top teams of that period have provided me with lasting memories.

I was lucky enough to move on from those childhood days to have a long career with my club, Buffers Alley, and with Wexford. After a successful underage period in which we did well at minor and under-21 levels I was promoted to the senior team in the mid-sixties and did not have to wait too long to taste All-Ireland success in 1968. Our victory that year was very sweet and made it one that sticks out in my memory.

We began the year being eliminated from the National League in a play-off for a semi-final place against Tipperary. The preparations for the Leinster championship began with local club games, inter-county challenge matches and training in St Patrick's Park, Enniscorthy.

First up were Dublin in the Leinster semi-final. They were quite a strong team at the time having done well at minor and under-21 in the previous few years. Our campaign got off to a very good start with a pretty convincing win which put us into the final against Kilkenny, the reigning All-Ireland champions, and after an epic struggle we came out on top by the minimum margin of one point.

As Galway played in the Munster championship at that time and Antrim did not have a senior team, the win over Kilkenny saw us through to the All-Ireland final against Munster champions Tipperary, the fourth time in the 1960s for the teams to clash for the Liam MacCarthy Cup. The score stood at 2-1 in Tipperary's favour and we were determined to make it 2-2.

Our minors got the day off to a terrific start with a fine win over Cork. And the big Wexford following looked forward to more of the same in the main attraction on the hurling calendar. Naturally, Tipperary had other ideas and completely dominated the first 30 minutes – the duration of games at that time was 60 minutes. Although Jack Berry scored a Wexford goal shortly before half time the Premier County went to the break leading by a comfortable eight points.

After some harsh words from manager Padge Kehoe in the dressing room we came out for the second half prepared to give it everything. An early point settled us and I got a goal which closed the gap to four points; we were back into contention. About midway through the half I was fouled and Paul Lynch drove the resultant '21' to the back of the net and the teams were level, something which had seemed impossible 15 minutes earlier.

When I got another goal to put us into the lead, and Jack Berry notched up his second, we added on a couple of points to go eight ahead – a turnaround of 16 points with time running out. Tipperary did hit back with two late goals but we had done enough to make it 2-2 in the Wexford v Tipperary All-Ireland series of the sixties winning by 5-8 to 3-12.

To finish off the year on a high, Buffers Alley won our first ever Wexford senior hurling title when we beat Faythe Harriers by a single point in the county final. What a memorable end to a memorable year. It was magic all the way.

# MICK DOWLING

## There's no place like home

**MICK DOWLING** has the unique record in Irish amateur boxing of winning the Irish National Senior Championship title at bantamweight for eight successive years, 1968 to 1975. He boxed 60 times for Ireland and competed at the 1968 Mexico and 1972 Munich Olympic Games. He is also the proud owner of two European bronze medals.

The Kilkenny man is one of Ireland's most respected boxing coaches having served as a member of the National Coaching Committee for ten years. He is senior coach of the Mount Tallant Boxing Club and IT Tallaght boxing squad.

More recently, he trained the Leinster rugby squad in boxing conditioning and is an RTÉ boxing analyst. He was Texaco Boxer of the Year in 1968, 1969 and 1970, only one of three boxers to win such an acclaim in three successive years.

I came into boxing in a glorious era for the sport: our boxers had won four medals in the 1956 Olympic Games in Melbourne and the 1960s brought great promise. I remember going to training in the National Stadium in an old Ford Anglia car in 1965/66 and hearing 'scalpers' cry out "anyone buying or selling a ticket?" The crowds at the Stadium were huge in those years – nowadays people are more attracted to social activities and leisure pursuits and do not have the same interest in boxing, except on major occasions.

I loved going to the Stadium, even with butterflies in my stomach. Fighting out of the Arbour Hill Club, I won a national title very early in my career in 1967 against John Finn from Tramore Boxing Club in Waterford. This launched me into international competition while working in the Gresham Hotel. Following a victory over German southpaw, Horst Rascher, at the National Stadium I was selected on the Irish team for the Mexico Olympics in 1968. I reached the last eight which was a huge highlight for a young boxer who was only two and a half years in the sport. I was just nine minutes away from a bronze medal, at least, but two warnings against Eiji Morioka of Japan killed off any chance I had of taking the decision.

I retained my national title in 1969 and took part in the European Championships in Bucharest where I defeated Igor Killagin of Russia inside the distance. He was one of the best boxers of that time, but I hit a good day and had him down for the count and the fight was stopped in the second round. Not many people beat Russians and I was very pleased with that performance. Next up was an East German, Reinhard Schulz whom I stopped in the first round with a good right hand. My semi-final was against a Frenchman, Aldo Cosentino, later their national coach, and he won on a split decision.

I then had offers to turn professional and I trained in Manhattan where the promoter could not understand why a little curly-headed lad from Ireland would refuse such an opportunity. However, I liked home, I liked Ireland and being from a big family it was important to me to be close to home.

Another of my best achievements came in 1971 in the European Championships where I had a wins on points against Antonios Houliaras of Greece and Jose Luis Otero from Spain before going out with a bronze medal when losing on a split decision to Alexandr Melnikov, a classy Russian fighter.

In the Munich Olympic Games in 1972, I fought my way to a quarter-final with Cuba's Orlando Martinez. Again, I was only three rounds away from bronze, but, after nine minutes of total action by both of us, Martinez got a split decision and I was out. The Cubans were then coming into their own as a major force in international boxing. Of course, the Munich Games were totlally overshadowed by the kidnapping and terrible massacre of Israeli athletes, coaches and officials by Palestinian guerrillas belonging to the Black September organisation, something I will never forget.

John Finn from Waterford was my oponent in the national final in 1973 and I had to be at my best to win. I respected John greatly as he never ducked a division to avoid meeting me, and he is still one of my best friends. By that time I was getting tired but I continued on and retained my title in 1974 and gave it one last throw of the dice in 1975 when I won again defeating Terry Hanna, a tough fighter from the Immaculata Club in Belfast.

Emily and I had married in 1973 and our first child, Lisa, was born on 18 May 1975. Family responsibilities became a piority and I retired a few weeks after her birth. Despite media reports that I had been selected to fight against Britain I had called it a day. And by that time, in 10 years of top-class boxing, I was never beaten by an Irish or British boxer.

I had travelled the world with a sport I loved and my interest then turned to coaching. I set up the Mount Tallant Club which has been running for 27 years. Emily founded Sportsworld Running Club and Lisa owns a gym where she runs pilates, personal training, and boxing conditioning classes which are very popular. My son, Mark, is a full-time cyclist with a superb level of fitness. Stephen is a keen young boxer with loads of ability and Julie is a keen marathon runner.

We are all involved in sport in a variety of ways: I enjoy putting something worthwhile back into a sport that gave me many oportunities in life but if I were to pick my favourite sporting occasion it would have to be All-Ireland hurling final day with Kilkenny playing the best of the rest for the glory of taking the Liam MacCarthy Cup to the Marble City and to the towns, villages and townlands on both sides of the River Nore.

# ANGELA DOWNEY

## Singing and dancing in the rain

**A**NGELA DOWNEY, along with her twin sister Ann, starred for the St Paul's club and Kilkenny county camogie teams for over 25 years. She won 13 Leinster senior titles with Kilkenny and 12 All-Irelands from 1974 to 1994, including seven-in-a-row from 1985 to 1991.

She also holds eight National League medals and was Texaco Camogie Player of the Year in 1986 and was an automatic choice on the Team of the Century. Angela has 22 county medals and six All-Ireland Club titles.

She is one of a family of five children of Shem and Brigid, is married to Ted Browne from Limerick and they have two children, Katie and Conor. Her leisure interests include gardening, walking and golf.

As you can imagine, any sporting career that spans more than a quarter of a century is bound to contain a plethora of memories – some good, some not so good. Some of my favourite memories include marching behind the Artane Boys Band on All-Ireland final day with my four year-old daughter Katie as our mascot, winning seven All-Irelands in a row, travelling as a guest to the Skydome in Toronto with the All Star hurling and football teams, and how could I ever forget a most memorable 'This is your life' evening hosted by Micheál Ó Muircheartaigh attended by friends and rivals from the four corners of Ireland.

Without doubt I have had a great innings on the camogie field from colleges, to club, to county. I was privileged to be a member of a very successful St Paul's team while playing alongside some of the most talented and skilful players that ever graced a pitch in either hurling or camogie. I won club and county honours at a very young age with both St Paul's and Kilkenny. Winning 12 senior All-Irelands and five Club All-Irelands with St Paul's, in hindsight, is no mean feat.

When I reflect on such memorable and heroic victories and, indeed, some defeats there is little doubt that the club All-Ireland of 1994 with Lisdowney is the sweetest of all. Why? Well – Picture the scene.

Venue: My native parish pitch at Ballyragget on a cold November day.

Objective: To win a first Club All-Ireland title with neighbouring Lisdowney and smash hot favourites Glen Rovers' (Cork) ambitions of winning their third All-Ireland club title in a row.

Throughout the game I was being policed and, I may add, curtailed by Glen captain Sandie Fitzgibbon. As half time approached and with only four points registered on our scoreboard, I remember gathering a ball about 45 yards out. I got past a couple of tackles and shot hard from 20 yards. The sliotar ricocheted off Mary Ring (Yes! Christy's daughter) but I snatched it again. I sent a cute hand pass to the corner of the net but Mairead O'Leary made a superb reflexive save. I said to myself, "It's not going to be your day, Angela" and I'm sure few among the home following gave us any chance. With 14 minutes of the second half gone we were 1-13 to 0-6 in arrears. Finbar McCarthy from the Glen was heard reporting live to Cork local radio and advising his listeners, "Glen Rovers now lead by 10 points. There is no way Angela Downey can pull this one out of the fire for Lisdowney." I then scored four goals and we proceeded to devastate our more illustrious opponents and reigning All-Ireland champions by 5-9 to 1-15. The Glen girls departed the scene with heads bowed, totally dejected and bewildered. We sang and danced and went berserk in the rain.

So why does this rank as my greatest sporting memory? Well, for a few reasons.

No 1. A turnover of 15 points in 14 minutes: 1-14 to 0-8 became 1-15 to 5-9.

No 2. I was by then a 37-year-old mother and should have been well withdrawn into the shadows of retirement.

No 3. By any standards this was a victory born out of indomitable spirit and pride. Each and every girl played her heart out to bring honour and glory to our parish against a club team that included ten inter-county stars in their team. The fact that the venue for this was my homeland of St Patrick's Ballyragget – the very pitch on which I played my first primary school game – was the icing on the cake.

No 4. To witness the sheer pride and joy, delight and ecstasy among both players and supporters of a tiny rural parish having slain the Goliath of camogie are memories that one only dreams of. That November day, our dream became a reality.

# JOHNNY DOYLE

## Joy unbridled on winning Kildare and Leinster titles

**J**OHNNY DOYLE from the Allenwood club has been a tower of strength for Kildare senior football team since 1999. He won a Leinster medal in the Millennium year, has two interprovincial medals and was top scorer in the All-Ireland championships of 2008 and 2010.

He won a Kildare senior medal in 2004 and has a county under-21 medal. Johnny has also won an Agricultural Colleges All-Ireland. He was chosen as Kildare Footballer of the Year in 2004 and 2005. His talents are many and varied: he holds an All-Ireland Colleges cross country medal and won several boxing medals.

He was named as a 2010 Vodafone GAA football All Star and has captained his county for five seasons. The popular Lilywhite player is noted for his association with many charity and fundraising events.

When asked to contribute to this book and add my best sporting memories I thought "Yes, that's no problem, that's easy enough" but as I sat down to put pen to paper it wasn't as easy as I thought. From a very early age I was introduced to sport. Well, one sport... Gaelic football and that came from an influence that remained with me throughout my life, my dad. Sport was a very big part of out family life and many Saturday afternoons were spent in the company of Brendan O' Reilly and *Sports Stadium* on RTÉ television. The voices of Jimmy Magee, Mick Dunne, Fred Cogley and the great Micheál O'Hehir were often heard blasting out of the TV as we jumped around the sitting room to cheer our heroes on.

I have so many great memories of great occasions in Irish sport down the years; John Treacy winning his Olympic medal in Los Angeles in '84; Barry McGuigan and his world boxing title in '85; Stephen Roche winning the Tour de France in '87; the Boys in Green in Italia '90 led by big Jack. I also remember Anthony Daly banishing the curse of Biddy Early in '95 and Dennis Taylor winning the world snooker title with the last black in '85. So, to pick one highlight is next to impossible, and I'm not going to pick one; I'm going to pick two, and surprise, surprise, they are both GAA-related and very close to home.

It was a magical time around the plains of Kildare in the summer of 1998 when Mick O'Dwyer's mighty men were on the march to try to win the county's first All-Ireland final since 1928. Now, around these parts we are world famous for horse racing where we produced some of the best trainers and jockeys the world has ever seen. However, nothing grips this county like Gaelic football and for a county that has had many lean years, the people of Kildare are unbelievably passionate about their football. Three great games with Meath in the 1997 Leinster championship whetted the appetite and while Kildare didn't progress, it certainly heightened expectations.

From early 1998 there was an air of anticipation around the county. Attendances were up for the O'Byrne Cup and this continued throughout the league. By championship time the bandwagon was in full swing and what a first round it was against Dublin in Croke Park. This was the real test; Dublin were the bogey team that we came so close to beating in previous years but just fell short. This time we were ready. This was our year.

The game ended in a draw and we could have won it but we lived to fight another day. And what a day that was! A point to spare. The county went mad because the mighty Dubs were gone and the Lilywhites were on the march.

The only problem for us in Allenwood was that our local hero, Ken Doyle, broke his arm and was out of action for a few months. Laois were easily accounted for in the next match. We were back in the big time. Leinster final here we come! The flags and the bunting went up and the county was on a high. For the first time ever young lads proudly wore Kildare jerseys in the streets.

We headed for Croke Park to bring home the Delaney Cup for the first time since 1956... a lifetime. This time we faced Meath who were All-Ireland champions just two years previously. I got my ticket for Hill 16 which Kildare took over for the day.

The game was in the balance with about two minutes to go when Dermot Earley won a kick-out from Christy Byrne. He sent the ball towards the Nally Stand. Martin Lynch caught it and sent a wonderful pass across to big Brian Murphy on the 13-metre line, and BANG! 'Murph' rattled the net. Croke Park erupted. Were the years of hard luck stories finally over? The game finished 1-12 to 10 points. Kildare were Leinster champions – what an unbelievable feeling.

As the crowds spilled on to the hallowed sod I met grown men in tears. Kildare went on to beat Kerry which saw Ken back to give a man-of-the-match display as an added bonus. However, they fell at the last hurdle when losing to Galway by four points in the All-Ireland final. To witness Glenn Ryan lifting the Delaney Cup that day was a very special moment, one I'll never forget. It was the highlight of a great summer for Kildare supporters, and it's one of my greatest sporting memories.

The second sporting memory is a lot closer to home and a journey I was proud to be part of. The year was 2004 and the event was the Kildare senior championship. Allenwood is one of four clubs in the parish of Allen situated in west Kildare near the Offaly border. 'The Blues' was formed in 1956 to accommodate the influx of people who came to work in the ESB and Bord na Móna at the time.

The club was successful very quickly winning the junior A championship in 1961 and the intermediate championship in 1962 but had to wait until 1971 to get to our first senior final which we lost to neighbours Carbury.

When we began the 2004 campaign we seemed to be as far away as ever from landing the Dermot Bourke Cup. The format of the championship had changed. There were now four groups of four with the top two teams from each group heading for the quarter-finals. We drew with Raheens in our first game and beat Celbridge in the second. The third and final game was against Round Towers which we lost, 2-9 to 1-7. Our year looked to be over but we scraped into the quarter-final on three points.

Clane were our victims in the quarter-final and, without noticing, we were in a semi-final against the mighty Sarsfields. The game was fixed for Saturday 11 September, the day our captain, Johnny Wiltshire, and his wife to be, Julie, were to be married. After a bit of negotiating with the county board, the game was fixed for 4 p.m. and John (or maybe it was Julie) agreed to bring the wedding forward to a 1.30 p.m. 'throw-in' in Allen Church.

We were definitely the best dressed football team to ever arrive at a game as we came straight from the church in our swallowtail coats to St Conleth's Park. The bridal party were treated to champagne and the groom played a starring role as we took down the mighty 'Sash'. Off we went to the Keadeen Hotel to celebrate a wedding and a county final appearance. What a day!

The final was against St Laurence's, another club still looking for their first county title. To make matters more complicated, my better half at the time (now Mrs Doyle), was a staunch 'Larries' woman and her nephew was a vital part of their forward line. Life got very awkward for the next few weeks!

Siobhan wasn't too heartbroken when Allenwood were crowned Kildare senior champions for the first time two weeks later. It's hard to explain the emotion on that day as old men wept with joy to see 'the Blues' finally crowned kings of Kildare. These were the 'die-hards' who formed the club in the old wooden hall back in the '50s and kept it going in the early years. And this was the team's ultimate tribute to these men.

On a personal note, Kildare's fortunes have improved greatly in the last few years. It has been nice to play in three All-Ireland quarter-finals and a semi-final in four successive years. However, I'm facing 2012 in the hope that my greatest sporting memory is yet to come.

# PÁRAIC DUFFY

## Forty-one years is a long wait

**P**ÁRAIC DUFFY has been Director General of the Gaelic
Athletic Association since 1 February 2008. Prior to that he
was the GAA Player Welfare Manager and is a former
chairperson of the Monaghan County Board.

He chaired the national Coaching and Games Develepment
Committee between 2003 and 2006. He also headed the GAA
Games Administration Committee from 2000 to 2003. He was the
International Rules Tour Manager in Australia in 2001 and also
took charge of two Junior Tours.

Páraic played at senior level with Castleblayney Faughs and was
a selector of the Monaghan senior team between 1983 and 1987.
He held several officer positions in his native county and was
principal of St Macartan's College, Monaghan. He and his wife
Vera have a daughter, Nuala, and two sons, Mark who plays with
Scotstown and Paul who is involved in the Clanna Gael Fontenoys
club in Dublin.

My best sporting memories all relate to Monaghan. Growing up in
Castleblayney, I can recall, as a child, racing onto the pitch in Ballybay as
the Faughs won another senior championship title. As a teacher in St
Macartan's College there was huge excitement on days of memorable
victories but one year encapsulates the joy and passion that comes with
success on the GAA fields. That was 1979, the year that Monaghan ended
the county's long 41-year wait for an Ulster senior title and 27 years
without a provincial final appearance.

The excitement that marked Monaghan's Ulster final victory over
Donegal in Clones on 22 July 1979 came to my mind in the aftermath of
Dublin's victory over Kerry in the 2011 All-Ireland final. For Monaghan
people, the most loyal of GAA supporters, it marked the end of a 41-year
famine and it was celebrated with as much euphoria as the All-Ireland
win by the Dubs.

At the beginning of the year there was little reason to think that the 1979 season would be any different to those that had gone before but Scotstown's success in reaching the All-Ireland club final – they lost to Nemo Rangers in a snowstorm in Croke Park – provided a St Patrick's Day boost to the county as a whole.

In the early part of the year the form of the team in the National Football League was mixed but a winning Dr McKenna Cup campaign provided a timely morale booster before the onset of the Ulster championship. Wins over Tyrone, Fermanagh and, most notably, a fancied Armagh team, underlined the improvements already underway under the management team headed up by Seán McCague, who was later to become President of the GAA. McCague was Monaghan's Mick O'Dwyer and Brian Cody all in one and was to lead Monaghan to a National Football League title and three Ulster championships. The 1979 success came after a particularly depressing period of county team performances and there is no doubt that it was McCague's inspirational personality and tactical shrewdness that was the key driver of success in 1979.

Down were first up in championship action and a robust and committed approach at Castleblayney helped Monaghan record a 0-14 to 0-10 win and a ticket to the semi-final. The quality of opposition in no way declined thereafter with Armagh waiting in the wings at Breffni Park on a day when Monaghan produced their best performance of the championship to win on a scoreline of 2-10 to 2-8. I remember standing on the grassy bank on that afternoon and watching in amazement as Monaghan produced football of a quality I had never witnessed from a Monaghan team before.

With Donegal accounting for Derry on the other side of the draw, the scene was set for a first ever final meeting of Monaghan and Donegal in a game that took place in Clones. I will never forget the build-up to that game. The county was awash with Monaghan flags and Donegal support was lost among the packed crowd in Clones on a beautifully sunny 22 July.

Monaghan players drew obvious inspiration from their passionate support and with Kieran 'Jap' Finlay scoring 1-9, decades of failure ended in a 1-15 to 0-11 victory. I will always remember the emotional scenes as referee, Hugh Duggan, now a key figure in San Francisco GAA circles, blew the final whistle as we witnessed Monaghan being crowned Ulster champions for the first time since 1938.

No fewer than five civic receptions followed in the county's five towns on the Monday night and the win gripped the county in the weeks that followed – in part helped by the semi-final it set up against an all-conquering Kerry team. We may have over celebrated because our All-Ireland semi-final fate was to be a hefty hiding from Kerry but even that couldn't take away from what had been a fantastic season.

As county PRO, I was fortunate to have a bird's eye view of the season and to see at first hand how an outstanding manager could draw the very best from some of the most committed GAA players I have ever met; Paddy Kerr, Gerry McCarville, Nudie Hughes, Eamonn Tavey and captain Brendan Brady to name but a few... and provide some of my best sporting memories.

# BERNARD DUNNE

## Hard work pays off at O2 title fight

**B**ERNARD DUNNE was born in Neilstown, Clondalkin, County Dublin on 6 February 1980. He boxed at amateur level for Ireland recording 119 wins in 130 fights and winning 13 Irish titles. He was never beaten by an Irishman in his amateur career.

He began his professional boxing career in December 2001 in the United States winning his first 14 bouts while based in LA. Bernard then moved back to Ireland and won the IBC Super Bantamweight and the European Super Bantamweight titles. On 21 March 2009 he defeated Panamanian Ricardo Cordoba for the WBA Super Bantamweight world title in a contest chosen as ESPN's Fight of the Year.

Bernard announced his retirement from boxing on 19 February 2010. He is a regular contributor to many radio and televison programmes. He is well known for his work for the Bernard Dunne Charities and he published his autobiography, *Bernard Dunne, My Story* in 2009.

It was my dream from childhood to win a world boxing title and it really took off in earnest when I lasted only 86 seconds against Kiko Martinez in 2008 after he knocked me out. It was a devastating blow to my ambitions after being on a high when I thought the world was my oyster. People said I had difficulties, that doubts crept in, and I had to take stock of my team and my management. I had no doubts about myself; one defeat does not change a boxer overnight. I decided to get back on the horse and achieve my lifetime ambition.

My next fight was against Felix Machado at Breaffy House in Castlebar. There was an unusual sense of apprehension on the night, a weird atmosphere. People were not sure what to expect – whether I'd be my old self or be cautious and wary of being caught again. I won that fight and two others after that and then had the offer to box Ricardo Cordoba who was world super bantamweight champion at the time. This was a huge opportunity for me as he was one of the best super bantamweights of that era. He was very experienced for a 24-year-old and had boxed several of the best fighters in the world.

I was getting ready for the big challenge, my confidence was high and I was looking forward to making the most of my opportunity. Mike McGurn put me through a severe physical training programme and pushed me to the limits of my endurance. Harry Hawkins was my boxing coach and we worked together in Belfast for 12 weeks, a very long time to be in isolation, away from my wife and children and on a routine of training, eating and resting. It was constant; I kept my head down, concentrated on the job in hand and pushed myself as far as I possibly could as I knew that I would need extraordinary determination to win the title.

The media were not very optimistic about my chances of success and gave me little encouragement or hope: I was painted as a lamb going to the slaughter! I actually never read the papers but I gathered from the line of questioning from reporters at various press conferences leading up to the fight that they really gave me no chance. That suited me fine as that meant there was no real pressure on me and I could just relax and focus on what I wanted to achieve. I knew I could achieve my goal and when you think like that, anything is possible: I knew I was capable of beating anyone.

I returned to Dublin the Wednesday before the fight determined to go to war, and so it turned out. Just before the fight I was standing behind the screen waiting to make my entrance when Cordoba stood down the hall from me shadow boxing. When I walked out the crowd went wild: it was a crazy scene and set the tone for the fight. There were so many Irish supporters it lifted my spirits even higher. I got a great buzz from that, and the adrenalin flowed.

As I walked to the ring I gave my dad the 'knuckles' and Harry kept telling me what to do: "Keep doing what you always do. Focus on every three minutes; each three minutes is a new fight and you have to concentrate on that, forget about what went before." It's like concentrating on the next ball, the next puck of a sliotar. The fight would be 12 three-minute rounds, each round a fight on its own.

When the bell went there was no tapping around, no preparatory work at all. We just got into a battle and went at each other. I caught him with a peach of a left hook, my best punch ever, and thought the fight was over in round three. He got back on his feet and I could not believe it. It took a super-human effort to do so and I wondered how he came back: like in any sport, you know when you have hit the spot, and I had done that. Later I was glad he had got back on his feet as the fight became a classic and had it finished in three rounds that would not have been the case.

In round four we clashed heads and I had blurred vision from that moment on. I was dropped twice in five and after the second knockdown I had no idea where I was. It was only when I looked up and saw that my mother was not looking at me that I realised I was on the canvas. It was like an out-of-body experience. I had a full conversation with myself about what I was doing and knew if I didn't get up that my boxing career was over and if it was what was I going to do next. I knew I was capable of more so I got up but Cordoba wanted to end it there and then and attacked me like a whirlwind. He jumped all over me. But thankfully he couldn't finish the job.

When I went back to my corner Harry kept telling me to concentrate on the next three minutes, a new fight, and that was all that mattered. The strains of 'The Fields of Athenry' rang round the arena and that lifted my spirits again. I raised my hand in the air and got the crowd going. The fight took a whole new swing again in round six and I'm sure Cordoba could not believe I was coming back out to fight him. I put my hand in the air to let the crowd know I was still there and they went absolutely crazy.

I kept getting stronger and stronger from this point and by round eight I was right back in the fight. In round 10 he made a huge effort to end the fight and get out of there with his belt. He threw more punches in that round than in any other. Again I fought back and countered his attacks as much as possible.

Round 11 really changed my life and fulfilled my dreams. We were both tired but I caught Cordoba with a quick combination that sent him to the canvas. Like a true champion, he got back to his feet. We met in the centre of the ring and I caught him clean again with a left hook which sent him sprawling on the floor. Again he got up but seemed in serious trouble at this stage and looked as if he could be stopped but the referee decided to allow him to go on. I chased him down and just tried to really let my hands fly and end the fight. However, he got away from me and I could hear my coach shouting at me to get after him. I pinned him on the ropes over by his corner, got low and threw a straight right hand and a left hook. By the time the left hook landed he was already on his way down and I was about to be crowned word champion.

The crowd were ecstatic as I celebrated my victory but I took time to check on Cordoba who was not moving while being attended to by the medics.

I was world champion in front of a wild and excited crowd in the O2 Arena. I had achieved everything I set out to do and it justified all the training, the sacrifices of being away from family and friends and giving up my social life. For all my team and everyone who helped me it was payback time, and how they enjoyed the moment.

The Ireland rugby team had won the Six Nations Grand Slam earlier that day so it was a double celebration for the country, a great day in Irish sporting history. I celebrated their win and I know they celebrated mine.

I believe that nobody should be a victim of circumstances: if you believe in your dream, go for it. Look for the perfect event to achieve your ambition and work hard to make it happen. I know: I had my boyhood dream as young lad in Neilstown and I worked hard to become champion of the world.

# ADRIAN EAMES
## Two Sundays, two summers

**S**LIGO native Adrian Eames is a producer and presenter with RTÉ Sport. He joined Mid West Radio in July 1990 as host of the Breakfast show and was the first voice heard on independent radio outside of Dublin.

Adrian worked with North West Radio and Century Radio before moving to FM 104 in 1993 as a sports reporter and he joined RTÉ in the summer of 1998. He commentated on his first World Cup in 2010 and has commentated on the Champions League final. In 2008, he headed up RTÉ Radio's coverage of the Olympic Games in Beijing, which won a PPI Radio award.

He presented *Saturday Sport* before taking on the *Sunday Sport* programme. Adrian has reported and commentated on soccer and Gaelic games for radio and television and will be in charge of radio output of the London 2012 Olympics.

It would creep up on me without any great warning and usually just a few hours before the 'off': A Connacht Championship Sunday. My father would say: "Do you want to go the game?" knowing full well what the answer was going to be. At the time I mightn't have had a clue who was playing, but the one thing I did know was that wherever it was happening and no matter who was playing, I wanted to be there!

Being raised in Sligo and reared on a diet of Sligo Rovers matches, I would always know when there was a game on in the Showgrounds. My dad brought me to those matches on the bar of a bike and so I'd know that we were unlikely to be travelling to Cork to see Rovers playing Cork Hibs, so "Which game is that?" I'd ask, while already getting ready to go. "Leitrim are playing today. There is a bus going and there's a place on it if you want to go," he'd reply. Those were the days when only the All-Ireland semi-finals and finals were televised live. So, as a sports-mad youngster, the thoughts of going to a big match in somewhere like Carrick-on-Shannon or Hyde Park was too good an opportunity to turn down; besides, there was also the possibility of getting some Taytos and maybe a bottle of Coke!

So my father, who left Rossinver in north Leitrim for work in Sligo in the forties and myself would head off on the bus listening to the rest of the excited travelling customers talking with such confidence about football, that they must surely be right on all issues: "Such and such a player shouldn't be playing because he's useless," while I listened wide-eyed about the really good player who "for some reason" wasn't being given a chance. Perplexed faces all around the bus, including one busily munching crisps.

I especially remembered the talk about Mickey Martin, as if one man alone could drive a team to glory, as if he held the key to make that day special for Leitrim. By the time we reached Carrick, Mickey had taken on all the attributes of a god, given the plaudits bestowed upon him on the bus from Sligo. And being a keen young sportsman myself, I watched out for this "brilliant player" and, sure enough, the gospel of the travelling bus was correct. He was exceptional but more often than not Mickey and Leitrim ended up losing out.

It didn't bother me hugely as I was young and I was from Sligo and I had other fish to fry, with Mickey Kearns and his colleagues in the championship, while the Rovers were always striving, like Leitrim, to make a breakthrough. Nonetheless, I kept a place in my heart for Leitrim when it came to the championship. Summers would roll by and each passing year would see Leitrim departing the Connacht campaign, beaten but always proud.

Mickey Martin had departed the senior scene by the time 1994 came around and Leitrim once again set about mounting a campaign, beating Roscommon by a point and then Galway by a similar margin after a replay before taking on Mayo in the final in Hyde Park.

It was a game I had to attend so I headed from Dublin to Roscommon and eventually secured a coveted ticket for the Hyde. Leitrim made a terrible start by conceding a goal in the first minute, but there was a great resilience in John O'Mahony's team that day and they simply refused to be beaten. They'd had too much of that down through the years and it wasn't going to happen, not on that day and not in that summer.

One of the enduring images of that day is the post-match scene, when Leitrim supporters swarmed onto the pitch to celebrate – and boy did they celebrate! Young and old, they were all there. There was the palpable sense of an outpouring of emotion. Joy, absolutely, but tinged too with years of pent-up frustration, not just to do with crushing heartbreak on the playing fields, but perhaps also reflecting the mood of a county which traditionally suffered from the blight of unemployment and emigration.

One of the other great moments from that July day was the picture of a beaming Leitrim captain, Declan Darcy, holding the Nestor Cup alongside Tom Gannon, who led the county to their only previous Connacht success in 1927. It was a special snapshot on a special day.

And I was simply delighted to be there to savour it all. In a way I was there for my dad and maybe in a way for some of those who travelled on that bus back in the seventies, when defeat was likely to be the result at the end of the journey.

It was a day for all those who backed Leitrim and of course for all those who toiled without getting a reward, lads like Mickey Martin.

I'm sure Mickey would have loved to look back on a Connacht senior success, but it wasn't to be.

I know that in the modern day sporting success is deemed to be everything. At least that's what we are continuously told. 'Sport is for winners, losers are nowhere' goes the mantra. The Leitrim winners of 1994 are in the record books. They will always have that.

But there are others who became heroes, one day, one summer, on a bus to Carrick.

# DERMOT EARLEY

## Watch the breaking ball

**D**ERMOT EARLEY JUNIOR, a captain in the Irish Army, held a regular midfield place on the Kildare senior football team from 1987 until injury curtailed his involvement in 2010. He won two Leinster medals – in 1998, when the Lilywhites went on to All-Ireland defeat to Galway, and in 2000 when they defeated Dublin in a replay.

The 33-year-old represented Ireland in the International Rules series in 1999 and 2001 on tour to Australia and in 2000 and 2006 in Ireland. Dermot won two All-Star awards for his performances in 1998 and 2009 and has three county medals with his club, Sarsfields.

A son of the late Lt General Dermot, he will be remembered for many a year for his brave display in the Kildare versus Antrim qualifier game in Newbridge on the day his father was laid to rest in June 2010.

Having had the honour of playing for Kildare since 1997 I have been fortunate to have so many happy memories each time I have pulled on the all-white jersey. My senior inter-county debut against Meath on 6 July 1997 is something that I'll never forget, nor will I forget Kildare's great Leinster final win in 1998, and the privilege of playing in the All-Ireland final later that year even though it ended in disappointment after we lost to an excellent Galway team. However, the memory that really sticks out for me all through the years is the All-Ireland semi-final win against Kerry in 1998.

After winning Leinster that year and bridging a 42-year gap to claim our first provincial title since 1956 I didn't think it could have got any better. As Leinster champions we were up against Kerry, the reigning All-Ireland champions, in Croke Park on 30 August 1998. I remember the build-up to the game which had huge media emphasis on the fact that Mick O'Dwyer, the former Kerry player and manager, was pitting himself as Kildare manager against his old team. On top of that, his son Karl, a former Kerry player, was also playing full forward for us that day.

Looking back I think that all the attention on Micko helped us get on with the job in hand as players, and training for the few weeks before the game was ferocious with players gunning for places on the team. We also had the added novelty of training in front of big crowds in Newbridge, something that had never happened before.

The week before the game, Niall Buckley, who was our best player and arguably the best player in the country at that time, pulled a hamstring. We knew as players that he wasn't right because he wasn't training that week and was getting treatment instead but we all thought he was going to make the game.

The morning of the match we were seen off by a big crowd at the Johnstown Inn where we always met and the number of cars with white flags that we passed on the way up the N7 was astonishing. When we got to Croke Park about an hour and a half before the game Micko told me in the dressing room that Niall failed a fitness test and that I was going in at midfield in his place. I remember thinking to myself I would be marking Darragh Ó Sé. I left the dressing room which was under the new Cusack Stand and made my way up to the seats to seek out my mother and father. I would often get some last-minute advice from my father before a game and felt I needed it a bit more that day. I told him Niall was out and that I was going in at midfield and he said: "Watch the breaking ball…don't mind the clean catch in such a minefield, the breaking ball is most important. The very best of luck," and off I went to get ready.

It was a hot day and we ran out to a huge roar. I remember walking in the parade and looking at the sea of white in the crowd of 65,000. It seemed every Kildare person was in Croke Park that day. The game itself is a bit of a blur and it was played with a ferocity and intensity I never experienced before. It became even more of a blur when my head collided with Glenn Ryan's knee before half time and I got slightly concussed. We went in at half time five points to four ahead. I can't remember much of the team talk at half time but the eagerness to go out for the second half was evident on the face of every player. We stretched our lead out to five points mid way through the second half but Kerry came back at us. I remember catching a ball from a Christy Byrne kick out which seemed to hang forever before coming down in a crowded midfield. It was something I always dreamed of, catching a kick out in midfield in Croke

Park in front of a full house against the top players. My dream came true on this occasion. When I landed my momentum took me forward and I was fouled just short of the 45m line in the Kerry half of the pitch. My exuberance from the catch and the slightly concussed head made me want to take the free and put it over but Karl O'Dwyer persuaded me to give it to him and he duly sent it over. Martin Lynch then scored a cracking point as he was falling to leave it 12 points to 1-7. Kerry had a goal that would have levelled it but Denis Dwyer was in the small square and it was disallowed. The last five minutes seemed to go on forever and Kerry scored two points to leave the margin at one point. As Anthony Rainbow was attacking down the left side of the pitch under the old Hogan Stand the referee blew the final whistle. We had won!

It was a euphoric moment; I remember sinking to the ground only to be surrounded by a crowd of Kildare supporters who had made their way onto the pitch. I didn't really see that many players on the pitch such was the number of supporters but when I finally made my way to the tunnel I met Anthony Rainbow where we just hugged each other and kept saying, "We're in the All-Ireland final, we're in the All-Ireland final." As I made my way to the dressing room door a TV camera was placed in front of me and a reporter asked me: "What's it like to be in an All-Ireland final?" When I heard those words the emotion of the day caught up with me and all I managed to say with tears in my eyes was: "Ah stop, it's incredible."

We didn't manage to beat Galway that year in the All-Ireland final but the memories of the semi-final day and the pride and passion of that team will forever stay with me. I have had some great memories since but, unfortunately, through no lack of trying with the current Kildare team, we have yet to have the experience of winning the Sam Maguire Cup... but 2012 is only around the corner!

# DESSIE FARRELL

## Sport matters

**D**ESSIE FARRELL, born in 1971, won an All-Ireland senior football medal with Dublin in 1995 and has six Leinster championship medals. He represented Dublin at minor and under-21 levels and captained the county under-21 hurlers in 1992.

He won three Dublin football titles (1999 to 2001) and a Leinster medal in 2000 with Na Fianna. Dessie collected an All-Star award in 1995 and in 52 championship appearances for Dublin he scored three goals and fifty-eight points. He also played representative hockey with Leinster and Ireland. In 1989, he won a Leinster Colleges soccer medal, and a Gaelic football medal with St. Vincent's CBS, Glasnevin.

He currently manages the Dublin minor football team and is CEO of the Gaelic Players Association, the official representative body for county hurlers and Gaelic footballers. He recently graduated with an MBA from DCU. His autobiography, *Dessie Tangled up in Blue*, was published in 2005.

Maybe it's the primitive rawness, the naked ambition stripped bare, but for me boxing has always been the ultimate athletic challenge.

My interest in sport was nurtured by my parents, both of whom were steeped in Gaelic football through their own backgrounds in Donegal and Kildare. But while I was obviously drawn to football from a very young age many of my earliest iconic sporting memories and indeed inspirations came from inside the ring.

As a child of the 1970s, I grew up during a golden age of boxing. Ali was the universal icon but I was too young to experience, first hand, the impact of the big fights against Foreman and Frazier in 1974 and 1975.

The 1980s heralded an incredible era of middleweight contests and the performances of Sugar Ray Leonard, Thomas Hearns, Roberto Durán and Marvin Hagler were the backdrop to my own development as a young footballer and hurler.

However, the impact of an Irishman taking a world title belt in front of my own eyes was profound and I can recall the sense of sporting ecstasy when Barry McGuigan defeated Eusebio Pedroza for the WBA featherweight crown in 1985. I must admit that it was a feeling I experienced again when my old neighbour, Steve Collins, and Bernard Dunne went on to replicate Barry's success.

As someone whose life has been committed to our indigenous sports, I have always looked on somewhat enviously at Irish athletes prevailing on the international stage. Indeed I'm often reminded that my path crossed with Padraig Harrington during a schools Gaelic football match while former Irish international Kenny Cunningham was a school friend and a team mate of mine in Na Fianna.

The exploits of the likes of McGuigan, cyclists Sean Kelly and Stephen Roche, the great Irish soccer team of the late 1980s and early 1990s, and snooker players Alex Higgins and Dennis Taylor were hugely motivational, even for a young Gaelic footballer getting his first taste of life in a Dublin jersey.

Of course these memories are eventually dwarfed by the privilege of winning an All-Ireland football medal with Dublin in 1995 but I've little doubt that many GAA players are inspired by the success of not only great athletes in their own sport but also by their fellow country men and women in other sports.

The recent successes of our golfers, amateur boxers and rugby teams are a case in point and, along with the continued success of Gaelic football and hurling on the national stage, they are also testimony to the potential for sporting excellence in this country. And I say potential because any time I'm drawn to reminisce about sport I'm also inclined to think of how much better things could be in Ireland if we gave sport a more prominent role in our society.

For sure, the various governing bodies and agencies in Ireland have been hugely successful in developing sports.

However, I believe that they are let down by the lack of status for sport within society and particularly in our educational system, specifically at primary and secondary level where it remains outside of the formal curriculum. So why not establish sport right at the heart of the classroom?

This is done in other countries. In Northern Ireland and in the UK pupils can take PE Studies at A level. For some reason we don't afford the same recognition to sport in our education system. I believe if we did introduce sport and exercise as a formal examinable subject in our secondary schools, sport and physical exercise would be taken more seriously at primary school level too. This might in turn go some way towards our children receiving the recommended 60 minutes per day of physical activity per child.

Thankfully, we can study subjects like music, drama and art in our secondary schools – but why not sport – with both a theoretical and practical component? Why, as a society, do we not see the need to afford this discipline the same status as others?

Our educational system is predicated on academic ability. It has a hierarchical structure; at the top is mathematics and languages; in the middle are the humanities and at the bottom are the arts. Sport doesn't even register in real terms; for example, there is no exam and the subject isn't accounted for within the CAO system.

As we know, intelligence can be measured in a whole host of different ways. There are so many hugely talented, brilliant and creative people who think they are not valued, simply because the thing they are good at and passionate about is not valued. This is wrong. Our education system should encourage diversity and creativity, not stymie it. A half hour or 40 minutes of PE in a week for a primary school child is shameful. Most will not argue but the appetite to change this sedentary existence for many children is not there. I am not an expert in this area and a little knowledge can indeed be a dangerous thing, but it is my understanding having spoken to some people who are well versed on these issues, that so much more could be done to improve things. Simple things like the introduction of a fundamental range of movement to school pupils at the earliest age is known to assist children with their perception of their own competence in sport which has a significant impact on keeping them involved in sports as they grow older.

I have spoken to many people recently on the subject of upgrading the positioning of sport in society and our education system, and there are very few dissenting voices. Actually I haven't heard one. If there was a willingness to place sport on a higher plane in this country, particularly in the education system, the positive implications could be immense. These benefits are universally accepted; assisting in addressing ever-increasing health issues such as obesity; tackling social problems; combating poor self-esteem and self-confidence while improving academic achievement and lifelong participation in sport, providing greater social capital, social cohesion and community wellbeing along with other important economic benefits, employment and so on.

For sure, we do have experience of many of the above benefits already but only to a limited extent, especially when you consider the potential if the status of sport was elevated in the manner suggested.

While we think we are a sports-mad nation, I believe the reality is different. As a nation we like to observe more than participate. Statistics with which I won't bore you will back this up. We don't allow ourselves to be compared with other true sporting nations like Australia, blaming the weather here. But yet in Canada and in the Nordic countries where their climate is very difficult, they put us to shame in relation to where sport is positioned on their social agenda. Then we justify our ambiguity towards sport due to the lack of facilities and resources. But this too is a smokescreen. In Finland, because of health issues we are now experiencing, the schools introduced an exercise break in the classroom a couple of times a day with dramatic effect.

If there is 'the will' there is always a way.

This is not about an elitist pipedream aimed at hot-housing talent (which would also be an indirect benefit), it is about recognising and taking seriously the critical role that sport and physical exercise has to play in society with its inherent health and developmental benefits from the beginning, while laying the foundations for a lifelong commitment to sport and physical activity resulting in greater individual and collective happiness and wellbeing.

To take it a step further – why is that children from socially disadvantaged areas are not provided with the same access to sport as others? The parents of these children often cannot afford membership fees to local sports clubs or enrolment fees to swimming or judo classes. Young parents with large families, trying to feed hungry mouths have bigger priorities than bringing their child to the athletics club, to soccer or basketball training or to a football or hurling match.

But if sport was properly embedded in the education system, this would move some way towards a level playing field – where our most vulnerable children would not be discriminated against in this way. For many of these children, even though the schoolbooks may not be the answer to a better life, providing the opportunities to engage in and enjoy sport in a comprehensive rather than a tokenistic manner gives them a fighting chance to see life through a different lens, perhaps inspire them to take a better route through life. Many of the contributors to this book got that opportunity; surely the time has to come to ensure that more of our children get that same opportunity.

For such a small country, our impact on the world sporting stage has been phenomenal while our own indigenous games rank among the greatest amateur sports in the world. However, if we can harness our love of sport in Ireland by making it more important, then I believe we will be helping the next generation to create a better future than we can envisage currently. We will be cementing the importance of sport at all levels by positioning it at the heart of childhood development.

Ultimately, to bring about real change we must convince the politicians, the bureaucrats and the policy makers that the future wellbeing of our society depends on this urgent intervention. Some would say this is an impossible challenge, but hope is part of the human condition. I and many others like me desperately hope for this change. But to hope is not enough. We must act.

I know there are so many more people who share this view. In the GPA, because sport has been good to so many of our players, we want to give something back, if you like, our very own Corporate and Social Responsibility Policy (maybe less corporate and more social!). We are looking at ways to influence positive change in this regard. This may amount to nothing but then again it may be the catalyst for a proper debate on the issue or indeed the beginnings of a movement of like-minded people who want to enhance the lives of our citizens through a greater engagement with sport.

We all know how uplifting sport can be; personally I only have to recall Barry McGuigan's triumph or think of John O'Leary and Paul Curran lifting the Sam Maguire for Dublin in '95, if ever I doubted just how uplifting. Even now coaching youngsters or watching my own children playing their games is what does it for me. Everyone who has played and enjoyed sport at whatever level can give testimony to its values and benefits. A child's love for sport should be nurtured, not impeded or denied.

Sport matters – in times of difficulty it is often a touchstone for recovery. So let's ensure our children experience more of it and value its importance from the off so that society can reap the benefits in the future.

# BERNARD FLYNN

## Winning is great... but look after your body

**B**ERNARD FLYNN is 46 years old, married to Madeline and they have three children, Jessica, Billy and Rachel, all of whom were born in Mullingar, where he has resided for 20 years. It's a hard one for him to swallow at times when he sees them clad in maroon jerseys!

He played for the Meath senior footballers from 1983 to 1995 winning two All-Ireland titles, five Leinster titles, three National League titles, a Centenary Cup medal in 1984, and a Leinster under-21 title.

Bernard also represented Ireland in the Compromise Rules International series against Australia in 1987 and 1990.

I first came onto the Meath senior panel in 1983. It came on the back of my club, St Colmcille's, with which I have many great memories, winning the Meath junior championship that year. Sean Boylan attended our medal presentation function. It was an indication of his enduring class as a leader. He invited myself and Bobby O'Malley onto the senior county panel. It took some time for it to click with me just exactly what the man was about. In later years I'd come in the door and my mother would tell me how he had called in earlier for a cup of tea and chat. He was building that unity and camaraderie among the group, and he started it at a stage when it went unnoticed by many of us. I feel that's something we've lost in Meath in recent years, but it was a hallmark of Sean's era.

He'd be the first to admit that in the early stages his knowledge of football wasn't as rounded as it might have been but his loyalty to the players and man-management skills were exceptional. I only worked under one manager at senior inter-county level and I'm privileged that it was Sean. Such a solid human being.

One story that sticks out in my mind about him was in the mid-1980s, before we made the breakthrough in Leinster. We were training on the sand dunes on Bettystown beach. I always found the physical training difficult, but this was particularly barbaric. At one stage I stopped to get sick and allowed the rest of the lads to run ahead. I thought I had timed my stop so that it was well out of Boylan's eyeline. I was wrong! He waited until the lads came back around and stopped the whole training session and admonished me in front of everyone for giving up and letting my team mates down, and he was probably right. He insisted that it shouldn't happen again, and it didn't. From then on, even if I came in last, I finished out every run we did. It was a pivotal moment for me.

When I look back on my football career, some games are only a blur and then others are crystallised clearly in my mind. If I have one regret, it would be that I didn't take proper care of my injuries, something I've paid a price for in later life. No one forced me to do anything though, and I take full responsibility. However, one bit of advice that I would give young players now – look after your body.

I won about as much as I lost and, typically, some of the defeats stand out more than the victories, none more so than the 1991 All-Ireland final defeat to Down after all we had gone through that year. Ten championship games, including four against Dublin, and then to lose so narrowly was heartbreaking. I still find it hard to talk about it to this day.

On the other side of that, to be involved when we won in 1987 and 1988 was special. The Centenary Cup win in 1984 and a Leinster title success two years later were significant stepping stones for what came after. In between, we suffered a harrowing defeat to Laois in 1985 which made us all sit up and take stock of where we were going as a county. The levels of fitness, application and dedication just weren't good enough. Although I still cringe at the savagely difficult training schedule we were subjected to thereafter, we simply had to do it and never looked back.

As I said, failing to go all the way in 1991, having also lost the final the previous year, brought a horrendous feeling and we never recovered from it. Winning the National League in 1994 was a false dawn. We were finished.

Early the following year I was forced into retirement on foot of advice from Dr Pat O'Neill, who told me I'd be a cripple if I played on. I just thought of some of the great men I had played with: Joe Cassells, Colm O'Rourke, Mick Lyons, Phil Smyth, Liam Harnan and Gerry McEntee to name a few. I had to close the chapter on that phase of my life.

Having relocated to Mullingar by then, I continued to play with the Shamrocks and won four county titles in succession from which I took great enjoyment. Before I finished with St Colmcille's, we won the intermediate title in Meath in 1988 after a replayed final in which I scored 1-11 out of our total of 1-12. It brought such joy to the likes of mentors Paddy Brannigan and Jackser Kavanagh, and my own father Noel, and meant so much to the local people in that small area just outside Drogheda. It was a massive occasion for us all.

When all is said and done, whether you win one All-Ireland or ten isn't what's important. It's the friendships you forge with team mates and opponents (many of them from Dublin, oddly enough) that sustain you more in later life.

I had a hip replacement a couple of years ago and it got me thinking. I had time to reflect and I changed my mindset somewhat. The procedure certainly wasn't a pleasant experience but then you think of Sean Boylan and Liam Hayes battling cancer. And John Kerins and Mick McCarthy from Cork who are no longer with us, and Mick Holden, too. Cancer also claimed Grainne Keigue and Edel Duignan, good friends of mine.

And then there's Jim Stynes.

I played against Jim in the 1987 Compromise Rules series, and played with him on the Ireland team three years later. We forged a lasting friendship and he often visited my home down the years when he was back from Australia. Given his well-publicised cancer battle, I had been trying to get out to visit him and finally managed to do so in late 2010 and spent eight days with him. Observing what he goes through on a daily basis and how he fights his illness so stoically was the single biggest life-changing experience that I have experienced. The economic downturn in recent years has had dire consequences for me in my business life, but I took great strength from watching Jim Stynes and what he is fighting against all the odds.

All in all, I'm one of the lucky ones. Things could be better just now, but then they could be an awful lot worse. There are plenty of reminders of that in the shape of Jim and the others I mentioned. My main concern now is just to get through the challenges I face in business and look after my body.

Because, ultimately, living a full and healthy life is more important that what you win or lose on the field of play.

# CLIONA FOLEY
## Swifter, stronger, higher

**C**LIONA FOLEY was born in Abbeyleix, County Laois and now lives in Kildare. After qualifying with a degree in Physical Education and English from Thomond College (Limerick) in 1982, she worked as a PE teacher for six years before obtaining a post-graduate diploma in journalism at DCU.

**She is a staff sportswriter with Independent News and Media (INM) since 1991 – primarily covering Gaelic games and athletics for the *Irish Independent* at present – and has covered a wide variety of sports in the last 20 years, including European and World Championships and the last two Summer Olympics. She hopes to extend her own personal Olympic appearance record to three in London 2012.**

As a child I had zero interest in dolls or collectibles of any kind but I can still vividly recall a series of Olympic replica posters and medals produced by one of the petrol companies in the early 1970s which my brothers and I slavishly collected. My own personal Olympic flame was lit by some sporting figures who still remain gobal icons.

These were the days before 24-hour sports broadcasting and we lived in 'two-channel land' so the rarity of these quadrennial glimpses only added to the glamour and intrigue held for me by Olga Korbut and Nadia Comeneci, Mark Spitz and Greg Louganis, Lasse Viren, Alberto Juantorena, Carl Lewis, Daley Thompson and the utterly absorbing track duels of Ovett and Coe and Budd and Decker. All my life I wanted to go to the Olympics.

Years later my dream came true when the *Irish Independent* dispatched me to cover the 2004 Athens Olympics. I have since also covered the Beijing Games and now London, whose proximity will induce severe Olympic fever in this country, is fast approaching.

When I finally made it I discovered the Olympics were not actually sprinkled with the fairydust of my youthful dreams, largely due to my occupation.

Just before I departed for Athens an Irish athlete was uncovered as a drugs cheat, which meant that, even en route, I was filing copy of the most depressing kind. On arrival I quickly learned that, for any sportswriter, an Olympic Games is exactly like any World or European Championships, just scaled up to unfeasible proportions.

It is 20 non-stop days of dawn rises and midnight finishes, racing through mixed zones and security queues desperately searching for fresh angles in a huge range of sports, often filing copy on your knee in cramped media shuttle buses as you dash from one sport to the next.

There are few spare minutes left to admire your bird's-eye view of this extraordinary sporting behemoth that has, since the mid-1970s, been tainted by drugs scandals, security scares, corruption and such a commercial imperative now that it includes beach volleyball and BMX cycling.

Don't get me wrong. It is still enthralling and an absolute thrill and privilege to cover the epic stories and battles that emerge; the equivalent for any sportswriter of being dropped into a war zone, with all the challenges and adrenalin that entails. But if it is the absolute purity and wholesomeness embodied by that original Olympic motto – 'Swifter, Higher, Stronger' – then Tullamore Harriers Athletics Club, on the first Saturday in June, is the place for me.

The All-Ireland Schools' Track and Field Championships embodies everything that inspired me to become a sports journalist. The contestants come from the four corners of Ireland and have already been 'top three' in their event and age-group in the Connacht, Munster, Leinster and Ulster finals. Some of them are already members of athletics clubs and well on their way to becoming future senior internationals and, possibly, Olympians. But others are just naturally sporty kids who, having been persuaded to represent their school have discovered, to their delight, that they are not half bad at this running, throwing and jumping lark.

The event comes bang slap in the middle of a tough time in any Irish teenager's life; a few days before the Leaving and Junior Certs begin, yet provides the perfect antidote to those academic pressures. The spectators are largely family and friends and if the day is fine little tents quickly pop up on the outfield, rugs, flasks and sandwiches come out and it assumes a festival atmosphere.

The crowd invariably includes former and current greats of Irish athletics who make the pilgrimage annually to see what the next generation promises. If they are spotted by Michael Hunt, the avuncular president of the schools' athletics association, they are inveigled upon to present some medals and happily do so before slipping back into the crowd. That is the beauty and randomness of a day which is also a mammoth feat of organisation.

It involves 800 teenage competitors and 106 separate events, starts at 9 a.m. and finishes with the 4x100m relays before 6 p.m., timed with military precision. Kit-Kat sponsored it for 46 years and have now, crucially, been replaced by Aviva, but most of the officials are current or former secondary school teachers who are, technically, already on their summer holidays. The local club, and others across the country, provide additional officials; all of them also volunteers and unsung heroes. Nowadays the Irish Milers Club – another voluntary organisation – runs a couple of 'paced' guest races on the programme, adding to the feel of a championship T&F meet.

Virtually every final produces a narrative worth telling and the challenge, always, is squeezing as many into too few column inches.

Ask any Irish athlete of note, from any generation, how they performed, and whom they beat – or by whom they were beaten! – at the 'Irish Schools', and they will immediately recall it, particularly at the senior grade. Many of them will also confess to scanning the results every June to see how the next generation compares and if their 'schools' record has survived.

That first Saturday in June is a magnificent rite of passage and a barometer, not only of the state of Irish athletics but of the nation. In the past decade alone the noticeable increase in young immigrants involved confirms the nation's burgeoning diversity and the important role that schools, and sport, can play in their integraton.

Every year a new generation rocks up to Tullamore to run, jump and throw, to try to do it better than ever before and to see if that will be good enough to beat their peers. Few emerge as national champions but all surely learn something about themselves in this championship arena which, like most underage sport, is untainted by cynicism or corruption or drugs scandals. Nine hours of non-stop athletics fly by, leaving even the spectators breathless and exhausted. Yet somehow you depart hugely energised by the sheer honesty, enthusiasm and optimism of youth.

Seb Coe, searching for a theme for London 2012, settled upon 'legacy' and that is exactly what the Irish Schools Track & Field Championships has created. Visit this, our own annual mini-Olympics, some time soon to feel your own heart soar swifter, higher and stronger.

# EDDIE HARTY
## My special Grand National

**E**DDIE HARTY (EP) spent his entire life in the horse industry, as did his father and grandfather. He rode at the top level as an amateur and professional jockey, was a show jumper, and took part in three-day eventing.

In the 1950s he developed an equestrian ranch in California (later used to train the US three-day event team) and coached and trained riders of various standards. Eddie represented Ireland in equestrian events at the 1960 Olympic Games in Rome.

He became a professional national hunt jockey in 1961 riding for all the leading trainers including Fred Winter, Fred Rimell and Toby Balding for whom he won the 1969 Grand National. In l972 he began training under both rules and ran his own bloodstock agency, dealing with top national hunt and flat racehorses, shipping them all over the world.

The mounted bobby came slowly towards me. "Who won?" I croaked as he drew closer. His expression suggested he thought I was pulling his leg. Then his face spread into an almighty grin. "Why, you did, of course!"

The penny was still very slow to drop, until I remembered that the Grand National winner always gets a mounted police escort back to that hallowed winner's enclosure, under that old iron canopy. So, it must be true. I had ridden Highland Wedding to win the 1969 Grand National!

I knew how Sir Edmund Hillary must have felt when he became the first man to conquer Mount Everest in 1953. Not, of course, that I was the first to conquer the Everest of steeplechasing. Some lucky man had done just that every year since 1837, many of them Irishmen like me.

Forty years on I realise that Highland Wedding was the real Hillary. My role had been Sherpa Tenzing's, merely responsible for guiding my 'Hillary' to that triumphant ascent – of Aintree. Not that either of us was an Aintree virgin. By then a twelve-year-old veteran, Highland Wedding had finished eighth in 1966, missed out in 1967 and finished seventh in

1968. Owen McNally was his regular partner and would have been on board Highland Wedding's burly back in 1969, but for injury, every jump jockey's bugbear.

As for me, I had had my National misfires too. Knoxtown fell with me in 1960, as did Floater in 1961. Cannobie Lee and I had at least completed in 1962, albeit a remote eighth to Fred Winter on Kilmore. Sidelined through injury in 1963, I finished seventh on April Rose in 1964, when Willie Robinson and Team Spirit succeeded at their fifth attempt. Crocked again in 1966, I gave myself a real chance on Solbina in 1967. Unfortunately that was the National that will ever be remembered as 'Foinavon's Year'. The stewards took the unusual step of issuing a public announcement. "As a result of the leading loose horse running across the fence after Becher's (23rd) on the second circuit, there was a pile-up and Foinavon was the only horse to jump the fence first time. The remainder of the finishers were either remounted or put to the fence a second time."

Would Solbina have won? I am sure he would have. They had simply gone too fast from the start, so fast that Solbina, a classy two-and-a-half-miler could not lie up. We were just creeping into contention when I saw the melee ahead. I pulled to the very outside where there was room to jump the fence. The delayed gasp from the massed spectators on the embankment distracted Solbina. He got over the fence, somehow, but pitched so badly on landing that I had no chance of staying aboard. I caught him and remounted to finish a despondent sixth.

Having ridden Steel Bridge to finish tenth in 1968 I was thrilled to see him as my only danger coming to the last 12 months later. If Highland Wedding could not see Steel Bridge off I was in the wrong business. Thankfully, trainer Toby Balding had cooked this equine enigma to perfection, as he demonstrated by galloping home twelve lengths clear of Steel Bridge and Richard Pitman. Poor old Richard got done in the 1973 National when Crisp set out to make all under 12st. He would have won a distance, but for Red Rum mowing him down in those final heart-breaking yards, with just 10st 5lb on his back.

David Coleman assured BBC viewers that they were in for a treat when Eddie Harty got hold of the microphone. I don't know if he was correct. It was all a blur. Only when I got back to the Adelphi and got a chance to telephone my ailing father back in Clondalkin did it begin to sink in. Having said all the usual things, my father stuck me to the ground by saying how sad it was that 'Boss' Harty had not lived to see one of his descendants win the National. He was referring to his own father – Michael J. Harty of Alston, Croom – the first public trainer to set up shop outside the Curragh. All I knew was that 'Boss' Harty had not been around in my lifetime. Only later did I learn that my paternal grandfather had died as long ago as 1929, shortly after his son John H. Harty had died as the result of his mount throwing him against a stone marker post during a race on the Curragh.

'Boss' Harty had ridden winners at Nottingham and Manchester in 1894. Henry, one of his five jockey sons, had bought his own place, Fort Etna, out of his 1915 National riding fee, even if he had only got as far as the first because the starter let the field go as he was hacking back to line up. Two of my brothers – 'Buster' and the late John – had their Grand National thrills and spills too.

What makes the National so special? What has endowed it with an aura that overshadows every other steeplechase? For me it is the uniqueness of the course, its famous fences and the calls it makes on horse and rider alike. No other steeplechase remotely compares, not in these islands anyway. Another thing too, there is a romance attaching to the Grand National that the other 'championship' races just never have generated. Anywhere in the world the Grand National is guaranteed instant recognition.

If I had to live my life as a jockey all over again and was to be granted just one big win, it would have to be the Grand National. Of course it would have been lovely to have repeated that triumph as a trainer, like Fulke Walwyn, like Fred Winter. It wasn't to be. Smartside got as far as the first fence. Count your blessings in this game that tames lions. I certainly do.

# LIAM HAYES

## Meeting Thomas 'Hit Man' Hearns

**L**IAM HAYES won two All-Ireland football titles, five Leinster titles and two National League medals with Meath. One of his best-known performances was as captain of Meath in the thrilling four-game series in the first round of the 1991 Leinster championship against Dublin.

He played in the Compromise Rules Series of 1984 and 1987 against Australia. An author, publisher, journalist and commentator, he penned *Out of our Skins* which has been described as one of the best accounts of the experiences of a GAA athlete, both on the field and off.

Since 1995 Liam has spent his time as a publisher, having launched 11 national and regional newspaper titles. They include *The Title, Ireland on Sunday, Dublin Daily,* and the Gazette Group of regional titles, comprised of eight local newspapers in Dublin. He lives in Lucan, Co. Dublin with his wife Anne and they have four children.

First things first, let me publicly admit that I couldn't punch my way out of a paper bag. And even though Gaelic footballers, as a rule, are not asked to do any punching on the football field, it is regularly a requirement, both in defence of your own personal honour on occasions, and also in defence of the football team you might be playing with on a particular Sunday.

The team I played with most of my adult life – the Meath senior football team – luckily enough had men who could throw a punch or two faster and more accurately than I ever could. We got the name of being a 'Big, Bad' football team but, believe me, if you were playing Gaelic football in the 1970s and '80s, it was necessary to be both 'Big' and 'Bad' as the likes of Dublin and Kerry, around that time, were as tough and physical, as they were brilliantly skilful.

I threw some punches in my life, sure I did, but mostly I got punched, or threw big swinging right fists which never landed, or arrived much too late.

I remember being 13 years old playing for Skryne against Batterstown (yes, Batterstown!) and a 10-year-old kid pushed me in the chest. I marched up to him, and said 'Just try to hit me again!' And, of course, he accepted the invitation and sent me backwards with a left jab which had my nose spurting blood in several different directions.

I remember being 22 years old in Croke Park, lifting myself up off the ground, and Ray Hazley, a Dublin defender, standing over me telling me what he thought of me! And, for some reason, I decided, while still on my knees, to throw a punch at him. I lost that fight too.

I remember losing too many fights!

All my life, however, funnily enough, boxing has been my favourite sport – and therefore my favourite sporting memory comes from a boxing ring. But not a boxing ring in this country! Actually, a city in the United States which boasts of possessing the most famous boxing ring in the world!

In the 1980s, the middleweight division in boxing was dominated by four of the greatest fighters in the sport's history – Sugar Ray Leonard, 'Marvellous Marvin' Hagler, Thomas 'Hit Man' Hearns, and Roberto Duran. And they fought each other about a dozen times, with blistering, bloodied, unforgettable results.

On 15 April 1985, it was Hearns and Hagler who met in that magnificent ring in Caesar's Palace, and served up eight minutes of the most thrilling sporting action I have ever seen in my life – even though I was sitting in my home in Skryne, looking at highlights of the fight on the BBC, with my late dad, Jim, for company in the chair beside me.

At the ringside, the famous boxing writer Harry Mullan, later reminisced that his hands were shaking so much with excitement during the three rounds that he could not write anything down on the paper in front of him!

Hagler had 10 straight defences of his title behind him, nine of them by knockout, and with his opening shot of the evening Hearns broke his hand on the top of 'Marvellous Marvin's' shiny, bald head. But, the fight still did not stop for another eight minutes! There were more punches thrown in those eight minutes than in any other fight, ever, and midway through the third round Hagler, with his face covered in blood from a cut on his head, asked his corner-men: 'I'm not missing him, am I?' Hagler was not missing him, and won the fight, but Hearns, who possessed the fastest hands I have ever seen on a fighter (and, unfortunately, legs which could only be compared to a statuesque six feet tall model in high heels) was my favourite fighter, ever!

Hearns is the most fearless sportsman I have ever seen in my life.

And, 14 months after the greatest fight I had ever seen, I found myself in Caesar's Palace in Las Vegas, reporting on Barry McGuigan's failed attempt to retain his own World Featherweight title, when I got to meet the 'Hit Man'. I got one of his handlers to let me into his hotel suite, and I waited in a giant room outside of the 'Hit Man's' bedroom while he watched, of all things, a cowboy movie. I waited for 70 minutes until the movie finished.

The bedroom doors opened, and the man with the blackest eyes I have ever seen and with the fastest hands I have ever seen, sat down in the magnificent piece of furniture in front of me, and asked 'Who are you... and what you want to ask me?'

And... then... he smiled!

*Ronnie Delany, winner of the 1500 metres final at the Olympic Games in Melbourne, 1 December 1956*

*John O'Mahony and Joe Kernan share a joke after a Mayo v Galway National Football League match*

*Fiona Shannon, Antrim, triple World Open Singles handball champion*

*Dessie Farrell, Dublin, on the ball in the 1995 All-Ireland football final*

*Trevor Brennan who was capped 13 times for Ireland in rugby*

*Dan Shanahan, Waterford, with his daughter Chloe*

*Darragh Maloney, RTÉ sports presenter and commentator*

*Conor Niland on his way to victory in the 2010 Israel Open final*

*Paul Brady, Cavan, the only player to win the World Open Singles handball title on three occasions*

*John Delaney, CEO, FAI, congratulates Robbie Keane after the Ireland v Russia European Cup qualifier*

*Tony Ward keeps a close eye on his St Gerard's school rugby team*

*Ronan Sweeney, Kildare, concentrates on the ball*

*Páraic Duffy, GAA Director General with Eddie Keher, former Kilkenny hurler*

*Lar Corbett, Tipperary, signs autographs for admiring fans*

*Adrian Eames, producer and presenter,
RTÉ Sport*

*Mick Dowling, two-time Olympian and RTÉ
boxing analyst*

*Jimmy Keaveney, Dublin, winner of three
All-Ireland football medals*

*Noel King, manager of the Ireland
under-21 soccer team*

*Cora Staunton, Mayo, in full flight*

*Brian Cody jumps for joy at the end of the 2011 All-Ireland hurling final*

*Henry Shefflin raises the Liam MacCarthy Cup after the 2011 All-Ireland hurling final*

# JAMIE HEASLIP
# Into the Lions' den

**J**AMIE HEASLIP was born in Tiberias, Israel, while his father was on duty with the United Nations. He attended Newbridge College before starring at the 2004 IRB U-21 World Cup, when Ireland were runners-up to New Zealand and he was nominated for the IRB U-21 World Player of the Year Award.

Jamie made his Leinster senior debut in the Celtic League in 2005. His first Irish cap came in 2006 against the Pacific Islands and he was the 1000th player to be capped by Ireland. He was a member of the Ireland team that won the 2009 RBS Six Nations Championship and Grand Slam and a key member of Leinster's 2009 and 2011 winning Heineken Cup teams. He started all three Tests in the 2009 British and Irish Lions tour to South Africa. He is the only player to have been named in all Magners League Dream Teams from 2007 to 2011. Jamie was nominated for the inaugural European Player of the Year Award in 2011.

When I was first approached by Lorcán via my dad about writing a few words on my best sporting memory plenty started coming to the fore. I have been blessed with the opportunity to play a sport that I love dearly as a job. I would, like many of my friends, play on Saturdays and Sundays for Naas RFC regardless of the money. The reason I play is simple; I want to win. I don't know why winning is important; maybe it's innate, maybe it's nurtured as I've grown older. I'm a competitive git and this game is a true representation of what happens when every member of a team rows in together, and the feeling of winning and accomplishment from this is addictive.

The other side of the game that I love is the friendships that are forged like in any other team sport. Only your team mates truly know the 'blood, sweat and tears' that goes into training and preparing for matches. Not the pundits, not the supporters, not your family and friends. This friendship is something that endures. Some of my closest and most trusted friends are those with whom I first started playing rugby as a young eight year old in Naas RFC.

Enough about that though, now on to the sporting highlights. They go from winning my first All-Ireland with Trinity under-20s, to going from Division 3 to Division 1 in the AIL League with Trinity in three years and a nomination for the under-21 World Player of the Year in 2004 to being nominated for World Player of the Year in 2009. The highlight for me though has to be one particular season, not one single event.

In January 2009 the season was at its mid point. I was heading into the last round of the Heineken Cup group stage with Leinster and looking forward to the beginning of the RBS Six Nations. To complicate things there was the small matter of the impending British and Irish Lions Tour to South Africa at the end of the season. At this point in the season the pundits were dismissing Leinster's chances of landing our first Heineken Cup, and they were also writing off Ireland's prospects of capturing the RBS Six Nations Championship. The form book would have reinforced their scepticism.

However, in the Irish squad we focused on our goals and how to achieve them by breaking them down into tasks. We weren't worried about what was being said because that never seems to be good and is mostly written by people who aren't aware or informed of the team's strength and abilities.

In Leinster we scraped out of our Heineken Cup group before starting the Six Nations tournament with the small matter of the opening encounter against France, the defending champions. But, again, as a group we focused on our tasks in training and then examined what had to be done for the opening RBS Six Nations game. Confidence grew on the back of the result in no small part to our dedicated focus and hard work. By focusing on our tasks and goals as a group we overcame a 61-year gap to capture the Grand Slam and the championship.

The RBS Six Nations experience was brought back to the Leinster camp. This knowledge was invaluable especially in the tight quarter-final game against Harlequins. By applying the focus and hard work we progressed through the Heineken Cup. The final result is now in the history books.

For me the tip of the iceberg that year was the day I was selected for the British and Irish Lions. It was a tense day as nobody knew what squad was going to be selected. I watched the announcement from the café in our training complex with some other players and the sense of achievement when my name was called out was something I never felt before but this still wasn't the best of the day.

The best of the day occurred when I returned home from training to find my closest friends, some of them the guys with whom I first started playing rugby when I was eight, throw an impromptu party in my house. The highlight was when they presented me with a Lions jersey signed by all of them. One of my most prized possessions and one of the most humbling, yet proudest moments I've ever experienced in my sporting career.

# JACQUI HURLEY

## O'Gara and Dunne land blows for Ireland

**J**ACQUI HURLEY **is a sports presenter on RTÉ television and radio. She can regularly be seen delivering sports bulletins on the 6 o'clock and 9 o'clock news and also co-presents** *Sunday Sport* **on RTÉ Radio One alongside Con Murphy.**

**She graduated from University of Limerick with a degree in media and communications and worked for a year with CBS TV in Mississippi and in local radio before joining RTÉ in 2006.**

**Jacqui is a native of Cork and lived in Australia for several years. She is a keen athlete herself, represented Cork in camogie, was an international basketball player and has also managed the Irish under-16 women's basketball team.**

As a sports journalist, you are often asked by people what your favourite sporting memory is. Having witnessed so many great sporting occasions down through the years, I have a catalogue of events I usually reel through, which includes everything from being in Croke Park as a spectator for the Cork hurlers' All-Ireland win in 1999, to Munster's first Heineken Cup success in 2006, to Rory McIlroy's win at the US Open.

Memories of my own sporting achievements always come to mind – from winning county championships to playing for my county and country, being involved in sport myself has always made me appreciate the big occasions even more. From a personal point of view, there is nothing like the feeling of representing your county or country. Standing alongside your team mates, belting out Amhrán na bhFiann, is one of the most incredible feelings you can ever experience as a sportsperson and they are memories I will never forget.

Working at a sporting event is so different; you have absolutely no control over the situation and you spend so much of your time keeping your emotions in check so you can cover the story. Inevitably, there are moments when you lose yourself in the occasion and, for me, that was the case on 21 March 2009, when Ireland won the Six Nations Grand Slam in rugby and Bernard Dunne won the World Super Bantamweight boxing title.

I was sent to Young Munster Rugby Club in Limerick as part of RTÉ's coverage of the Grand Slam match against Wales in Cardiff. A close-knit club, home to Paul O'Connell and Keith Earls, I was welcomed with open arms. The plan was that if Ireland won the match the programme would come to me live with celebrations from the clubhouse. The drama of Ronan O'Gara's late drop goal and Steve Jones's missed penalty, coupled with the amount of drink taken by the supporters led to what can only be described as one of the funniest and most enjoyable live shots I've ever been involved in. I'll put it to you this way, it's the only time I've ever been happy to be licked on the face!

Sport is one the very few things that can unite absolute strangers. No other eventuality allows you to hug a person you've never met and dance around the room together, as if it were the most natural thing in the world. When that final whistle went, it was like watching Riverdance in Limerick! Great rivals, Cork Con and Young Munster had just played in an AIL Cup final at the grounds, yet they sat together, watching what has become one of the greatest sporting moments in our nation's history. Watching the scenes, both on and off the pitch, in the aftermath of that win is something I will never forget. Coming from where the Irish team were at that stage to win a Grand Slam was incredible and to win it in that fashion was even more remarkable. What followed that evening only added to the drama of the day.

Bernard Dunne was placed in front of Ricardo Cordoba, as a small obstacle en route to retaining his world title. What Cordoba didn't know was that he wasn't just facing Bernard Dunne at the O2, but 10,000 Irish people, already on a high from what they'd seen in Cardiff hours before. Around the country, people stayed in their seats in homes and pubs to watch what they hoped would become another part of Irish sporting history.

The fight would later be listed as ESPN's fight of the year, as Bernard Dunne eventually won in the 11th round. Having been knocked down four times in the fight, the only way Dunne could win was to knock Cordoba out. Driven on by the huge Irish support in the stadium as well as the hundreds of thousands of Irish people across the country, he finally delivered the knock-out blow which not only won the fight, but sent Cordoba to hospital. How he found the strength after 11 rounds, only he will know, but I'd like to think it was something to do with the goodwill and support of the Irish people that day.

For a country as small as we are, we really punch above our weight when it comes to sport. To have had two sporting occasions of that magnitude happen on the same day reads so well it could be fiction. Those of us who were lucky enough to watch history being made in front of our eyes on 21 March 2009 can testify to the fact that it was reality and it's a day that will live long in the memory.

# BERNARD JACKMAN

## Heineken Cup glory in Edinburgh

**B**ERNARD JACKMAN from Tullow, County Carlow was educated at Newbridge College, and at Dublin City University where he studied business and Japanese. After playing rugby for Connacht and Sale Sharks he played 99 times with Leinster from 2005 to 2010 winning a Magners League title (2007/08) and a Heineken Cup in 2009.

Bernard played for Ireland at U19, U21 and college levels, captained Ireland A and won nine full international caps, two during the 2005 tour of Japan and two more during the 2007 tour of Argentina. A member of Ireland's 2008/09 Six Nations Grand Slam squad, he featured in all five games.

He has coached Tullow RFC, Newbridge RFC and Coolmine RFC and was Director of Rugby and forwards coach of Clontarf RFC from May 2009 to 2011. He and his wife Sinead have two children, Ava and Ben.

Murrayfield in May 2009 was the scene for what was undoubtedly the highlight of my sporting career when Leinster lifted their first Heineken Cup with a narrow victory over English champions Leicester. I think it was the long journey that it took me and Leinster to reach that point which made the victory even sweeter. My career had been a series of ups and downs. Warren Gatland had selected me to tour South Africa with the Ireland senior international side in 1998 when I was only 20 years old. Despite having been in extended Irish squads as the third-choice hooker for most of the following years it wasn't until 2005 on an Irish tour to Japan that I managed to win the first of my nine caps for Ireland.

In 2003 following a two-year stint over in Manchester with the Sale Sharks I returned to Ireland to try and improve my chances of winning an international cap but none of the provinces had a contract for me so I ended up leaving the professional game for a year and getting a job as a medical rep and used the club game to force my way back into professional rugby in this country.

When I played with the Sale Sharks and Connacht for four seasons we were always in the lower level European competition, the Challenge Cup. Although it's a good competition in its own right it lacks the profile and the quality of the Heineken Cup and I was always envious of the Munster, Leinster and Ulster players who got to play year after year in it. When Declan Kidney signed me to play for Leinster in 2005 I suppose I fell into the trap of believing winning the European Cup was just a matter of when, not if, given the talent that was in the Leinster team at the time. Players like Malcolm O' Kelly, Brian O' Driscoll, Felipe Contemponi, Denis Hickie and Shane Horgan were world stars and Leinster were capable of playing sublime rugby. Yet we consistently fell short in the knock-out stages even when we were handed favourable draws.

My signing for Leinster coincided with Michael Cheika becoming the Director of Rugby at the province and he must take the largest amount of credit for helping Leinster become the high-performing organisation that they are currently at all levels. He was incredibly single-minded in his approach to success and he refused to let anything get in his way that might stop us achieving our goal. There were bumps and turns on the road but that happens in any organisation that needs to undergo change. We had to become a team that was more evenly balanced and by that I mean a team that had a pack that it could count on just as much as our multi-talented backline.

Mike Brewer played a huge role in building a pack of forwards that could stand toe-to-toe with any in Europe because the old saying still holds true in modern rugby that "the forwards decide who wins the match and the backs decide by how much". We also needed to spend as much time working on our defence as we did on attack and Cheika added a defence coach to our management team in former Irish international centre Kurt McQuilkin who improved our individual technique but also developed a system that we could rely on to keep us in games even when our attack was struggling.

Armed with a better all round side and an ageing team I think there was a feeling in 2009 that it was a case of now or never. In the early stages we limped out of our group following a very poor display away to Castre and we were one of the lowest seeds so we were handed an away draw to Harlequins in the quarter-finals. Our 6-5 victory in this game was crucial to helping create real self-belief as we had to defend our line for the majority of the game and despite being under huge pressure Cheika made no substitutions which is extremely rare in the modern game. Whilst the bookmakers and pundits didn't rate the performance, we knew how hard it is to win away in Europe with nearly eighty percent of the ties going to the home team. We also felt that as a team we were building a real steel about us. Munster were next up at Croke Park which was the most hyped game in Irish provincial rugby history. 82,000 fans came to Croke Park with most expecting a Munster win as they were the Heineken Cup champions and had hammered the Ospreys in their own quarter-final at Thomond Park.

Our game plan to really target Munster at the breakdown (which was an area that most teams let Munster do as they wished) worked a treat and a great set-piece try from Gordan D'Arcy and an intercept try from Brian O'Driscoll put us into our first ever Heineken Cup final.

To be honest, the hype and build-up to the Heineken Cup final was a piece of cake in comparison with what we had experienced for the semi-final. There was a lot of rubbish being spoken about how you have to lose a European final in order to win one but we didn't buy that for a second. We realised how hard it actually is to make a final and that this could easily be our only chance ever. Leicester were formidable opponents and they know how to win silverware year on year. They pride themselves on their physicality and we knew that this match was going to be the most physical of our careers.

We stayed at a golf resort on the outskirts of Edinburgh and it was ideal as it limited our distractions. However, on the bus to the ground we couldn't help noticing just how many Leinster fans had made the journey to support us and it gave the team a lift to see that they outnumbered the Tiger fans three to one. The game itself was incredibly tight and Brian O'Driscoll and Jonny Sexton kicked brilliant drop goals to put us in front. Jamie Heaslip scored the crucial try and although we had to defend a one-score lead for the final ten minutes we held firm. Having looked in from the outside to finally get to win such an incredible competition is a day I will never forget.

# JIMMY KEAVENEY

## When the Dubs came back to the Hill

JIMMY KEAVENEY is a member of the St Vincents Club in Dublin and began his inter-county career as a minor. He won three All-Ireland senior football medals with Dublin in 1974, 1976 and 1977 and was Texaco Footballer of the Year Award winner in 1976 and 1977.

He won two National Leagues, seven Leinster senior medals, 10 Dublin senior football medals, three Dublin senior hurling medals, two Leinster club championships and an All-Ireland club championship.

Jimmy scored a record two goals and six points from play in the 1977 All-Ireland final against Armagh. A regular visitor to the Listowel Races where he revisits old memories with Kerry players of his era, his other interests include golf, soccer, rugby, and sport in general. He lives in Portmarnock and has two daughters and two sons and enjoys spending time with his grandchildren.

My football career with Dublin began in 1964 at the age of 19. The county won the 1963 senior title and I was really looking forward to joining the All-Ireland champions.

I commanded a regular starting position from the beginning of my career and won a Leinster championship in 1965. Naturally, I thought it was only a matter of time before we would win another All-Ireland. We had several experienced players on the team such as brothers Lar and Des Foley, John Timmons, Mickey Whelan and Paddy Holden.

I still felt that success was just around the corner but this was not the case. We went downhill and did not contest any major league or championship finals after the 1967 League final defeat to Galway. In 1972 Kildare beat us in the Leinster championship and I lost all interest in playing for Dublin and decided to retire. I was getting more enjoyment playing football and hurling with my club, St Vincents.

I still went to Dublin hurling and football games and attended the 1974 Dublin versus Wexford Leinster football championship match which Dublin, an average team, won. I went off and met a few of the lads in Meaghers in Ballybough for a few pints and went home. The following evening Kevin Heffernan phoned and said: "Jimmy, we want you to come back down to Parnell Park for a bit of training. I want to try to get you into some sort of shape for the championship." So, knowing Kevin - I had played with him - if he wanted me back he would have got me back one way or another. After hesitating for a few moments I told him that I'd be down the next night.

I heard later that on the way home from the Wexford match with his wife Mary and Lily Jennings, Kevin said he needed a good free taker. Lily's ten-year-old son Terence said: "Why don't you get Jimmy Keaveney? He's knocking over points every Sunday with the club." And that led to the phone call the next day. I went down and started training in Parnell Park on Tuesday and Thursday nights and was picked to play against Louth. We won that game by 2-11 to 1-9 and beat Offaly next and then won the Leinster final against Meath by 1-11 to 0-13.

That year we started to get a crowd back to watch Dublin football. In 1974 there was no great soccer team in Dublin. Shamrock Rovers had gone down and rugby wasn't as popular as it is in 2011 so the Dublin sporting public jumped onto the Dublin bandwagon. Hill 16 was a sea of blue and navy and numerous banners proclaimed the might of 'Heffo's Army'.

I thought we'd done very well to win the Leinster title but that we wouldn't go any further because we were playing a great Cork team in the All-Ireland semi-final. Cork had won the 1973 All-Ireland and being a good friend of Billy Morgan I was delighted for them and I knew many of the Cork players. I wasn't really confident of beating them but Kevin introduced Saturday morning training. Normally, if we had a match, players would get together and have a chat about the game the next day and rev everybody up. We'd done our little bit of work-about in Parnell Park on the Saturday morning and Kevin took the meeting after training. He spoke about Cork and how confident he was that we would beat them. He really lifted our spirits to a fierce height and we believed we would annihilate Cork. So, I thought to myself that Kevin could be right and we could beat the 1973 All-Ireland champions.

The Cork team were staying in the Grand Hotel in Malahide on the night before the game. Ann Cogan and Mary Morgan, twin sisters who are married to Frank Cogan and Billy Morgan, were staying in my house in Portmarnock. But Frank wasn't on the Cork team, much to everybody's surprise. So, we got up the following morning and went to Mass and Ann asked me if it would it be okay if she rang Cork to see if Frank came up for the game. I said: "No problem, go ahead," so she rang and got no answer. Mary said to Ann that he could be playing in the final. I said: "Hold on a sec girls, you haven't won the semi-final yet!"

We went out and played Cork and it looked like we were going to get beaten. We played well and won the game by a couple of points. After the match I was coming out of the dressing room and the first people waiting for me were Mary Morgan and Ann Cogan. I couldn't believe it, but fair play to the two girls.

We were in an All-Ireland final and I never expected after retiring in 1972 that I would play in an All-Ireland final, or even get close, and here we were now on the brink of history and the prospect of Dublin winning an All-Ireland. We were playing Galway, and this was a very good Galway team although they had lost two All-Irelands in 1971 and 1973. Galway were more than holding their own from early on. We unluckily conceded a penalty that Paddy Cullen saved and we held on and won by 0-14 to 1-6 before an attendance of 71,898 on 22 September 1974.

I couldn't believe it! Here I was at 29 years of age, and we weren't a young team by any means! We had Paddy Cullen, Tony Hanahoe, Gay O'Driscoll, Sean Doherty and myself who were around 28 or 29 years of age. We'd been there for about 10 years and now we were All-Ireland champions. It was something beyond my wildest dreams but to me that was the greatest day in my whole life. I'll never forget it. I threw myself on top of David Hickey when the game was over. I think I nearly killed poor Davey! We had done something that I never thought could happen. Some of the younger lads might say beating Kerry in an All-Ireland semi-final or an All-Ireland final were their highlights but we'd been there so long that we never thought we'd have the opportunity of getting to an All-Ireland final and playing in one. It all added up to my greatest sporting memory, thanks to Kevin Heffernan and a wonderful Dublin team.

# EDDIE KEHER

# It all started on the village square

**E**DDIE KEHER made his debut on the Kilkenny senior team in the replayed All-Ireland hurling final against Waterford in 1959 and retired in 1977. He scored seven goals and 74 points in 10 All-Irelands, winning on six occasions. He won nine Railway Cup medals, three National Leagues and 10 Leinster titles.

He was selected on the Century and Millennium Teams, was a nine-time All Star under two different schemes and was 1972 Texaco Hurler of the Year. He was leading scorer 11 times between 1963 and 1976, was highest scorer in an All-Ireland with 2-11 in 1971 and had the highest points tally in a final with 0-14 in 1963.

In 298 senior games with Kilkenny Eddie scored 211 goals and 1,426 points, 35-320 of this in 49 championship matches. He lives in his native Inistioge with his wife Kay.

If you are a GAA player, the one thing that you can never hide is your age, so it is always best to come out with it straight away! When GAA people wonder about someone's age, the first question they ask is: "When did he play minor?" (under 18). A quick calculation will then get the result!

God willing, I am going to hit the magical age of 70 towards the end of 2011, and the reason I bring that up at all is that those who know will confirm that the memory grows dim at that stage of one's life! So, rather than focusing on one particular event, I propose to do a sketch of the many memories that I still hold dear.

My earliest hurling memories go back to my own village of Inistioge, and the village square in front of our house at the time, and watching the 'big lads' playing hurling there. At the age of four, we (the young lads) dared to venture out there when they were gone to try our skill at this fascinating game. When the 'big lads' returned, the cry went out: "Hold the ball, the big lads are coming," and we scarpered! However, we discovered in time that they weren't so bad, and they were the ones who gave us our first coaching lessons in how to hold the hurley properly, and how to hit the ball left and right, etc. And they continued to check on our progress and encourage us.

In time, we became the 'big lads', and passionate games were played by throwing in the hurleys and, blindfolded, someone picked two teams by throwing them to each side. "I'm Jim Langton," "I'm Christy Ring" were calls ringing out before the ball was thrown in, as we tried to imitate those heroes.

As we got more sophisticated, matches between the 'Up Streets' and the 'Down Streets' were arranged beforehand and were played with passion and competitiveness. The inevitable row broke out when the vanquished disputed the legality of a player who lived on the border of the dividing line. Eventually, the match to settle all arguments was arranged when the 'Up Streets' agreed to give us the disputed key player, but the match would have to be played at an 'Up Street' venue, Dobbyn's Park. They would get Nick White, an adult who lived in High St, to referee the game. But the carrot offered to us was that Nick (who played cornet in the local brass band) would parade us around the field, like the Artane Band in Croke Park before the game! We lost, due to some dubious refereeing decisions!

We graduated in time to play on the local school under-14 team in the Kilkenny Schools League, and the winning of my first medal at the age of 10 in 1952 is a very fond memory. We beat a city team, St John's, in the final, which was a big achievement for a small village. I won my second medal in that competition in 1955 against Lisdowney.

Our club, the Rower-Inistioge, progressed over the next decade, winning the junior championship - after many attempts - in 1963. We were now in the senior grade against the really big guns, and we finally reached the top in 1968 by beating what was probably one of the best club teams ever in Kilkenny, Bennettsbridge, to win our one and only senior championship final. It was a wonderful feeling at that time that those of us who battled together from the days on the square had finally reached the top. We subsequently had several narrow defeats in finals and semi-finals but could never win another championship. Star-studded teams like James Stephens, the Fenians, and the Shamrocks had emerged to make victory in the Kilkenny championship an almost impossible task.

My own hurling career went in parallel with our club success. I won my first All-Ireland with St Kieran's College in a thrilling All-Ireland Colleges final against St Flannan's, Ennis in 1957. We had previously won Leinster junior and senior titles, but it was a wonderful feeling to win my first All-Ireland when that competition was revived in that year. We won again in 1959 against Tipperary CBS.

Meantime I had succeeded in getting on the Kilkenny minor panel in 1956 and got my first Leinster minor medal, with three more on the field of play in the following years. What a thrill it was to wear the famed 'black and amber'. We had no All-Ireland success in that grade, but after losing the minor final in 1959, I couldn't believe it when I was drafted into the senior panel for the 1959 replay against Waterford on 4th October, 10 days before my 18th birthday. Here I was, training in Nowlan Park with my heroes, Ollie Walsh, Sean Clohessy, Johnny McGovern, Paddy Buggy and Denis Heaslip. When Johnny McGovern got injured after 15 minutes of the game, I was called in to get my first taste of All-Ireland senior hurling.

I managed to score two points in the second half, but we were well beaten by a great Waterford side.

I had been tried in a couple of Walsh Cup games beforehand and must have won the confidence of the selectors to give me a chance in the All-Ireland final. In that first Walsh Cup match, I have a very fond memory of the late, great Des Foley of Dublin coming especially over to me during the 'warm up' to wish me good luck.

As I write my mind is flooding with many more wonderful memories, like my first senior All-Ireland success in 1963 and being captain of the All-Ireland winning side in 1969. I got that honour because of our club success in 1968. It was such a thrill to accept the MacCarthy Cup on behalf of Kilkenny, but especially for my club considering that four of the team were from my beloved Rower-Inistioge, lads with whom I had soldiered on the village square during my boyhood and teenage years.

# EOIN KENNEDY

## I still smile about my first All-Ireland win

**E**OIN KENNEDY from the St Brigid's GAA Club in Blanchardstown is the holder of 25 All-Ireland senior handball titles, 15 of these in Senior Singles – eight 60x30, one 40x20 and six hardball – and 10 Senior Doubles titles with Egin Jensen, four 60x30, one 40x20 and five hardball.

Eoin has represented Ireland winning the 2006 World Men's Open Doubles title with Tony Healy of Cork in Edmonton, Canada and retaining it in Portland, Oregon with Michael Finnegan from Cavan in 2009.

He won the International Collegiate Singles title representing DCU in 2001 and holds USA (1999) and Canadian (2001) Open Singles titles. He has three Men's Open Irish Nationals Singles titles and was Irish Player of the Year All Star on six occasions. A keen follower of Dublin GAA teams, he lives less than 100 yards from Croke Park Stadium.

Sport, and in particular the game of handball, has always been an integral part of my life. Growing up, I was encouraged by my parents to participate in as many different sports as possible. As a result, I played and competed in Gaelic football, hurling, soccer, tennis, athletics, badminton, basketball, table tennis and handball until my mid-teens – needless to say, I had plenty of half-days from school!

Aside from competing, I have wonderful memories of watching the big sporting events of the era. I can clearly remember the excitement of watching Italia '90 as a 10 year old with my friends on a big screen in Castleknock Tennis Club and subsequently standing amongst the crowds on O'Connell St trying to catch a glimpse of my heroes on the open-top bus. I can also still recall the disappointment I felt leaving Croke Park after Meath had pipped Dublin by a point in the fourth and final game of the epic 1991 Leinster first-round tie.

While these were hugely influential sporting events at the time, it was perhaps inevitable that given my family history I would end up focusing on a different sport, that of handball. My grandfather, Paddy Kennedy from Boyle County Roscommon, won an All-Ireland Junior Doubles title in 1942 while my dad, Eugene, was also a strong player winning numerous overage All-Irelands over the years. Every September on the eve of the All-Ireland hurling and football finals, my dad would take me and my younger brother, Brian, to Croke Park to watch the All-Ireland 60x30 handball finals where Kilkenny's Michael 'Ducksy' Walsh reigned supreme. While there were many fantastic games, I remember the 1992 final particularly well with 'Ducksy' winning his 8th title-in-a-row by beating Meath's Walter O' Connor in a very tight, tense match in front of a massive crowd.

I had started playing handball regularly three years earlier when my local GAA club, St. Brigid's in Blanchardstown, built two new courts in 1989. I took to the game fairly quickly and went on to win several underage All-Irelands as well as underage World and USA titles. Some of the toughest games I had during that time were training matches against my brother Brian who would use a racquet while I would play with my hands. Brian represented Ireland in tennis at underage level so he had a serious smack of the ball – hard to beat that for training! Brian was also a good handballer and together we won a minor All-Ireland doubles title in 1998 when Brian was only 14 years old, still a record to this day.

As a young lad watching 'Ducksy' win title after title, I never dreamed that one day I would end up facing him myself in a senior final. As it turned out, in 2001 'Ducksy' was still the man to beat and by All-Ireland final day he was the last man standing between me and my first All-Ireland senior 60x30 title. I got off to a tremendous start against him winning the first game 21-2. However, in the second game, he improved dramatically and I tightened up a little bit and stopped going for the rally-ending killshots. I lost narrowly 21-19. 'Ducksy' used all of his experience in the decisive game and beat me 21-14. I was gutted but I had learned a valuable lesson and vowed that if I ever got to another final I would be far more offensive and aggressive in my play.

The following year, in 2002, 'Ducksy' and I were back in the final again. A few weeks before the final, he announced that it would be his last year playing senior handball (thankfully he later rowed back on this decision and is still playing at senior level). As a result of this as well as Kilkenny being in the All-Ireland hurling final the following day, a massive crowd travelled up from Kilkenny. I'd say close to 800 people crammed into the Croke Park handball centre that night. The heat was intense and the atmosphere was the best that I have ever experienced as a player. As in 2001, I started quickly and won the first game 21-6. I knew the second game would be tougher but I quickly gained control and managed to win it 21-12.

The feeling after winning the final rally of the match was incredible – pure elation. Before the presentation of the Purcell Cup, my dad came into the alley and I remember embracing him and saying, "We did it". I had won on the court but it was the years of coaching and support from my parents, the many thousands of miles that they had travelled driving me around the country to training and matches, and the financial support that they had given me to compete in international competitions that had helped me achieve my goal. It felt brilliant to have won in front of so many friends and family and to have the opportunity in my victory speech to thank people who had helped me over the years like my former juvenile mentors, Michael McCloskey and Shea O' Reilly. There were huge celebrations in the Croke Park handball centre that night. While I have gone on to win many more titles, from a personal perspective that night is my outstanding sporting memory – even now, I can't help but smile when I think about it!

# JOHN KENNY

## Swimming and motoring... it's just not cricket

JOHN KENNY is a Broadcaster/Journalist with RTÉ primarily with sport but also as a DJ with RTÉ's digital radio network 2XM where he presents *The JK Experience.* Born in Dublin, he started broadcasting at 18 when he left Terenure College and worked Radio City, the Big D, South Coast Radio in Cork and the original Q102 before joining RTÉ in 1986.

He has covered three Olympic Games and presented a number of radio documentaries including *Ten Years of Jordan Grand Prix, Olympic Years, The Dirty Dozen, Ireland's Motorsport Legends* and the award winning Doc On One *Heroes of the Caribbean.*

He has also worked with the BBC on their legendary *Test Match Special,* two Cricket World Cup finals and wrote *The Dirty Dozen, Ireland's Motorsport Legends,* published by O'Brien Press. He is the motorsport columnist with the *Irish Daily Star.*

This is my second stab at writing a 'My favourite Sporting Moment' as a number of years ago I also contributed to another book of a similar title compiled by the legendary Seán Óg Ó Ceallacháin in which I described Gary O'Toole's silver medal performance in the men's 200 metres breaststroke at the European swimming championships in Bonn, West Germany in 1989.

In truth, Seán was looking for stories outside of the usual GAA, soccer and golf anecdotes. He had plenty of them. So when he approached me to write something for his collection, he asked for a contribution from one of the so-called 'minority' sports I cover such as swimming, cricket and motorsport. I was happy to oblige with the O'Toole story.

Not only was it a fantastic success by an Irish swimmer in a sport that had yielded no Irish international success to that point, but it followed a difficult period in Irish swimming. O'Toole remains to this day a man I respect, admire and remain friends with, I'm glad to say, and to have shared in his greatest moment in Bonn when he finished runner-up to Britain's Nick Gillingham from lane eight in the men's 200 breaststroke final on a hot evening at the Rommerbad University complex, is still very fresh in my mind.

O'Toole also had the audacity to beat Hungary's Joseph Szabo, the then Olympic champion in the event, and the pictures of his leap across the lane ropes to celebrate with Gillingham, who incidentally had equalled the world record of American Mike Barrowman, were seen across the world.

O'Toole and Gillingham were good mates, so much so that the Englishman turned up at O'Toole's 21st birthday party a few weeks later. I know. I was there. He has gone on to become an orthopaedic surgeon and provides fantastic analysis for RTÉ Sport's Olympic swimming coverage.

That trip to Bonn to see O'Toole's success was actually my first sojourn abroad for RTÉ having joined as a freelance sports journalist just two years earlier. I was sent primarily because I was covering swimming for Radio Sport at the time, more by accident than design.

I needed the work.

RTÉ Sport only had slim pickings for me in those early years and I supplemented that by occasional programmes on 2FM as well as working as a DJ in nightclubs the length and breadth of Ireland.

I was initially sent to the 1987 National Swimming Championship in Bangor, County Down where the likes of O'Toole and Michelle Smith competed and chanced upon a niche in the market.

The sport has taken me to three Olympic Games and in 2008 I had the privilege to work as the RTÉ TV commentator in Beijing along with Olympian Nick O'Hare with O'Toole back in studio when Michael Phelps took his historic eight gold medals.

As with covering swimming, it was likewise with motorsport.

I was cajoled into reporting on the 1988 Leinster Trophy meeting at Mondello Park in County Kildare and watched Mika Hakkinen, a future Formula One world champion, win the famous old trophy that weekend. So I took up that mantle as well.

I still report on motorsport for RTÉ Radio (occasionally for TV as well) and have written a book on Ireland's Motorsport Legends entitled 'The Dirty Dozen' for O'Brien Press which came out of a radio series back in 2006.

Motorsport too has taken me around the world.

When Jordan grand prix was in its heyday, Gallagher's, the team sponsors, took journalists to at least two grand prix a year and in 1999 I was one of only a handful of Irish at Magny Cours in France to witness Jordan take one of their four grand prix wins.

Funnily enough, that wasn't one of the sponsorship trips.

I was on the other side of France with my family that weekend when I got the daft idea to drive 250 miles accross the country with my then 16-year-old daughter Danielle to see Heinz Harold Frentzen win on a dark gloomy afternoon on the Magny Cours circuit. It was made all the more memorable by the fact that it took us 350 miles to drive back as we took a wrong turning and the car got back to our holiday camp site running on the smell of petrol fumes!

Cricket is another one of those sports that I cover, not just for RTÉ, but occasionally for the BBC as well. I found myself in the West Indies in 2007 and had the privilege to work for the BBC's legendary *Test Match Special* on BBC Radio 4 for the entire Irish world cup campaign, including that memorable win on St Patrick's Day 2007 when Ireland beat the mighty Pakistan.

I actually kept all the commentaries and interviews from that period and ultimately made the RTÉ Radio Doc On One *'Heroes of the Caribbean'* which won an award at the New York Radio Festival Ceremony in 2011, an award of which I'm extremely proud.

If you would like to relive that brilliant summer you can hear it at http://www.rte.ie/radio1/doconone/irish-cricket-ireland-icc-world-cup-2007-cwc-07.html

To pick out one particular event for this book has been difficult as I have witnessed some sensational events, including the Croatia versus Yugoslavia soccer match in Zagreb in 1999, a game played in an incredibly hostile atmosphere just after the Balkans War.

Other memories which spring to mind include Dublin beating Galway in the 1974 All-Ireland football final, a game I watched supporting the Dubs with my brother, Noel, sitting, I kid you not, in the Galway dugout.

Another memory was watching my beloved Manchester United beat Juventus in the Roy Keane inspired Champions league semi-final second leg on another hostile night in the Stadio Del Alpi in Turin, also in 1999.

The pity was I missed the final!

# JOE KERNAN
# Lesson learnt and applied

JOE KERNAN played for Crossmaglen Rangers senior team for 20 years and the Armagh senior team for 17 years. He won five county senior titles with his club and three Ulster senior titles with Armagh, and scored two goals in the 1977 All-Ireland final defeat to Dublin.

He won two All-Star awards in 1977 and 1980 and holds four Railway Cup medals. Joe managed Crossmaglen Rangers to five Armagh under-21 and senior club championships and three Ulster and All-Ireland club championships.

He became manager of the Armagh seniors in 2001 and led them to four Ulster championships and the county's only All-Ireland win, in 2002, and a National League title in 2005. An estate agent and mortgage broker, he is married to Patricia. Four of their five sons are on the Armagh panel.

One of the greatest lessons I took from my playing career into management came about when our county senior team reached the All-Ireland semi-final in 1980.

Three years previously, in 1977, Armagh had reached the All-Ireland final for the first time since 1953. Together with some of the experienced players on the team I approached the management team to suggest that we bring in someone who had the experience of winning All-Irelands to see if the knowledge they gained by their success could help bring us as a squad to the next level.

To our disappointment, this request was frowned upon by the management team and the county chairman, their reason being that they felt this would undermine them and they did not want anyone 'stealing their thunder'. Needless to say, we lost our All-Ireland semi-final but this experience stuck with me for a long time.

When my playing days were finished and I had moved into management, Crossmaglen Rangers won its first Armagh county senior title for 10 years in 1996. Later that year we progressed to win our first ever Ulster club title and brought the club into uncharted territory. At this stage I was preparing the side for the All-Ireland club semi-final and it brought me back to my own playing days and how I felt let down when our request was refused way back in 1980: this time I was going to make sure that I did not have any regrets or make the same mistakes with my players. The way forward was to take in the right people when I felt their expertise was needed. This started a practice which stood to me throughout my managerial career with both club and county. By March 1997 Crossmaglen Rangers had delivered our county's first ever All-Ireland club title.

Through time I was able to call upon many successful sportspeople like Colm O'Rourke, Martin McHugh, Eamon Coleman, Sean Boylan, Sean O'Neill, Tommy Dowd, Mick O' Dwyer, Brian Cody and Paul O'Connell to address my squads and not only did the players benefit from listening to their experiences but I also learned and enjoyed having them in.

I am very lucky to have been involved in All-Ireland success with both my club and county. Winning with Crossmaglen Rangers was something special because I was born and bred in Cross and had played for my club since I was a child. I had watched all these young men come up through the underage ranks and now I was in the fortunate position of leading them to Croke Park to fulfil their dreams. A few years earlier nobody would have thought this would be remotely possible. Even now that 15 years have passed, the club has continued to grow and teams are still delivering All-Ireland titles. It makes me very proud to know that I was there at the very start when the seeds of success and self-belief were sown. To see my own sons now being part of successful All-Ireland club winning sides with Crossmaglen gives me even greater satisfaction.

Taking over the Armagh senior side in 2001 was also very special. It was heartbreaking to see them go so close to All-Ireland glory in the previous three years but from the minute I took the job I knew that winning an All-Ireland title was a realistic objective. I honestly believe that if you hurt enough there is always more inside a team and inside every individual, and that certainly was the case with this bunch of Armagh players.

People say that the day we won the All-Ireland against Kerry was the most special of all but to me the semi-final against Dublin was equally special. The way the game finished on a knife edge only added to the occasion and when the ball ended up in the hands of John McEntee and the final whistle blew, there were many tears shed as we had qualified for our first All-Ireland final in 25 years.

An All-Ireland final against Kerry is the day all players dream of but the last 12 minutes of this match typified what the Armagh team was all about; edge of the seat stuff, no scores, end-to-end football, tackles, breaking ball fought for as if it was the last breath a player would draw. I will never forget the welcome sound of John Bannon's whistle as the ball ended up in Geezer's hands: you would think it was meant to be. We had reached the Holy Grail and Kieran McGeeney would be accepting the Sam Maguire Cup on the Hogan Stand for the Orchard County. Happy days!

# NOEL KING
## Born to manage

**N**OEL KING played soccer for Dundalk, Shamrock Rovers, Home Farm, Bohemians, Valenciennes, Derry City, and Limerick, winning every FAI and League of Ireland playing honour.

His first player manager position came in 1986/7 leading Derry City to the LOI First Division title and Shield. He returned to Shamrock Rovers in 1989 as player manager reaching an FAI Cup final against Galway, before leading Limerick to a 1992 League Cup win. In 2001/02 he was caretaker manager in Shelbourne's Premier title win. In 2003 he led Finn Harps to a Premier League play-off against Derry.

As Ireland women's senior manager Noel led the girls to a UEFA high of 15th, a FIFA world ranking of 25th and a first UEFA European Finals play-off against Iceland in 2008. He led Ireland's U-17 girls to a European final in 2009 losing gold to Spain on penalties. He was appointed Head Coach of the Irish men's U-21 team in 2010.

At seven years of age I dreamed of becoming a soccer manager.

Back then I was the official Home Farm mascot and had an access all areas pass as my dad Kevin and uncle Nicky managed the team together.

I listened and watched and enjoyed it so much, I promised myself I would become a football manager just like them. They were brilliant. I, too, wanted to pick the team, decide the tactics, analyse the players and the teams' performances and discuss football in the finest detail all day long, in the house, the car or even the pub.

In late 1985 I left Valenciennes FC in France where I was playing and accepted the job of manager of Derry City FC.

At 28 years of age I was presented with an opportunity to fulfill a boyhood dream. It was my start as a full time manager. Thank God two of the most experienced voices in my life were still alive and giving advice: "Getting a job is one thing, but keeping it is an entirely different proposition. So keep your head down and keep grafting."

Derry City had been absent from the Irish League (Northern Ireland League) for 13 years but had recently been accepted into the League of Ireland. They were attracting crowds of 3,000 to 4,000 but after seven outings, they had not won a league game and, as fans do, they demanded change.

My first game as manager in the Brandywell was a 2-0 loss to Sligo; it wasn't encouraging. A draw in Bray the following week gave us a point, but we were still rock bottom. It was time to make changes. Adding players such as Da Gama, Da Silva, Gauld, Devlin, Bradley and Gorman to existing players like Doherty, O'Neill, McDowell, Mahon, Quigg and McGreadie made a difference. We got our first league win at Monaghan and zoomed up the table to finish the season an amazing fourth place.

An FAI Cup fixture against the Garda in February 1986 brought the glare of the world media to Derry. One might have thought that with players from Scotland, Zaire, Brazil, England, Dublin and South Africa they might be the focus, but none of it.

There were no RUC (northern police) personnel inside the ground on match day. The Brandywell was self-policed by local supporters, still a unique arrangement in world football. So when the Republic's police force crossed the border to play in the Brandywell, the irony was felt everywhere. The country held its breath in fear of trouble. Thankfully, the match passed off peacefully. We won, 5-0 in front of a full house.

The next month we lost the quarter-final of the FAI Cup 1-0 away to Cork, but Derry was still buzzing with crowds continuing to grow and games selling out.

The FAI Shield final in 1986 was Derry City's first FAI final competition. It was also my first FAI final as a professional manager. It was regarded as a minor cup and is now a defunct competition, but to Derry City supporters and officials it was all that mattered. I felt exactly the same.

Longford Town provided the opposition and with over 6,000 red- and white-clad Derry supporters travelling to the Showgrounds in Sligo, the occasion was colourful and the pressure immense, despite having a 3-1 advantage from the first leg in the Brandywell.

History was made. Owen Da Gama hit a hat-trick and on the final whistle of a 6-1 aggregate victory the crowds spilled onto the pitch creating amazing scenes of celebration, the likes of which I have never witnessed before or since. It was party time and people were singing, crying and dancing. The players were mobbed.

En route home to Derry, a cavalcade of hooting cars and buses was formed, a mile long some people said. If we had won the Champions League the celebrations could not have been more genuine. That day is a sporting favourite of thousands, including me.

And how appropriate it was, as Derry City's won their first FAI trophy, that the fans had successful football back in their lives, and on a personal note my journey as a trophy-winning manager had started. The following year we won the league title and promotion.

Twenty-five years later, on 1 September 2011, history was repeated in the same Sligo Showgrounds when I managed Ireland to a 2-1 victory over Hungary in the UEFA u-21 Championship: the dreams of the seven year old live on.

# JOE LENNON

## Producing a video of Gaelic football skills

J OE LENNON began playing Gaelic football at St. Colman's College, Newry and with Aghaderg Club, County Down. He won three All-Ireland championship and three National League medals – one of each as captain in 1968 – in an 18-year career with Down, represented Ulster six times and played for the Combined Universities.

He qualified as a secondary teacher in 1961 and graduated from Loughborough College of Physical Education with First Class Honours in 1964. In 1971 he was conferred with an MSc in Recreation Management at Loughborough University of Technology.

After teaching for 25 years at the Franciscan College, Gormanston and following comprehensive research on the evolution of the GAA rules of play, he was awarded a PhD at DCU in 1998 for his thesis – Towards a Philosophy for Legislation in Gaelic Games. He organised the first Gaelic football national coaching course in 1964 and later wrote *Fitness for Gaelic Football* and *Coaching Gaelic Football for Champions*.

It all began in low key at a meeting of the Coaching Advisory Council held in Croke Park in 1987 when an item on the agenda read simply – A Coaching Video for Gaelic football. The chairman, Joe McGrath, all the members of the committee, and Lorcán Ó Ruairc, secretary, were present.

After a long discussion it was decided to proceed with the project. What was not so clear was who was going to take on the responsibility of getting the video made. Each member of the committee declined to do the job until it came to me. When I was asked, I said I would be interested, but made it clear that I had never done anything like this before, and thought that the project would be shelved.

However, when committee member Fr Donncha McCarthy said: "Give it to Joe Lennon. He does not know how to do a bad job", I did not know whether to feel grateful for his encouraging remarks or that I had let myself into something that could turn out to be a success or a terrible failure. The committee assured me of their full support, and I knew that Lorcán Ó Ruairc was a superb administrator and would make an excellent programme manager.

I had to get some ideas together quickly, and it soon became clear that we would need a lot of support from a whole variety of sources. Early on, I got permission from Gormanston College to use their playing fields which are very scenic and would provide a great setting. I was a member of St Patrick's GAA, Stamullen, and the club readily agreed to the use of their grounds for part of the shoot.

I needed some accomplished coaches, and as I am an Ulsterman I selected one from each of the other provinces - Michael Ned O'Sullivan, Kerry; John Tobin, Galway and Paddy Clarke from Louth. All agreed without hesitation.

Early on too, I decided to use local young players and asked four clubs if they would each send 10 players – a few under 16s, some minors and one or two seniors - to Gormanston College for a four-day shoot. They all agreed wholeheartedly. O'Neills very kindly supplied four sets of playing gear and some footballs.

While this planning was in progress, I consulted Louis Marcus, a professional film maker, who recommended Anner International Post Production Ltd. for the project. I had begun writing the script soon after accepting the task, and invited the coaches to make suggestions for the script and the format.

When discussing the project at home one evening, I said that some music could help to enliven the video. My son, Darren, told me that there was a 'fabulous' band playing in Drogheda several nights a week and that Eric Sharpe, a near neighbour, was playing. I went to listen to Jump the Gun, and though I don't claim to have much of a musical ear, I decided to ask if they would be willing to produce and play the theme music. They agreed.

Things were going very well. I had the venue, the players, the coaches, the kit and, now, the music. Avonmore agreed to sponsor the video.

The coaches met several times to discuss the script. We decided to take the skills in turn and go through the coaching routines that we would use in practice.

I was delighted at how well the players adapted to the task. They got on very well – never a word of criticism of one another though there was a good deal of 'slagging'. One of the players turned out to be a real comedian who kept us all in tucks of laughter.

When we got down to shooting the sequences, I was delighted that one of the cameramen, Gerry McArthur, had worked in RTÉ Sport. He had a real feeling for the game and what we were trying to achieve.

The basic plan was to select each of the skills in turn, and select a group of players and a coach who would do a coaching session with them. The coaches took turns in running the sessions. Although the routine had to be adapted to meet the needs of the cameramen, nothing of the coaching content was affected. And we were blessed with good weather.

The shoot was completed on time, and Lorcán Ó Ruairc arranged for the whole group – players, cameramen and helpers – to go to Croke Park to watch an All-Ireland semi-final. It was a great day out.

But now the serious work had to start. I contacted Slane Recording Studios to see if they would record the music that Jump The Gun had produced, and to record the song Confidence that I had written. The music was named The Solo Runner. I did not realise that these musicians worked odd hours! We often left Slane Studios as dawn was breaking. I then had to go and do my day job that started at 9.00 a.m.

When we had the music on tape, I went to Anner studios where we laid down the footage. This was a fascinating process that I quickly learned to do and appreciate.

RTÉ supplied me with master tapes of games played in Croke Park. After each coaching sequence was laid down, a selection of the skills performed in big matches was added to reinforce the coaching points made.

This was the real 'making' process. I had the raw footage from the shoots, the music from Jump the Gun and the excerpts from championship games to back up the coaching.

From here on in I was on my own. The process of putting all this together was new to me but I soon learned what had to be done. Importantly, I learned that it was up to me to decide what went in and what was scrapped. I was determined that I would only include what I felt was totally relevant. After about three months, I finally had a video that was something like I had imagined.

All the 'tops and tails' were added – the acknowledgements to the artists, the cameramen, the clubs and their players, Lorcán and, of course, the coaches without whom this would not have been possible.

At about this time, Jump the Gun won the National Song Contest with Take Him Home, and would represent Ireland in the Eurovision Song Contest. Events were getting very exciting.

The GAA funded the launch on 9 March 1988 and the video got a good reception. I was very much aware that all the praise for the video was from our own team and association. However, I wanted to find out what the general public would think of it and perhaps how the industry would rate it.

The video was entered for the Irish Television Awards (ITVA) for Irish non-broadcast videos. I was quite unaware of the various sections of The Irish Non Broadcast Videos competition – The 3M Award of Excellence, The PVL Sales and Marketing Award, The Ampex/Eorotek Public Relations/Information Award and The JVC Training Award. This is the section in which our video was entered.

When I got an invitation to the Gresham Hotel for the presentation to winners on 18 October 1989, I was quite excited for I did not think I would be invited unless the video had done well. I invited all the coaches. John Dowling, GAA president, attended.

As the evening proceeded and the prizes for the various categories were awarded, the temperature rose. Finally, the judge came to the Best in the Category for Training. The chair of the adjudicating committee went to some lengths to compliment several entries and then said: "I don't know anything about Gaelic football but, for me, this video is by far the best entry in the category."

I felt as happy and proud as when I had won my All-Ireland football medals. For here were we, a small group of amateurs with literally no experience in the field of producing training videos coming first in quite a prestigious competition where all the big companies were competing.

I got a very nice congratulatory letter from GAA Director General, Liam Ó Maolmhichíl. I will always regard this video *Gaelic Football Skills* as one of my most important achievements in Gaelic games, and perhaps my most valuable contribution to the development of coaching Gaelic football.

# OLIVE LOUGHNANE

## World silver in Berlin... but my daughter kept me grounded

**O**LIVE LOUGHNANE was born in Cork on 14 January 1976 but grew up in Carrabane parish near Loughrea, County Galway. She represented Ireland at the Olympic Games in 2000, 2004 and 2008 finishing 7th in the 20k walk in Beijing, inside the Olympic record. She will compete in her fourth Games at London 2012.

Olive also represented her country at the World Championships in 2001, 2003, 2005, 2007, 2009 and 2011, winning the silver medal in Berlin in the 20k walking race in 2009. She was awarded Irish Sportswoman of the Year, Athletics Ireland Athlete of the Year and won a Texaco sports award in recognition of that achievement.

She attended secondary school at St Raphael's College and St Brigid's Vocational School in Loughrea and obtained a BComm from NUIG. She lives in Coachford, County Cork with her husband Martin Corkery, who manages her career, and their daughter Eimear.

For as long as I can remember, I loved sport. As a young child I lapped up the Tour de France and the Dublin Horse Show. Sunday afternoons were spent glued to the All-Ireland hurling and football championships. I got up at 6.00 a.m. to watch the boxing from the LA Olympics. As I got older I became interested in golf and rugby. When I am away training and competing, news of Irish sporting success inspires me and makes me up my game. When Padraig Harrington was winning his third major, the US PGA in 2008, I was preparing for the Beijing Olympics. I literally had my head in the clouds 2000m above sea level in the Pyrenees. Internet coverage was patchy to say the least, so my husband patiently described the unfolding drama down the phone.

However, the sport which I have always followed the closest was athletics. I watched Eamonn Coghlan win gold at the World Athletics Championships in Helsinki in 1983. I roared as an eight year old when John Treacy shook off Charlie Spedding in the 1984 Olympics to claim silver. I was inspired by Sonia O'Sullivan's mental toughness to come back from disappointment in the 3000m to take silver in the 1500m at the World Championships in 1993. Catherina McKiernan was a cross-country and road legend.

In my first brush with competitive athletics, the parish sports, I didn't cover myself in glory. I was small in stature. Despite my best efforts I failed to get on the podium in a class of four girls. The consolation lollipop did nothing to heal the disappointment. I stuck to the task and it was the only year I failed to make the top three! I joined the athletic club in Loughrea when I was 12. I loved the buzz of competing. I was lucky to have a good group of girls around the same age. In winter we ran cross-country in the mud, snow and ice. In summer we ran on the track. There was a great team spirit. Every summer we competed in the National League, a competition where the club fields somebody in all the events – sprints, middle distance, throws, jumps and, of course, walks.

We were a small club so everybody got stuck in and did their own events plus two others and the relays, the idea being that even if you finished last, the club still got one point. The 3000m was my event, the hammer and the walk my add-ons. I got the solitary point in the hammer but surprised everybody when I finished second in the walk. I wasn't quite as shocked as everybody else because I had done some sneaky training. I had decent endurance from cross-country and I liked the technical nature of the event. I met the national event coach after the race and he suggested I might like to a bit of event specific training.

That was 1994. One thing led to another and I qualified to represent Ireland in the women's 20k walk at the Olympic Games in Sydney. This was my first major championship. Since then I have competed at five World Championships. In March 2011, I qualified for my fourth Olympic Games. There have been many great memories. Qualifying for my first Olympic Games is a stand-out day; finishing seventh in the Olympic Games in Beijing inside the old Olympic record is another. However, nothing compares to the buzz of taking silver at the World Championships in Berlin in 2009.

The race took place in the heart of Berlin. It started at the Brandenburg gate and proceeded down 'Unter den Linden', one of the main streets in Berlin. We covered ten 2k laps. I'd love to be able to tell you I was inspired by the historic location. The truth be told, I went there to win a medal and the location was a bonus. Before the Olympics in Beijing, my thoughts were: "it would be nice to win a medal". In Berlin my attitude was: "there aren't three people in the world better than me today, I will win a medal". The race began at one o'clock. It was 28 degrees when we started and 32 when we finished. I wasn't intimidated by the heat.

I had trained in a little town near Granada in Spain where 28 degrees was a 'fresh' day. I was very comfortable for the first 30 minutes. At 7k there was a surge and I found myself back in sixth place. I reeled in the others and by 13k I was back in the top three. At 14k I felt I couldn't walk another step but I knew that difficult moments like this were bound to come. I ploughed on. The Russian girl, Olga Kaniskina, was clear. For the last 30 minutes it was a battle between the Chinese girl, Liu Hong, and me for silver and bronze. I continued to surge and with 1800m to go I broke free and pushed home for silver. There were thousands of spectators on the course. I was sandwiched between two athletics superpowers so I had the neutrals roaring me on. Of course the Irish were loud enough to be heard above all others! The tricolours waving gave me that extra push for the last 6k.

When the race was over I was whisked off to the press conference. I had a quick stopover in the team hotel to shower and then on to the medal presentation. One of my first calls was to my three-year-old daughter, Eimear. She was staying with her granny in Cork while I was away. She was at the swings when I called. "Mammy won the silver medal", I said. "I know mammy, well done mammy. I'm going to go back to the swings now mammy." There's nothing like a small girl to keep you grounded.

# STEVEN MCDONNELL

## When Sam came to the Orchard County

**S**TEVEN McDONNELL from the Killeavy St Monnina's club has been an ever-present corner forward on the Armagh senior football team since 1999. The highlight of his career to date is his county's All-Ireland victory over Kerry on a scoreline of 1-12 to 0-14 in the 2002 All-Ireland football final.

He received All-Star awards for his performances in 2002, 2003 and 2005. He holds seven Ulster senior medals and one National League Division 1 title. In 2010 he captained Armagh to a National Football League Division 2 title defeating Down in the final.

Steven was named captain of the Ireland International Rules team in 2010 and was chosen as GAA Vodafone and GPA Footballer of the Year for his performances in 2003. He is married with three children and has a keen interest in soccer (especially Liverpool FC) and golf.

As a fan, 25 May 2005 is the date that will forever stay with me. The delight my beloved Liverpool FC brought me that night has only been bettered in the sporting arena by what Armagh achieved on that glorious afternoon of 22 September three years previously. I can still picture it now. The final whistle going, the ball in Kieran McGeeney's hands as John Bannon blew the whistle, and not knowing what to do. Honest. We were delirious with delight but we were frozen stiff because of it. It was only when the crowds came onto the field and we were hoisted into the air that we began to really celebrate. Thousands upon thousands of fans flooded the field and yet somehow when I was thrown up onto a couple of shoulders the first people I saw were my brother Kevin and a couple of my friends. It was even beyond being surreal!

We had beaten Kerry. I'll say that again. We had beaten Kerry, the county that made football look like they were born to play it. And yet we felt we owed them one. We felt we should have beaten them on the two occasions we played them in the 2000 All-Ireland semi-final. We couldn't let this one slip away. We kicked the first two points that day and it developed into a tit-for-tat affair before Kerry hit a real purple patch before the break. If the truth be told, they could have been further ahead. After bursting through the middle, Eoin Brosnan drove a ball just wide of the post and Enda McNulty got his fingertips to a ball that had been destined to land into Colm Cooper's hands going one-on-one with our goalkeeper, Benny Tierney. Inches won us the game.

Kerry had gone into the break four points ahead of us, having scored 11 points. We were unlucky ourselves in that Oisin McConville had missed a penalty. Against a team practised in All-Ireland finals and knowing how to win them, the miss was seen as a huge psychological blow for us but we were made of sterner stuff. One of the things that sticks out at the end of that half was when 19-year-old Ronan Clarke went over to Oisin and put his arm around him and told him to lift his head. You didn't know how someone as young as Clarkey would react on the biggest of big days but he was sensational for us. One of the greatest defenders in the game, Seamus Moynihan, was marking him but he managed to score three points off him. His words of advice for Oisin did the trick too as he came out for the second half as if what happened beforehand didn't mean a thing to him.

Joe Kernan, of course, gave us that famous half-time speech where he managed to get his hands on an All-Ireland loser's medal and hit the four corners of the dressing room with it. Things hadn't been looking good for us but we had to give it a go. We couldn't come back afterwards wondering what might have been. We had to throw caution to the wind. We needed a goal; that's what we felt. And Oisin was the man to deliver it for us. It was the pivotal moment and to me signified just how special a player Oisin is. He could have easily struck it across Declan O'Keeffe but he did the unexpected, striking the ball at the Kerry goalkeeper's near side and hitting the net.

It was a superb move up the field and got us to within a point of Kerry. It was at that stage that I started thinking: "We're playing Kerry but we're so much in control." The next two points were just as memorable for us. Clarkey got the equalising score, looping around Moynihan and measuring his kick. It was then that the crowd really got behind us, cheering us on loudly and proudly. Kerry could feel it too and doubt seemed to creep into their game.

It's hard to realise now that the winning score was kicked 10 minutes before the end of the game. When I kicked it I certainly didn't think it was going to prove the difference between the teams. There was just too much time left. But so it turned out and it was the result of a move we had practised ad nauseam on the training field. Sometimes it worked for us and sometimes it didn't but we felt its percentages were good. Aidan O'Rourke put the most perfect ball in to me. It bounced just in front to give me the opportunity to twist and turn to kick it over the bar with my left foot. For that move we had rehearsed so much to come off when it mattered most was a testament to the work put in not only by us but by Joe Kernan, Paul Grimley and John McCloskey. It justified everything we had toiled for. The kick gives me shivers even thinking about it now!

For those last 10 minutes Kerry did all they could to break us but try as they might they failed. We weren't going to let them take this from us. Then that whistle blew and my, what a feeling! So many thoughts raced through my head but one kept reverberating: "We've finally done it".

One of the great statistics from that game was that the full-forward line of Diarmaid Marsden, Clarkey and myself scored 0-9 from play. For a team that was seen as too physical and too negative, that spoke volumes. On All-Ireland final day, when it mattered most, we showed the country that we were a real footballing team.

Up until the time of writing, it has been our one and only All-Ireland. With that great Armagh team, it should have been more. That's why it makes 2002 even more special. Making Armagh people smile, making our families swell with pride and getting the very best out of ourselves. In a nutshell, that is what winning an All-Ireland is all about. We did it. And the Sam Maguire Cup rested well and safely in the Orchard County for the next 12 months.

# EUGENE MCGEE

## Waistcoat not enought to stop Kerry in All-Ireland final

E UGENE McGEE started managing football teams with the UCD club in Dublin in the 1970s and won six Sigerson Cups in seven years, three Dublin senior championships and two All-Ireland club championships. He managed the Cashel club to win their first Longford SFC in 1977.

With Offaly he won three senior and two Leinster under-21 titles and the All-Ireland senior title in 1982. He was manager of the Ireland Compromise Rules teams in 1987 and 2000, losing 1-2 in Ireland and winning 2-1 in Australia.

As a journalist Eugene was Managing Editor of the *Longford Leader* for 23 years and wrote for the *Sunday Press, Sunday Tribune* and *Evening Herald*. He is a GAA columnist with the *Irish Independent* as well as doing radio and television work.

Eugene was conferred with an Honorary Degree by the National University of Ireland in 2009 for his achievements in journalism and sporting activity. He lives in his native Longford with his wife, Marian, and children Conor and Linda.

Today team managers, particularly in the GAA, often go to ludicrous levels to 'cod' the opposition, and the media, with wild goose chases about what they think will happen. "I can't see Johnny playing on Sunday, sure his ankle has swelled up like a balloon". "And Paddy Joe is still in trouble with that auld hamstring and you all know what hamstrings are like so don't bank on him even togging out for this match".

Then Sunday arrives with even the team's own supporters not sure what sort of a team will line out but when the National Anthem is being played it is plain to see that both Johnny and Paddy Joe are the pictures of health and singing Amhrán na bFiann with gusto.

In 1981 I was in charge of the Offaly football team as they were preparing to play Kerry in the All-Ireland final. Remember it was 1981 - not THAT final which took place in 1982! Offaly were dominating Leinster at that stage having eventually got the great Dublin team of the 1970s off their backs in 1980. And even though Offaly played Kerry in 1980, also in the semi-final, with that remarkable scoreline of Kerry 4-15, Offaly 4-10 and the great Matt Connor scoring 2-9, we in Offaly felt that there was a definite possibility that the five-point gap could be bridged in 1981.

There was extra motivation for Offaly footballers that year because on the first Sunday in September the Offaly hurlers had won the All-Ireland for the first time so the fans were almost demanding that the footballers complete the double, and of course Liam Currams was a member of both teams.

We had been progressing steadily towards our aim when about three weeks before the final I received a phone call from one of our selectors, the late Paddy Fenlon who was a veterinary surgeon in Edenderry. Vets get around the rural areas all the time and Paddy had heard the news quickly which he relayed to me: "Johnny Mooney is after falling off a tractor-load of turf at Fahy Hill and his shoulder has been dislocated".

Short and not so sweet, these words sent a chill through my body because I immediately realised that our chances of beating Kerry had been dealt, if not a mortal blow, certainly a very serious one. Mooney had been a teenage prodigy from his minor days and played in the 1976 Leinster minor final which Offaly lost narrowly to Dublin. He went on to win two Leinster under-21 championships and played, aged 19, in the 1978 Leinster semi-final against Dublin in Portlaoise which Dublin won narrowly. He had developed into a classic-style midfielder in the Mick O'Connell mould and was a really outstanding young player. He was due to be a key figure at midfield against the great Kingdom pairing at that time of Jack O'Shea and Sean Walsh, one of the best ever Kerry midfield duos. The other midfielder was Tomas O'Connor, also an outstanding high catcher in the days when high fielding was the most prized skill in football, but he was only recovering from a serious knee injury and was a high risk selection.

Not many people knew about Johnny Mooney's accident when he was helping to bring home the turf from the local bog but inevitably the word got out in his native parish of Rhode and following the first team training session afterwards the bad news was dispersed county wide. It was a devastating blow to the other players who were banking on Mooney taking on the Kerry midfield with some success at least. But it soon became clear that he was not going to be able to play despite the best medical attention. The psychological effect in the camp was serious.

But an All-Ireland final is a rare occurrence for any player so the rest of the panel decided that even greater effort by them was the best way to make up for Johnny Mooney's absence. However, not long after the game commenced Sean Walsh connected with a fair shoulder to Tomas O'Connor and it was clear that his ability to last the game was very doubtful.

And this was proven right, so with Offaly being in dire straits in the midfield area one of those gambles that every manager has to take at some stage was taken to replace O'Connor with Mooney. At least Mooney, who was clearly medically unfit for the task, did make his own piece of history when he appeared on the Croke Park pitch because he must be the only player ever to have worn a waistcoat while playing in an All-Ireland final!

Sports medicine was nothing as sophisticated in the 1980s as it is now and bandaging an injured shoulder was never a very useful exercise anyway. So the legendary masseur, Ossie Bennett from Kilkenny, hit on the idea of having Johnny wear a tight-fitting waistcoat under his jersey as protection for the damaged shoulder. To cut a long story short, it did not work.

Yet despite all the problems Offaly had in this game through injury they kept hanging in with Kerry for the greater part of the match and the Offaly defenders played heroically to stop that brilliant Kerry forward line, who scored 2-19 in the semi-final against Mayo, from scoring a goal. But then Jack O'Shea finished off any chance Offaly had near full time when he was at the end of a Kerry movement from one end of the field to the other to score one of the great goals in All-Ireland final history which is so often replayed on television to this day. Kerry won by 1-12 to 0-8.

Obviously the Offaly players got their reward, with a bonus, when they beat Kerry in the famous five-in-a-row final the following year. If I had thought about it at the time I should have presented Johnny Mooney's waistcoat to the GAA museum for posterity because I doubt if we will ever see another player wearing a waistcoat in an All-Ireland final!

# JIM MCKEEVER
# Beginnings and Endings

JIM McKEEVER played with Antrim minors in 1947, Derry minors in 1948 and Derry seniors - in 12 positions, mostly at midfield - from 1948 to 1962. He lectured in Physical Education at St Mary's College, Belfast for 35 years and managed the college football teams every year.

Jim won one junior and three Derry senior championships, played for Ulster for 11 years, winning two Railway Cups, and was selected for Ireland versus the Combined Universities for six years. He captained Derry to the 1958 All-Ireland final against Dublin and was named inaugural Texaco Footballer of the Year.

He managed Derry football teams, winning two Ulster senior titles, and trained his county's under-21 hurlers who won the 1993 Ulster title. Elected Derry GAA Chairman in 1997, he has served as Central Council delegate and on the GAA Coaching Advisory Council.

Married to Teresa, they have three daughters and two sons and live in Magherafelt.

Around 1940 a good football was a precious possession and most clubs were content to start the season with one decent one. My local club, Ballymaguigan, was more fortunate than most when an entrepreneurial member discovered he could negotiate an occasional football from US Airforce personnel, stationed on a local airfield, in exchange for fresh eggs, easily obtained in our rural parish. But even with an extra supply source, providing a ball for a schoolboy kick-around had a low priority.

So the regular action we schoolboys craved depended on one of us owning a ball. The owner would have status and the power to decide the location and timing of our football sessions. So ownership was an ambition for all of us.

I remember my first leather ball. Aged nine or ten, I assisted my father and a helper to drive cattle to Magherafelt fair, repeatedly sprinting past them to man entrances to fields or laneways and keep them on the road. It was the task for young boys while adults marshalled the cattle from behind. The repetition of 50-yard sprints followed by stationary rests was my first experience of interval training, which I came to know less pleasantly more than 10 years later.

The cattle sale must have gone well. I could scarcely believe that my pleading over a long period was suddenly successful when my father asked if I still wanted a football. Like most towns then, Magherafelt did not have a sports shop. Sport had a very marginal place in the national economy or in a family budget.

But in the saddler's shop, along with harnesses, bridles, saddles and leather belts a few brown leather footballs were for sale. My father put a ball in my hands, paid the five shillings and I emerged from the shop as happy as I have ever felt after the greatest of matches. By arrangement I travelled home in the car of a Unionist neighbour who was also a family friend. I know that later he quietly followed and commented on my football career but I'm not sure he knew he was there at the beginning.

He dropped me off at the end of Berryman's road where he went right and I went left to my home almost a mile away. That day it seemed much shorter as I bounced and caught the ball on the concrete road and tried a few controlled kicks, panicking if the ball went close to the swampy ground on either side.

In the next two years that ball absorbed so much energy, was the centre of so much interaction with my neighbourhood peers and for almost all of us launched an interest which endures more than 60 years later. Of that small group of about a dozen regulars, six were on the Ballymaguigan team 20 years later which won the club's only senior championship, five played for Derry county, two played in an All-Ireland senior final, two represented Ulster, one played for Ireland, three managed senior county teams and one has sponsored both a club and a county team.

Pat McFlynn, a future President of the GAA, was a newly qualified teacher who came to our school as a substitute when Master Young was ill. At the end of his period there he suggested playing a game against Magherafelt schoolboys and it was fixed for us to travel. On the agreed midweek evening a group of about a dozen of us cycled, mostly on borrowed bicycles, the four miles to Magherafelt. We had a football but no jerseys, no togs and only a few had football boots. Refereed by Pat

McFlynn, the only adult present, the match had the kind of informality of our own group practice games. We knew nothing of the opposition except that one of them was John Maguire, brother of Sticky Maguire, Derry's best footballer, a player of rare brilliance whom all of us had seen play. He was a star on the first Ulster team to win the Railway Cup. With his brother as an opponent we knew we were mixing with quality and it added to the excitement. We had no team talk, no consideration of tactics or defence systems, but we played with unabashed passion and high enjoyment. Who won? I have no idea. But it was my first match.

Almost a quarter of a century later I played my last match. In 1965 I was selected as one of the 14 hurlers and footballers to be guest players in the Cardinal Cushing games in New York, Hartford and Boston. I hadn't played seriously for almost two seasons but this was too good to miss. So with my former midfield partner, Phil Stuart, I had a few sharpening-up catch-and-kick sessions.

The games were important to our hosts and to Irish American spectators and we played them seriously but it was the off-field events which were memorable. Each day we were guests at some location and quickly learned that the Irish had a comprehensive network of contacts. Our visit coincided with the World Fair in New York with many large pavilions, each with a spectacular exhibition representing an important country or a world perspective. When we arrived at the fair on a hot sunny day we found long queues at each pavilion. But our guide had contacts at the pavilions most interesting to us and each time we were ushered in by another entrance. It was VIP treatment we were not expecting but for which we were grateful. On another day we travelled, by special bus, to Washington and at the famous Senate building we were introduced to the speaker, Senator McCormack, and were photographed with him. However, the highlight of the New York part of our tour was being greeted individually in Gaelic Park by Bobby Kennedy, who was at that time electioneering in New York. His brother, the President, had been assassinated two years earlier, and it was impossible not to sense a vulnerability and an exceptionalism in the presence of this small man. I have remained fascinated by him.

The Hartford part of the tour in midweek was expected to be the least exciting but was memorable in three distinct ways. Firstly, it was my initial experience of playing under floodlights which came on at half time. I had forgotten they were on until at the end of the match I walked into darkness on my way to the dressing room. Secondly, I was fascinated to learn that the park we played in was overlooked by the factory where all the 'Colt 45' guns, familiar to followers of cowboy films or Wild West novels, were manufactured. And Connecticut sure wasn't cowboy country. The final recollection from Hartford is of a regrettable missed opportunity. There was a shortage of hurlers for the hurling game. When the organisers were searching for players I was tempted to volunteer, drawing on my hurling experience as a boarder for five years in St Malachy's College in Belfast where about half of my fellow boarders were hurlers from north Antrim or the Ards peninsula in County Down and who painfully inducted me into the art. But I hesitated and missed the opportunity no one should miss, of hurling alongside Christy Ring, the greatest hurler since Cúchulainn.

Christy was one of the hurlers on tour and I had become quite friendly with him but to have hurled with him would have been a boast for life. In the years since then I particularly missed the accolade, when invited as guest speaker to a football-cum-hurling club. My credentials as a footballer are generally accepted but for the hurlers I relate the story and present my claim to fame as having "almost hurled with Christy Ring".

In Boston for our final game we met Cardinal Cushing and he watched the most competitive game of the tour. I had been progressing towards match fitness in the previous two games and resolved to rejoin the Derry team for the championship. Derry were expected to beat Antrim in the first round, playing at a home venue on the day of our game in Boston. So, imagine my disappointment when towards the end of our game in Brookline Baseball Park, the championship results from Ireland were announced over the public address system, and Derry had lost. I immediately knew that I was playing the final 15 minutes of my football career and I tried to be involved in every second of it.

As a postscript to the tour, I learned on my return that the Ministry of Education in Belfast had refused to allow me time off to travel and deducted 14 days salary which included two Saturdays and two Sundays. When many years later I retired they further informed me that I had lost 14 days pension contribution and for almost 20 years I have been a little poorer each month. In 'our day' we really were amateurs and I have no regrets. The genuine friendships, the integrity of not being a 'bought' sportsman and the rich, irreplaceable memories are ample compensation.

# CATHERINA MCKIERNAN

## Cathy Freeman's 400 metre final at Sydney Olympics

CATHERINA McKIERNAN, born 30 November 1969 in Cornafean, County Cavan, won four successive world cross country silver medals (1992-1995) and a gold at the European Cross Country Championships in 1994.

She won numerous road and cross country races in Europe and America during her career, and ten national track and cross country titles. She was twice an Olympian, in 1992 and 1996, but because of injury she had to miss the 2000 Olympics in Sydney. She won the 2004 Great Ireland Run but a lack of fitness forced her to pull out of the 2004 Olympics in Athens.

Catherina also won Berlin, London and Amsterdam marathons as well as Lisbon and Paris half marathons. Her time of 2.22.23 in Amsterdam is a national record. She is married to RTÉ radio presenter Damien O'Reilly and they have two children, Deirbhile and Patrick.

Despite the many happy memories I have, thanks to my own running career, when I am asked for a favourite sporting memory, there is little to compare to the night I was in the Olympic Stadium in Sydney in 2000 to witness Cathy Freeman's sensational win in the 400 metres final.

I should have been competing in Sydney too but a series of niggling injuries in the months following my assault on the world record in the 1998 Amsterdam marathon put paid to my participation in what should have been my third successive Olympics.

There was a considerable amount of pressure on me following my Irish record-breaking win in Amsterdam to go on and win gold for Ireland in Sydney. The bookies had me marked down as a dead cert and as the media build-up to Sydney began in earnest, everyone believed the bookies, except one person, me!

I knew that I wasn't in the right shape and the mental pressure was no doubt feeding into the physical niggles which interrupted training and competition. I made my decision to pull out of Sydney. Everyone thought I would be devastated. To be perfectly honest, it was an immense relief. I know that sounds selfish considering that so many sports and athletics fans would have loved to have shared the joy of watching me compete and possibly win a medal in Sydney, but it was better to pull out rather than go there and break down as can happen to athletes at Olympic Games. There was no point in thinking everything would be alright on the night. A tough and brave decision was needed and I made it.

No amount of medical care could have got me right for Sydney. Now I know that the body was telling me: "Listen, we have had 10 really good years on the road, it's time to call a halt". And although it took another four years to wind down, a halt I did call in 2004.

But back to Sydney and that famous night. I was there courtesy of RTÉ Radio who took me along to the Olympics as an analyst. I was a somewhat reluctant pilgrim but looking back it was a great opportunity.

Cathy Freeman was the darling of the Aussies. She was under pressure to deliver gold in her own backyard to a sports-mad Aussie audience. She even piled on the pressure by participating majorly in the opening ceremony, something I never liked because of the sheer length of time and the energy-sapping experience it is for participant athletes.

It was night time, which added to the atmosphere. The build-up had been immense all week. Everywhere you looked, there were billboard signs with Freeman's immediately recognisable face. She was on every newspaper, on every TV station. The expectation was palpable everywhere you looked. Having been the star of the opening ceremony, she carried the weight of the nation on her shoulders from day one.

She entered the stadium for the final of the women's 400 metres, having lost out narrowly in Atlanta in 1996. And so there was an element of unfinished business to be added into the mix of this intriguing story. She emerged wearing what I remember as a very unusual looking spacesuit and had a hood pulled up round her head. If she wanted to play down the occasion, the spacesuit didn't lend itself to that. In fact in its own way, it injected even more suspense into the occasion.

As the finalists took to their marks, the nervousness of the crowd could be felt. Everyone went quiet until the gun went. Then the roar began. Every screech and bellow acted like a combined harness to get her round the track. Into the final 100 metres and she still had work to do. It's difficult to explain the emotion as she strode home: goose pimples, hairs on the back of the neck sort of stuff. Then with about 50 metres to go, the fairytale ending was almost complete. She crossed the line and the emotion, the pressure vanished from her - sheer relief. She had done it. Amazing. You could not have scripted it.

The 1996 disappointment in Atlanta was vanquished. The tension of the opening ceremony, the rising expectation... and the deliverance. She slumped to her hunkers and it took a moment for her to realise what had happened. Then the emotion; tears followed by happiness as the crowds all over the stadium cried and cheered and waved their flags. You couldn't but share in the emotion as she took off around the stadium waving the Aussie flag and the Aboriginal flag, adding even more spice to an already fantastic story.

I was there too for Sonia O'Sullivan's 5000 metres silver medal which was another fantastic moment and a great sporting memory as we cheered her down to the line against Gabriela Szabo. And I have had some great achievements and successes on the world stage myself but for some reason, to this day, when I am asked what is my favourite sporting memory, I can never bypass that night in Sydney and Cathy Freeman's 400 metres gold medal. Magic.

# JOEY MAHER

## When 'Opportunity Knocks', take the ball on the hop

**J**OEY MAHER was one of the key players in the popularisation of handball in modern Ireland. He amassed 22 All-Ireland titles in hardball, softball and 40x20 over five decades and was well known and respected on the international stage where he won eight titles during three decades.

He spent several years in Toronto where a career highlight was his victory in the 1967 World Open Singles final in New York representing Canada.

Joey played at the opening of numerous courts throughout Ireland and attracted vast numbers of supporters who admired and appreciated his wide range of talents as well as his sense of humour on and off the court. He lives in Drogheda with his wife Doris and they raised five children (Michael, Linda, David, Robbie and Eddie, RIP) and have 13 grandchildren.

In October 1963, Eamon de Valera was safely ensconced in Áras an Uachtaráin as President of Ireland, the Russians and Americans had entered into a space race, 'the comely maidens were dancing at the crossroads' and handball was played in concrete open-topped alleys at the street corners of many a town and village in Ireland. I was a foreman painter and decorator and as a formidable handball player had a successful competitive year, culminating in winning a place at the first World Handball Championships held at the Athletic Club in New York City. This prestigious club was noted for its glossy-painted handball courts on its upper floors, far removed from the concrete alleys of my native Drogheda.

My mother cautioned me as I took a taxi to the airport to play in the championships: "You should be careful and not fall out of the handball alley", she said, as she had read in the *Irish Press* that the NY Athletic Club

*Celebration time for Harry Hawkins, Brian Peters and Martin Donnelly, sponsor, after Bernard Dunne's world title win on 21 March 2009*

*High fielding by Jim McKeever of Derry in the 1958 All-Ireland football final v Dublin*

*Martin Breheny, Irish Independent Gaelic Games Editor*

*Dermot Earley, Kildare, All Star winner in 1998 and 2009*

*Micheal Corcoran, RTÉ rugby commentator and sports broadcaster*

*Jockey Pat Smullen and trainer Dermot Weld with Stunning View at the 2009 Galway Races*

*Jamesie O'Connor of Clare keeps his eyes on the sliotar*

*Philip Browne, Chief Executive Officer of the IRFU*

*Joe Stack, RTÉ sports presenter and broadcaster*

*Cliona Foley, staff sportswriter with Independent News and Media*

*Saoirse Mullan from Thurles holds the Liam MacCarthy Cup while Tommy Walsh, Brian Hogan, Michael Fennelly and Jackie Tyrrell enjoy the moment at Our Lady's Children's Hospital, Crumlin*

*Jack Sheedy, former Dublin footballer and manager of Moorefield, Newbridge*

*Brian Carthy, RTÉ Gaelic Games Correspondent*

*Olive Loughnane with her 2009 Texaco Sports Star of the Year Award*

*Colm Cooper, Kerry, shows his skill as he shoots for goal*

*President Mary McAleese with Joe Lennon, Down's 1968 All-Ireland winning captain*

*Steven McDonnell leads the Ireland International Rules team at Croke Park, 30 October 2010*

*John Kenny, RTÉ broadcaster and journalist*

*Jacqui Hurley, RTÉ Radio and TV sports presenter*

*Jim O'Sullivan, GAA writer with the Irish Examiner*

*Mary O'Connor, Cork, raises the O'Duffy Cup after the 2009 All-Ireland camogie final*

*Tony Doran who starred for Wexford from 1967 to 1984*

*Trevor Ringland, right, former Ireland rugby international, with Basil McCrea, MLA (left), and Tom Daly, former Ulster GAA President*

*Liam Sheedy, Tipperary manager, shows his delight after the 2010 All-Ireland hurling final*

*Eimear Cregan, Ireland's most-capped hockey player*

*Eamonn Cregan, Limerick All-Ireland hurling winner, 1973*

*Eugene McGee, GAA columnist with the Irish Independent*

was 20 storeys high. Although the Irish team did not win the championships we attained a respectable third place at the competition. And this would open many doors in my future career.

Shortly after I returned home, I was contacted by Inspector Ed Chalmers of the Canadian Metropolitan Police Force. He had been at the World Championships and had seen me playing. Canada had secured the hosting of the next championships in 1967. Chalmers with the support of Magistrate Joseph Addison, Commissioner for Handball in all of Canada, suggested I might go there and learn the Canadian game, and consider the possibility of becoming a policeman in the city of Toronto. Handball is a big game in Canada and they probably knew I could win a world championship for their country.

So, early in 1964 I left Ireland with my wife Doris and our three children, Michael, Linda and David to embark on a new career and a new life in Canada. The years which followed proved fruitful, as I studied to become a policeman and competed at all levels of handball in our new-found home. I was successful in competitions in many parts of Canada and the USA. I took a big chance going there. If Ireland had got the World Championships at the time, I wouldn't have gone. The courts were different. We had only the big courts then and I never saw a 40x20 court until I went to Toronto.

The police department gave me a lot of time off to represent the force. I played in a lot of tournaments representing the Toronto police against the Chicago police or the New York police. They wanted me there because they were being beaten in a lot of sports but they were nearly always sure of winning the handball when I represented them. At the time old 'Mother' Haider was our inspector and wouldn't let me go to represent the police. Next thing, the Chief, James Mackey, rang up looking for me when I was on traffic duty at Saint Charles and Eglinton. The sergeant said: "You have to go to the airport. Go home and get your bags". Says I: "The inspector told me I'm not to go", and I kept directing the traffic. Then the inspector himself had to come down and he told me to go to play handball.

Focusing primarily on the World Championships which would take place in October 1967, I set out to win the Canadian National Singles title. A win in the final over Barry Leech of Toronto qualified me to represent Canada at the championships in Toronto.

After a successful run through the preliminary rounds, I played competitors from Mexico, Australia and Ireland until finally confronting Carl Obert from the USA in the final. He displayed great skill on the court in his use of natural and reverse 'hooks'. This was no surprise as he and his two brothers, Oscar and Ruby, had won in excess of 100 American titles. I was fortunate that I was well tutored in reading a 'hook' and I defeated Obert, whom I would respect as one of the great players, in two straight sets 21-3 and 21-6. It was officially recorded that I was striking the ball at 150mph!

With the world handball title now secured, I decided to return home. In the years that followed I kept a healthy interest in handball, playing, competing and coaching all over Ireland. I had the great pleasure to coach Walter O'Connor the current president of GAA Handball Ireland who, in his own right, wearing the Meath jersey, has won many All-Ireland and international titles. I also coached and nurtured Peter McAuley, another great handball champion, who wore the Louth jersey. My eldest son, Michael, brought the first All-Ireland minor championship title to Louth.

Handball took a back seat when the Maher Family - myself, three sons and a daughter - won 'Opportunity Knocks' on ITV with Hughie Green. I was playing handball and playing in the band and I was out all night on the road. My training suffered and I could not keep up the standard of fitness required to compete at top level any longer.

Reviewing a handball career stretching over 60 years, I have made many, many friends in all parts of the country and in other countries. I still work out each day, commencing with an early morning swim of 20 lengths. Not bad for a man of 77 years! I would highly recommend that all young men and women take up handball as a means of keeping fit and healthy and I am delighted to see the game is enjoying a revival and getting stronger every day. Handball gave me countless wonderful moments in life and I am a firm believer in its potential as a game for life, and as a lifelong game. It offered me great opportunities and one of my greatest memories is going to work and live in another country, playing the game I love and winning a world title.

# DARRAGH MALONEY

## Offaly versus Kerry, 19 September 1982

**D**ARRAGH MALONEY presents and commentates on soccer and Gaelic games and boxing for RTÉ Television and Radio. He joined RTÉ in 1995 and has worked on the GAA hurling and football championships, three FIFA World Cups, three UEFA European Championships and three Olympic Games.

Darragh presents *Premier Soccer Saturday* on RTÉ2 and the nightly sports show on RTÉ Radio One, *Sport at 7.*

I have been fortunate to have been at many All-Ireland finals but my first will always be the best.

My family is steeped in the GAA and in particular, Offaly GAA. My dad, Pat, is from Offaly and he brought me to their matches from an early age.

In 1982, I was nine years old and we were visiting my grandmother in Rialto in Dublin on All-Ireland final Sunday. Dad was going to the game but was not planning on bringing me. I think I threw a bit of a 'strop' because I wanted to go and before I knew it, I was on the bus heading to Croke Park. Back in those days, you did not need to buy tickets in advance for the standing areas of the ground and if you were there early enough, you could pay in at the turnstiles. That is what we did as we took our places on the Canal End.

Offaly were the underdogs on the day. They were up against the side who were chasing history. No team, in hurling or football, had ever won five All-Ireland titles in a row and Kerry were as close to certainties to do it. They were regarded as the greatest team ever with the likes of Pat Spillane, John Egan, Eoin Liston, Mikey Sheehy and Jack O'Shea expected to guide them to victory.

Offaly also had some incredibly gifted footballers but they were not considered to be quite good enough to deny Kerry. Matt and Richie Connor, Johnny Mooney and Sean and Brendan Lowry were all heroes of mine but few could see them stopping Kerry.

It started to pour rain during the game and the Canal End was packed. When you are only nine, big crowds always look intimidating but the crowds were the biggest I have ever seen. With everyone standing, I could not see so I sat on one of the crush barriers.

My memory of the match is a little hazy. Offaly had won All-Irelands in 1971 and 1972 but the team faded and Dublin re-established their grip on Leinster football.

Offaly brought Eugene McGee in to try and turn things around and he did a sensational job. Their dream was to win Sam Maguire and every year they got closer and closer. They finally got the better of Dublin to win Leinster but lost to Kerry in the 1980 All-Ireland semi-final. The following year, Offaly made it to the final but Kerry beat them again and they were expected to lose again when the sides met 12 months later.

The "Five-In-A-Row" song was being played on the radio while one Kerry supporter had printed "5-In-A-Row" tee-shirts and was hoping to make a fortune after the game (they could be close to priceless now!). All they had to do was turn up and win the match!

The teams were level at half time but Kerry were a point in front when they were awarded a penalty right in front of where my dad and I were on the Canal End during the second half. If they scored it, the game was as good as over. However, Offaly goalkeeper Martin Furlong saved the kick taken by Mikey Sheehy and the place went crazy.

Kerry did recover from the shock to take charge again and were well in control heading into the final quarter. Offaly rallied and got back to within two points with just one minute to go. I have watched the match countless times over the years and Micheál O'Hehir mentions on several occasions during the second half that there had not been a goal. He talks about Offaly players "diddling and dawdling" in the moments before the ball is kicked towards substitute Seamus Darby and even says "You would think they were winning". Darby eased Tommy Doyle out of the way (many say he pushed him) and his shot drifted over the head of the Kerry goalkeeper Charlie Nelligan and nestled in the back of the net.

The place went crazy but the match was not over. Kerry had a chance to create one more scoring opportunity but Offaly's Sean Lowry caught the ball and the final whistle blew. Sean now lives close to where my father grew up and even though he left Croke Park with that ball, he is not completely sure where it is now.

There was no 'Plan B' in Croke Park in 1982 as everyone wanted to be out on the pitch. My dad and I did not even feel the rain as we were both soaked. Players were being carried shoulder-high but I will always remember seeing two of the Offaly lads, brothers Pat and Mick Fitzgerald, rolling around on the ground hugging each other, celebrating, as if they had not seen each other in years.

The defeat for Kerry ended their shot at history and they were caught again by another late goal in the Munster final the following year against Cork. The loss against Offaly completely shattered them but they recovered to win three more All-Irelands from 1984 to 1986.

The Offaly team were also shattered by their experiences but in a very different way. They had aimed to beat Kerry ever since Eugene McGee took over and each year they got closer. When they did eventually beat them, their goal was achieved and the hunger disappeared a little. Offaly lost the Leinster final in 1983 and by 1984 were a pale shadow of that great team which denied Kerry their place in history.

# VALERIE MULCAHY
# When I realised my dream

**V**ALERIE MULCAHY is a PE and mathematics teacher who holds five All-Ireland senior medals, six NFL Division 1 and one NFL Division 2 medals, two club All-Ireland medals with Rockbán and one O' Connor Cup with University of Limerick.

She was chosen on the ladies football team of the decade, won three All-Star Awards, was Texaco Award recipient and Vodafone Player of the Year in 2005, and *Tatler* Sportswoman of the Year and golden boot award winner in 2008. She was All-Ireland final player of the match in 2005 and 2008 and *Irish Star* player of the match in the 2005 and 2009 finals.

Valerie's interests include cycling, shopping, eating out, tasting different foods, going for walks, spending time in the Jacuzzi and sauna, and resting. She has played many sports including soccer, basketball, tennis and camogie - which she still plays with her club.

There was a time when I would have settled for just one All-Ireland medal. Now that I have transitioned between having never played on All-Ireland day in Croke Park to winning five All-Irelands in a row I find myself wanting even more. As I now have five All-Ireland medals I realise that it's not really about the medals at all... there is something more that makes me hungry for success.

Maybe it's the memories that I will have and cherish for the rest of my life, the bus journey to Croke Park on All-Ireland final day with our Garda escort, or the feeling of elation after the final whistle. Maybe it's the satisfaction of hard work paying off, the sense of achieving my goals and dreams, the feeling of being indestructible and the sense that I still have more I can give.

More and more in ladies football the only day that seems to matter is All-Ireland final day. It's an unfortunate side effect of the sexist nature of sport, particularly in an intimate country like Ireland. A season's efforts can be utterly futile if you don't make it to the All-Ireland final, the one occasion in the calendar that gets adequate exposure.

It seems ironic then that out of all of the greatest moments in my career my most treasured memory is of a semi-final day in O'Moore Park in Portlaoise against Mayo, and that second when the final whistle blew. In the years running up to this match Mayo were the team that were living my dream. They were the team who stole our first national title in the league earlier in the same year having caught up to us after we led by six points at the half-time whistle, the same team that knocked us out in the quarter-final in 2004, causing us to doubt our abilities at the beginning of what is now our seventh year as a unit. It was the year we had been so fortunate to have somehow attracted Eamonn Ryan who, for me, is the best the country has to offer in terms of a coach, a facilitator and a motivator.

It was 2005, O'Moore Park on All-Ireland semi-final day. We were four points down with 17 minutes to go and it looked like both time and dreams were slipping away from us. I was sitting in the stand having being withdrawn from the starting team due to an ankle injury which hadn't healed on time. The nervousness I felt watching from the bench far exceeded any nerves I had felt on the pitch. I was feeling the crush of helplessness and was sensing that I was about to watch our dreams and aspirations come crumbling down around us. I knew in my gut that I could do something or influence the outcome somehow if I could just get off the bench... and then I got the call to warm up. I finally entered the fray with 15 minutes left and I knew that I could make a positive difference. The opportunity arose in the form of a free kick from an acute angle and although I was fresh on the pitch I felt a rush of confidence and I knew that I could get it. I stepped up and we moved up to being three points down. Another free ensued and once more I just had a feeling that I could get it. Time was visibly counting down on the stop clock and then came a third free... one point down. It seemed like out of nowhere the underdogs were fighting for survival.

And then something took over, some sense of belief we had never felt before. The momentum noticeably began to shift and we weren't the only people that felt it. The Mayo goalkeeper panicked and kicked the ball into our hands. We equalised and were getting palpably excited. Juliet Murphy, the captain and inspirational leader of our team, gained possession from a ball flicked down to her and steadied up, scoring with 29 seconds remaining on the stop clock. Mayo won their kick out and carried the ball downfield to the scoring zone. Then everything just slowed down and for what felt like minutes we managed to hold them back... and then the referee blew the final whistle, the sound that makes your heart pound and your breath flutter. It was at that moment I realised I was going to fulfil my dream of playing on All-Ireland day in Croke Park. I was going to stand on the grass, look up at the crowd and savour the moment that I had been playing out in my mind for what seemed like my whole life. I knew then that no matter what I achieved in the future I had experienced the intensity of a feeling that I would probably never feel again.

# CON MURPHY

## That goal, English fans and a round of drinks

**C**ON MURPHY, RTÉ sports presenter, has anchored the station's radio Olympic coverage from Atlanta, Sydney, Athens and Beijing. He was also part of RTÉ radio's award-winning commentary team on the Ryder Cup at the K Club in 2006. He says the Ryder Cup was one of the most enjoyable broadcasting experiences of his life along with the 2002 World Cup Finals in Japan and Korea – despite the Roy Keane / Saipan affair.

He has presented football, golf, rugby, hockey, basketball, athletics and horse racing on RTÉ Television, and has fronted *Monday Night Soccer* every Monday for the last four years.

He is rumoured to be an avid Shamrock Rovers and CD Tenerife fan, and his favourite group are "Jarabe de Palo" from Barcelona. Apart from his sports presentation, Con also co-presented *Crimecall* on RTÉ television for six years.

In 1977 into 1978, I remember my dad telling me that even if he had to sell the car, we would go to the World Cup in Argentina if Johnny Giles's Irish team qualified for the finals. Alas it wasn't to be, the campaign spoiled by some very dodgy refereeing decisions, and some bad luck as well. Argentina would have to wait!

Fast forward to 12 June 1988. It's hard to believe as I write that it's 23 years since the Republic of Ireland made their first appearance at a major soccer finals, and after such a long wait I suppose it was almost inevitable that the Irish should face the old enemy, England, in their first match of the Euro '88 Finals in Germany.

The venue was the Neckarstadion in Stuttgart. It was in my pre-broadcasting days, and I was there as a fan with my dad, and a friend Rob. Even in that dearer airfare era, Germany was still a much easier place to get to than Argentina, so cars did not have to be sold to fund the trip.

I'm a stickler for getting to any stadium very early before the start of whatever event is due to take place, and this day was no different. In 1988, English football hooliganism was alive and well, and with "No surrender to the IRA" being a common chant from the so-called 'hard men', we decided to get to the stadium even earlier than normal to avoid any potential trouble outside the ground, and were amongst the first to get inside when the gates opened.

It was a beautiful summer's day and from our position a few rows behind the dugouts, it was great to watch the stadium fill up over the next couple of hours. I've always loved being in stadia before games, from empty to full, and after the game back to empty. That day, the atmosphere built to an unbelievable pre kick-off crescendo. Even the Millwall fans seated behind us were pleasant!

Six minutes into the game, and an explosion of joy as Ray Houghton put the ball in the English net. This was the dream start to the game and the tournament, and not a Carlsberg in sight. I'm sure we've all seen, many times, the famous shots of Jack Charlton rubbing his head having banged it off the dugout roof, but I remember watching it from the other angle behind the dugouts, and laughing and cheering at the same time.

As every Irish football fan probably remembers, what followed was an excruciating 84 minutes (and a couple more for injury time), with Packie Bonner performing heroics, and the English strike force denied time after time. I almost couldn't breathe with the tension. In 1988 I wasn't used to a big clock behind the goal in the stadia I frequented, and it made it even harder to watch, when at every glance at the clock, I could see that only 30 seconds had passed since my previous look. It was painful.

Apart from repelling the English attacks, one of my other abiding memories from that day was at half time when the teams emerged for the second half. The big screen behind the goal was playing Robert Palmer's 'Addicted to Love' video, the one with the identical, black-dress-clad, and red-lipsticked models posing as band members; I recall Mick McCarthy stopping to have a look at the screen as he walked back onto the pitch. I was thinking to myself, forget about the models, Mick, just remember to kick Lineker!

Ireland somehow held on for the victory, thanks to Bonner, last gasp defending, the woodwork, and some poor finishing by Chris Waddle. What an amazing moment when the final whistle blew. Even our new friends from Millwall in the row behind us were magnanimous in defeat.

It couldn't have been better. I returned to the stadium some years later, when Ireland played Germany in the Euro 2008 qualifier during the Steve Staunton reign. Nowadays it's called the Mercedes Benz Arena, and I found it so changed from 1988 that it might as well have been a different stadium altogether. I was hoping there'd be something to remind me of that special day in June 1988, but time had moved on, and the terrace behind the goal where the Irish fans had made so much noise, was now all seated and with a roof overhead. Completely different.

Despite the change Stuttgart '88 will always have a special place in my memory.

To round off a great day, we drove to Heilbronn, about half an hour's drive outside Stuttgart after the game. We found a small bar and were enjoying a nice beer. A few heavy English fans came in, loud-mouthed, crude, and not very happy at the day's events.Thankfully, there was no trouble and they didn't stay too long, complaining about the price of the beer.

After they'd left the owner of the bar said..."Irishmen, those Englishmen have just bought your next round of drinks." Maybe the only over-charging I've ever approved of, and a nice way to round off the perfect day.

# CONOR NILAND

## The taxi driver and the Israel Open

**C**ONOR NILAND was born in Birmingham on 19 September 1981 and grew up in Limerick. He has played dozens of Association of Tennis Professionals (ATP) tournaments and is the top ranked Irish player.

He won the New Delhi Open in 2008, and his successes during 2010 including the Israel Open title put him into the top 200 at no. 165. On winning the ATP Salzburg Indoors he went to a career-high ranking of 129.

In 2011 Conor became the first Irishman to reach the main draw at Wimbledon since 1980 but lost in five sets in the first round. He also qualified for the main draw in the 2011 US Open but had to concede to world no. 1 Novak Djokovic due to illness during the first round. An Irish Davis Cup player since 2000, he studied English at University of California, Berkeley, before becoming professional in 2005.

I find you tend to remember your toughest losses more readily than your best days on the court, but my best sporting memory would be my win at the Israel Open in May of 2010.

I had been having a good season, having qualified for my first Association of Tennis Professionals (ATP) Tour main draw in Houston and winning a lot of matches on the Challenger circuit. My year had started with good tennis but not a big rankings jump, however. On the Challenger circuit, you have to win tournaments outright to really climb the rankings. I had been leading 6-2, 4-3, 40-30 in the last qualifying round in the Australian Open in January but lost in three sets. My opponent went on to play home favourite Lleyton Hewitt on Rod Laver Arena. That stung, but drove me on to keep giving myself those opportunities to play in the biggest events. I continued to get good results and trained well over the next few months and travelled to Israel in May for the $100,000 tournament.

The tournament was held in Ramat Hasharon, about 15 minutes outside of Tel Aviv, at the Israeli National Tennis Centre. Our hotel was in Tel Aviv, right by the Mediterranean Sea. Even with all its history, the city has a cosmopolitan feel to it. At the tennis centre, from my first practice, I immediately liked the courts. They were a slow, hard court which would be my preferred surface.

When it came to the matches, they were all tough and I had to come through some tight situations to win them. After my disappointing loss in Australia, coming through in those close matches was rewarding. I won four of the five matches in three sets, all in plus 30 degree heat. Off court, I had been just focusing on doing the little things that would help me win the event. My coach, Conor Taylor, was bringing up bags of ice to the room after the matches and I would sit in the bath with the ice and try to rehydrate!

My five opponents had all been ranked in the top 100 during their careers, and my second round opponent, Rainer Schuettler, was a former world no. 5 and a 2008 Wimbledon semi-finalist. I felt like I went up a level, in rankings and in confidence, with these wins and that helped give me a platform to push on for the rest of the year.

The final was perhaps the toughest match, against a good Brazilian, Thiago Alves, ranked just outside the top 100 in the world at the time. I came from a set down to win in three hours and eight minutes. Alves is a great competitor and we have a similar gamestyle, so it was a slog. So often in tennis you can have a good week but come up short in a semi-final or final and leave with regrets. To win it outright meant that didn't happen.

There was a big centre court and the final was well attended and was shown live on Israeli television. The Irish Ambassador to Israel was there with his family for the quarter-final and final. To play in a good atmosphere and win a close, exciting match made it a great experience. The organisers sent me a DVD of the final which is a nice memento.

What made the week even more memorable, and gave it a surreal twist, was that I was in a minor car accident on the way to the final. The tournament bus schedule didn't suit my planned preparation for the match so we decided to take a taxi to the courts a little earlier. We were in slowish traffic when our driver clipped the back of the car in front when trying to change lanes. We were not moving quickly so no real damage was done, but it was hardly the ideal pre-match scenario. We got out of the car and stood at the side of the road for a few minutes while the drivers exchanged details. The taxi driver didn't apologise to us for the inconvenience and we still had to pay him when he dropped us off at the courts. My coach and I just looked at each other, shrugged and got ready for the final - it kind of summed up our attitude that week. We were taking everything in our stride and let nothing at all get in our way of winning the tournament.

# CHRISTY O'CONNOR

## Rising fog heralds sunny day for St Joseph's Doora-Barefield

**C**HRISTY O'CONNOR is a journalist based in Ennis, County Clare, who has worked in the national newspaper industry for 14 years. As well as winning three county titles, two Munster club titles and one All-Ireland club title, he was a member of the Clare senior hurling panel for four years.

His first book, *'Last Man Standing'* was runner-up in the Boylesports Irish Sports Book of the Year in 2005. He has also written the *'GAA Quiz Book 1'* and the *'GAA Quiz Book 2'*. His last book *'The Club'* won the William Hill Irish Sports Book of the Year award in 2010.

His main interest is hurling and he feels lucky that he writes about it for the *Irish Independent* and the *Sunday Times*. He is married to Olivia and they have two sons, Thomas and Dáire.

The sweetest victory I ever tasted was our minor A win with St Joseph's Doora-Barefield in 1990. The final whistle was absolutely beautiful; the explosion of emotion, the kinetic charge of elation as myself and Seánie McMahon hugged one another in the goalmouth, and the absolute purity of the sense of satisfaction which followed. Beating our arch rivals, Éire Óg, Ennis enhanced the sensation because we'd been listening to their players in school for the previous two weeks telling us how much they were going to beat us by. They were reigning champions and hot favourites but we won an epic match by a point.

There's no doubt about it but that win was effectively the launch-pad for our All-Ireland club success nine years later – eight players from that minor panel in 1990 started the 1999 All-Ireland club final. It was the club's first minor title in 30 years and it heralded the beginning of a great odyssey for many Doora-Barefield players.

We never had a culture of underage success but winning that minor title infused us with the belief that we could go on to greater things. That minor win was pure elation. Winning an All-Ireland title is the ultimate achievement for a club. Yet the two are so intrinsically linked that they almost bleed into one memory.

On Wednesday morning, 17 March 1999, we boarded a bus outside our pitch in Roslevan and travelled to Shannon airport to catch an 8 a.m. flight to Dublin. On the bus journey to Shannon, I remember noticing a blanket of rising fog covering the plains around Dromoland Castle, which was a good indication that it was going to be a warm and sunny day. I thought the metaphor was perfect – this is going to be a beautiful day for our club.

When we landed in Dublin, the supporters and family who had travelled on the same flight made their own arrangements while we got on a bus to take us to our base in the Lucan Spa hotel. We had breakfast and a chat before going for a lie down upstairs. I was rooming with midfielder Joe Considine. Although the curtains were closed, the sun was shooting beams of light through the fabrics, the window was slightly open and we could hear the consistent drone of the passing traffic from the N4. It wasn't easy to switch off but we weren't concerned with sleep; a couple of hours before an All-Ireland final, we were subconsciously soothing our nerves by reminiscing about our days spent together in St Flannan's College.

After food and a chat, we went to the GAA field in Palmerstown for our puck around before a Garda escort led us into Croke Park. As the stadium loomed into view around Phibsboro, the bus suddenly broke down. As the driver tried to restart it on a couple of occasions, we were looking around at each other, wondering would we have to hike it up to Croke Park. At the third attempt, we could hear and feel the sound of the engine cranking into gear again. Saved.

We made our way under the old Hogan Stand and through to the old dressing rooms at the corner of the Hogan and the Canal End. Before we took to the field, our manager Michael Clohessy took to the floor. "A journalist rang me last week and asked me where is Doora-Barefield," he said. "Well, after today, everyone will know where Doora-Barefield is."

That victory put our club on the map but Doora-Barefield is in a totally different place now to where it was 12 years ago. Nearly two-thirds of the parish's population now live in a predominantly urban area. The communal loyalty to St Joseph's is still deep and persistent but it no longer pervades the parish's affection to the same degree it once did.

When people talk about Doora-Barefield, hurling is often the prism through which they view us. It is how many of us want them to view us. That stems from the pride we have in our club, our history, our heritage. Yet in our very own parish, the majority of our people certainly no longer view themselves through that prism of its flag-bearing hurling team.

There are a myriad of reasons why we have lost part of our identity as a senior hurling team and that's why we almost have to start again. To redefine our goals, reset our objectives. We just have to be patient now and keep working hard, keep coaching our kids with obsessive perseverance. And with so many other attractions now, we have to provide a structure for our young players to play games.

Our situation is not unique because numerous clubs have been affected in the last decade by the property boom and the difficulties urbanisation has presented. Conversely, many other clubs around the country have been faced with a totally different challenge in that emigration is threatening to wipe some rural clubs out. There is no easy fix; the only solution is to just work harder than ever before.

In St Joseph's Doora-Barefield, we still have a very competitive senior hurling team but we have to admit that dreams of winning an All-Ireland club title now only exist in a parallel universe. Yet we hope that we will get back to that glorious All-Ireland stage again some day. To live the dream again. To experience the most beautiful day imaginable.

# JAMESIE O'CONNOR
## For club, county and province

J AMESIE O'CONNOR lived in Ballinakill, County Galway before moving to Roslevan in Clare at 10 years of age. He attended St Flannan's College, Ennis - where he now teaches and coaches - winning Dean Ryan and two Harty Cup medals, and then NUIG, captaining the 1993 Fitzgibbon Cup team.

He holds Clare minor, under-21 and three senior medals as well as a Munster minor medal, two Munster senior titles and an All-Ireland club title. Jamesie made his senior debut for Clare in 1992 winning three Munster championships in 1995, 1997 and 1998 and two All-Ireland titles (1995, 1997).

He has four All Stars and was Player of the Year and Texaco Hurler of the Year in 1997. Married to Caroline with three children, Meadhbh, Sinead and Mark, he coaches his club teams, writes for the *Sunday Independent* and is an analyst with TV3 and Newstalk.

Trying to pick a single memory from a hurling career that gave me far more than I could have ever dreamed possible is an extremely difficult task. Obviously, most of the biggest highlights came during my time wearing the Clare colours, and two, in particular, spring to mind. Our first Munster final win over Limerick in 1995 was very special. We had been hammered in each of the previous two years, and in a county starved of success at provincial, not to mind national level, as players, winning a Munster title was all we ever dreamed of. In fact it had been 63 years since Clare had last been kingpins in Munster. Winning that game and seeing the emotion it generated, and what it meant to people, was like taking the shackles off an entire county. Older fans especially, who had supported us the length and breadth of the country and never thought they'd see the day, literally cried tears of joy. As a player, knowing that victory was ours in the closing minutes, as the Clare supporters readied themselves to invade the pitch, made it very, very special.

The second All-Ireland victory over Tipperary in 1997 was another personal highpoint. Champions in 1995, but defeated in the opening round in 1996, we had set out at the beginning of the year with the sole aim of winning a second title; something we had to do to get the respect and recognition we felt we deserved as a team. Failure to do so would mean the achievement of 1995 would always be viewed as a flash in the pan. To work and train so hard all year and then to realise that ambition in what was a pulsating match and an epic climax to the hurling season was extraordinarily satisfying.

It was sheer elation when referee Dickie Murphy blew that final whistle. I still remember vividly the atmosphere in the dressing room: amid all the euphoria there was a sense of calm and of deep satisfaction. If I could ever suspend time, then I think that's one of the places I'd like to go back to. Furthermore, to beat Cork and Kilkenny, and Tipperary twice, the three traditional superpowers along the way also meant no one could question the merit of the achievement. A further bonus was that on the way back to the changing rooms after the game, to avoid the throng, we walked around under the stadium. The various media had assembled outside our dressing room, and among them was my brother Christy, a journalist by profession. With only a year between us, we had grown up hurling and playing every other sport imaginable together, and I can remember the emotion and bond between us as we embraced, and feeling that it meant every bit as much to him as it did to me.

When you win a major final it's always a great feeling. When you play well on the day, it makes it even better. While I had plenty of bad days in the Clare jersey (some of those in the biggest of matches) those were two particular days when things went well for me on the field, and those are memories I'll always treasure.

During those successful years playing with the county, there were plenty of unsuccessful days playing with my club St Joseph's Doora-Barefield. The club had won two senior county championships in 1954 and 1958, but had slipped into the doldrums and were only playing junior A, the third tier at adult level, when my family moved to the parish in 1982. An under-12B medal in 1983 apart, successes were few and far between. However, in 1990, out of nowhere we won the minor A title and three years later had evolved into a powerful unit that easily won the county under-21 crown. The same year, the majority of that group backboned the team that won the county intermediate title and finally secured a return to senior ranks.

Four years later, and after four successive narrow defeats to local rivals Clarecastle, two of these in county finals, we were still waiting to win that elusive first county senior championship. With defending champions Clarecastle suffering an early exit in the other side of the draw, we obviously fancied our chances and duly made it to the final. Red hot favourites to beat Kilmaley, a side we had no history or bad blood with, we played terribly on the day, but still managed to fall over the line and come out on top. Relief was the over-riding emotion after the game, but considering it was the club's first title in 40 years, if anything the day was an anti-climax. On the Monday night after the game, we met the Kilmaley lads in town for a few drinks. It had been a very long, controversial and draining year with the county and talking to one of my Clare colleagues, Conor Clancy, the conversation centred on the upcoming Munster club semi-final tie with Waterford champions, Mount Sion. I told him I had no interest in it and was just looking forward to a break from the game. However, he reminded me in no uncertain terms that we had a duty to Clare to represent the county, and that Clare teams had won the previous three Munster club titles. His forthrightness got me thinking and, on reflection, he was dead right.

At that time, Mount Sion had an excellent team, which included household names such as Ken McGrath and Tony Browne, as well as a plethora of good hurlers and Waterford seniors such as Brian Greene and Brian Flannery. Having to travel to play them in their own back yard down in Dungarvan made the task even more difficult. Having learned the importance of belief in the previous few years with Clare, my fear was that the rest of our team would have doubts about our ability to go there and beat them, and that was something we spoke about on returning to training during the week.

On the day, although I was well marshalled by Brian Greene myself, and didn't play well, the rest of the team were outstanding. We tore into the opposition and completely outplayed them. I will never, ever forget the dressing room after that game. All the emotion, joy and exuberance that should have come out of us, but didn't, after the county final win, was released. Experiencing that with fellas I'd grown up with and hurled with since I was 12 years of age, including my brother and some of my best friends, is one of the greatest memories I'll ever have. In particular, I can recall hugging Ger Hoey, a great friend and golfing partner, who was corner back and one of the unsung heroes on the team. Ger, a bank manager, was hugely respected, and someone who did most of his talking on the field. He died tragically, aged just 41 in 2009, and all our lives are poorer for his passing.

When I think of Ger, my mind often wanders back to that day, and how lucky those of us inside that small and cramped dressing room were to experience that togetherness, friendship and sense of camaraderie that only sport can give us.

# MARY O'CONNOR

## Teamwork is the key to flying in unison

**M**ARY O'CONNOR, born in 1977 in Killeagh, County Cork is a camogie player and ladies footballer. She is National Director of Camogie Development. She won her first of seven All-Ireland camogie medals in 1997.

She holds nine National League medals, nine Munster camogie championships and county, provincial and All-Ireland club medals with Granagh-Ballingarry with whom she played while working in Limerick. She won five successive All-Ireland football medals, captaining Cork in their 2009 victory.

Mary has six Munster championship medals, three senior ladies club All-Ireland medals, was Camogie Player of the Year in 2006, and has three Camogie All Stars and one Ladies Football All Star.

My best sporting memories include being Capt John Ledingham jumping over fences in the RDS, being Michael Kiernan practising my conversions in Lansdowne Road with my orange rugby ball, being Sean Kelly in a time trial on my gold bike somewhere in the French Alps, being Christy O' Connor putting the winning shot in St Andrews, being Kevin Sheedy scoring a goal against England in a fan-filled stadium, being John Fenton scoring a goal from 70 yards off the ground, being Pat Spillane (headband and all) hook-kicking the ball over the bar in Croke Park, being Tom Cashman leading my team behind the Artane Band on All-Ireland final day, being Billy Coleman in my father's Ford Escort.

More memories are being Chris Evert playing her way to Wimbledon victory, being Daley Thompson winning Olympic gold in the decathlon, being Magic Johnson free-throwing my team to success under lights in my back yard, being Barry McGuigan defeating Pedrosa with my prized red gloves. Being Ger Cunningham unbeatable in the Cork goal, landing my puck-outs on the roof of my house, being Packie Bonner making that save against Romania between goal posts made of jumpers. What a save! And being Dennis Taylor beating Steve Davis to win the world snooker championship against all the odds.

The fact that I was all of these sporting magicians in my front garden, in my back yard and on my mam and dad's farm with a supporting cast of my six brothers and two sisters lent me the feeling of joy of doing something I loved. The fact is that I was not all that good at the aforementioned sports; in my mind's eye, in my glorious imagination I was super! The innocence of it all!

I also believe growing up in a large family taught me to be a team player ever before I became involved in organised sport. To make games work at home, everyone was needed but because I was second youngest I had to think how was I going to compete with my older brothers and sisters, I suppose I learnt quickly to think outside the box, to anticipate the next play.

Sport has given me a truck-load of memories, from the very beginning. From playing under-10 parish leagues with my local club Killeagh to playing camogie in Croke Park, the feeling of total freedom, of total enjoyment will never leave me and I fear it's a feeling I will never experience again once I give up competitive sport.

I learnt so much about life and living through sport, that to get what you want from sport takes hard work, determination, persistence, practice, resilience and being able to learn lessons from a win or a loss. As I grew older I found that to succeed in life, to be happy in life, takes hard work, the ability to be resilient, to learn from life what you can and move on.

As I look back now on my sporting career I can see that sport has been my friend, my teacher, my motivator and my X factor. It has also been an all-consuming desire, a tease, a torturer and an enemy to my sanity; but would I go back to live it all again?... in a heartbeat!

Our football coach, Eamonn Ryan, gave me the following inspirational short story, written by Dr Robert McNeish, at the start of one season with Cork. I read it and it resonated with me, and I went on to reread it on the eve of every Cork match thereafter.

### *Teamwork Lessons from the Geese*

As each bird flaps its wings, it creates uplift for the bird immediately following. By flying in 'V' formation the whole flock adds at least 71%

greater flying range than if each bird flew on its own. When a goose falls out of formation, it suddenly feels the drag and resistance of trying to go it alone and quickly gets back into formation to take advantage of the lifting power of the bird in front.

*Lesson: People who share a common direction and sense of community can get where they are going quicker and easier because they are travelling on the thrust of one another. If we have as much sense as a goose we stay in formation with those headed where we want to go. We are willing to accept their help and give our help to others.*

When the head goose gets tired, it rotates back in the wing and another goose flies at the point position.

*Lesson: It pays to take turns doing the hard tasks and sharing leadership. As with the geese, we become dependent on each other.*

The geese in formation honk from behind to encourage those up front to keep up their speed.

*Lesson: If we honk we need to make sure it is encouraging.*

Finally, and this is important, when a goose gets sick, or is shot down and falls out of formation, two other geese fall out with that goose and follow it down to lend help and protection. They stay with the fallen goose until it is able to fly, or until it dies. Only then do they launch out on their own, or with another formation to catch up with their group.

*Lesson: If we have as much sense as geese, we will stand by each other in difficult times as well as when we are strong; let us all try to fly in formation and remember to drop back to help those who might need it.*

# WALTER O'CONNOR
## I'm not losing tonight

**W**ALTER O'CONNOR, born on 3 May 1968 in Gormanston, County Meath, represented Ireland in the World Handball Championships in Phoenix, Arizona in 1991 where he won the 23 and Under title. In 1994, he won the World Open Singles title in Dublin.

In 1998, he became the first handballer from the Royal County to win an All-Ireland senior softball singles title and was only the second player to win all four 60x30 titles in the same year. He also has five All-Ireland softball doubles titles to his credit and holds two All-Ireland singles and five All-Ireland doubles medals in hardball.

Walter has three US Handball Association underage titles and was elected President of GAA Handball Ireland for a three-year term beginning in 2011. He is managing director of Envirogreen Building Services and Facility Management.

My journey started when I was two years of age. I sat on my father's lap and watched the world handball final between Joey Maher from Louth and Clareman Pat Kirby in Croke Park and thus began a love affair with handball. For as long I can remember I would make the pilgrimage to Croke Park every September the night before the All-Ireland hurling final to watch the senior softball singles final, and after seeing so many great players and marvellous games I really wanted to be a part of it and win a final some day.

As the years progressed I was getting better as a player until I became one of the top players in Ireland. I realised my dream in 1992 and reached my first senior final but standing in front of me was the legendary Michael 'Ducksy' Walsh who, even at that stage, was going for his eighth title-in-a-row. In fact he was just about to equal the record of another legend, Paddy Perry who achieved this in 1937. After two and a half hours, and having had a number of chances, I lost narrowly in the third game and my dream was shattered; I was heartbroken. I went on to contest four more finals and went very close in 1996 only to lose again in the third game after getting a very bad refereeing decision which I believe cost me the match. At this stage I began to wonder if I was ever destined to win this special prize which was claimed by a truly great champion.

At the beginning of 1998 I decided to give it one more go. This had to be it so I trained harder than ever before and lost nearly two stone in weight. As the year progressed my hard work was bearing fruit and I won two senior hardball All-Irelands before the softball season started. I was playing with great confidence and belief and I reached the senior softball decider again. A week before the final I played Paul Brady, an up-and-coming young player from Cavan, later to become triple world champion. He told me I was playing as well as I had played at any time in my career and that I should win; but after so many disappointments I was very anxious in the run up to the game.

A week before the final my dad was taken into hospital and as the days progressed it became apparent he wouldn't be able to attend the All-Ireland as he was very ill. Both of us were heartbroken; he had never missed any of my matches and it was as much his dream for me to win this title as it was mine. The big day arrived I went to see him in hospital before I went to the match and we talked about the game. Seeing him in the bed as I left made my resolve even greater.

The scene was set and I was standing in the court again six years after my first final, the National Anthem being played and Meath supporters roaring me on to bring the title to the Royal County for the first time. And again standing in front of me was the great 'Ducksy' Walsh.

I had a dream start, was playing well and hitting the ball very hard and accurately and, for once, I had the great man on the back foot. My confidence was growing and I won the first game – halfway there but still a long way to go. The second game started and again I was playing well and opened up a lead and screamed ahead 18-12; victory was only three aces away and my heart started to race but then, as all great champions do, 'Ducksy' engineered a great comeback and levelled the scores at 18-18. "Surely not again", I thought as I walked out to receive serve. At that moment I caught my mother's eye and saw her anxiety and at the same time I also thought about my dad and I said to myself: "I'm not losing tonight, Walter". I took 'Ducksy's' serve out immediately and got back in to serve and win those three vital points.

When I got the last point I didn't know whether to laugh or cry such was the relief. I finally had reached my Holy Grail. And what a great feeling that was! After I received the cup I didn't even change out of my playing gear. I went straight to the Lourdes Hospital in Drogheda to share this wonderful moment with my dad, Tom, my coach from childhood. When we got there he was asleep so I left the cup on the locker beside his bed and when he woke the next morning it was his dream come true also. What a great night and what a wonderful memory for me and my family.

# JOHN O'MAHONY
## Making memories for life

JOHN O' MAHONY was elected as a Fine Gael TD in May 2007 for the Constituency of Mayo and was re-elected in 2011. He is married to Gerardine and has five daughters. He was previously a secondary school teacher at St Nathy's College, Ballaghaderreen.

John served his club and Mayo GAA as a player, administrator, referee and team manager. As a player he won All-Ireland minor and under-21 medals. He managed the Mayo under-21 team to an All-Ireland title and Mayo seniors to their first back-to-back Connacht titles, and to a first All-Ireland final in 38 years.

He has guided Mayo, Leitrim and Galway to Connacht titles and took Galway to All-Ireland success in 1998 and 2001. He managed the Mayo senior team from 1988 to 1991 and in 2007, and Connacht and All Stars sides on many occasions.

Gaelic football has provided some of the greatest highs and lows in my lifetime. Managing Mayo senior footballers to reach their first All-Ireland in 38 years, leading Leitrim to win their first Connacht title in 67 years in 1994 and taking Galway to their first All-Ireland title in 32 years in 1998 have all been out of this world but for me training St Nathy's to an All-Ireland Colleges title in 2000 ranks right up there with the best of them.

Of course I will never forget the final whistle in Hyde Park in 1994 when 20,000 Leitrim people invaded the pitch to greet their heroes and as Mícheál Ó Muircheartaigh said in his commentary that day: "Thousands of Leitrim people are looking down from the veranda of heaven on a sea of green and gold." The memories of Padraic Joyce's goal and Seán Óg de Paor's sealing point in 1998 are as vivid now as they were then but to train an All-Ireland winning colleges team where I was introduced to Gaelic football is one of the sweetest memories in my involvement in Gaelic games.

I entered St Nathy's College in Ballaghaderreen as a 13-year-old first-year boarder in September 1966. The legendary Dermot Earley had completed his Leaving Certificate the previous year and was already making the headlines on the playing fields of Connacht and further afield. St Nathy's had won the Hogan Cup in 1957 and in the 1950s and 1960s battled for supremacy in Connacht with St Jarlath's of Tuam, St Mary's of Galway, Summerhill College, Sligo and St Muredach's from Ballina.

Boarding school was tough going in the '60s; the days were long, with class, study, prayers and football every day of the week. But if you got on the team it meant you got out of the college to play the other teams, and it was the only escape; otherwise you didn't see the outside of the school from September to Christmas.

In St Nathy's I was given a love of Gaelic games by all my trainers there, Fr Tom Flynn, Fr Michael Joyce and Fr Tom Lynch. I wore the green jersey with pride and left the college in 1971 with the ambition to play and win an All-Ireland with my native Mayo. I found myself back in St Nathy's in 1974 as a teacher and trainer of teams in the college. My proudest memory was being the trainer/manager of the 2000 All-Ireland winning senior football team that won the B Championship.

The final was against St Augustine's College from Dungarvan. It was played in O'Moore Park, Portlaoise and was a titanic struggle, the winning margin being two points in a game that ebbed and flowed for its entirety. It was a special day because past pupils came from far and wide to cheer for their alma mater, including some who hadn't been back in the school for 20 or 30 years. What seemed like thousands (it was in reality hundreds) invaded the pitch afterwards and celebrated as if it was in Croke Park on All-Ireland day.

For me, it was so sweet and fulfilling to hand on to others what was given to me many years earlier. I went into the dressing room afterwards and startled the players by reminding them that all of us involved would never be in the same room together again but would always have the unbreakable bond of having achieved something for our school together. Some of that team like Andy Moran – a 2011 All-Star award winner– Eamon Towey, Derek Moran and Sean Mangan have gone on to play for Mayo or Roscommon, and Joe McCann has starred as an All-Ireland handball champion and taken part in several world handball championships.

Others don't play football at all now and still others have emigrated to the four corners of the globe but wherever they are they will never forget that wonderful day in Portlaoise when Keith Mahon received the All-Ireland trophy on behalf of St Nathy's College. For me it was one of the greatest days of my life, and I treasure the joy of being able to repay my trainers and coaches, and pass on some of the values I learned from them in St Nathy's. That day in 2000 was one of my proudest memories.

# COLM O'ROURKE

## All things come to those who wait long enough!

C OLM O'ROURKE played senior football for Meath from 1975 to 1995 winning two All-Ireland senior titles in 1987 and 1988. He has five Leinster senior medals and three National Leagues. Colm was honoured as an All Star in 1983, 1988, and 1991.

He was named Players Player of the Year in 1991 and he became only the second player (after Jim McKeever of Derry in 1958) to be named Texaco Footballer of the Year without having won an All-Ireland medal in the same year, an honour bestowed on Bernard Brogan of Dublin in 2010.

Colm is a GAA columnist with the *Sunday Independent* and a *Sunday Game* analyst with RTÉ. He is Principal of St Patrick's Classical School in Navan.

When people write about great sporting memories they normally think of the biggest awards won. In my case the Leinster final in 1986 eclipses most others as it was the start of a great five or six years. In many ways I could say that I became an overnight success with Meath after 11 years trying!

When I started playing with Meath in 1975 the county side had just won the National League in the previous spring and so I was coming on to a team which appeared to have serious prospects going forward. Instead, the next decade was a disaster area for Meath football in general. It coincided with the great Dublin team of the late 1970s and Meath were reduced to the team who gave them a good game in the Leinster championship but won nothing.

So, it was a long time till 1986, and 11 years of disappointments at all levels. The only big day in that time was winning the Centenary Cup which was a novel open draw, a knockout competition introduced by the GAA to commemorate the centenary of the GAA's foundation in 1884.

There were a few other straws in the wind which suggested that maybe, just maybe, we were beginning to get on the right track. Central to that was the appointment of Sean Boylan as team manager. He immediately brought his own infectious enthusiasm to the job and created a great team spirit. Without him we would have won nothing.

By 1986 there were players like myself, Gerry McEntee, Joe Cassells and Mick Lyons who were getting close to thirty years of age, or even over it. There were others like Liam Hayes and Liam Harnan who were creeping close too but, more importantly, a few new players like Bob O' Malley, Bernard Flynn and Brian Stafford were beginning to show how good they were going to be.

On that wet, windy day in July 1986 there was a sense among many of us that our chances were running out so it was definitely a case of all duck or no dinner in that game. If we lost, the future looked bleak and the most likely scenario was that the older players on the team would either opt out or get dropped by whoever was in charge. So the stakes were high in that match.

The day itself was one of the wettest I ever played on. A mini-gale blew down into the Canal End and Meath played with it in the first half. Soon after the start David Beggy took off on a mazy run. He slipped and slid, got up and kept going until eventually kicking a point. He was one of many who was playing in his first Leinster final and it did not faze him or any of the others either.

The conditions continued to worsen, and the football was hard but nobody complained. That was the great thing about playing Dublin: what happened on the field was left on the field. The match was tight all through as scores were hard to come by as a storm of biblical proportions descended on Croke Park. With a few minutes to go Liam Hayes punched a ball from the middle of the field back in towards the goal. It fell right for me and I kicked it over the bar. This was the first time I was aware of a Meath roar in Croke Park. It was something born from the frustrations of 16 years without a Leinster medal and many defeats in finals – and of course there was no 'back door' then.

The football probably was not too pretty either. If it was featured on *The Sunday Game* now I would be critical of it but no Meath person, player or supporter cared what the standard was like. A great weight had been lifted off our shoulders and we went on to have five brilliant years at the top. But it all went back to that rainy day in Croke Park, the best day in many of our careers, and a night of wild celebration. The final score was Meath 0-9, Dublin 0-7. It is hard to credit that a Leinster final could be won with such a low score. Such can be the thin line that divides success and failure. On that day the luck swung in our direction and once we got on the merry-go-round of winning we did not want to get off. One great day in my life.

# JIM O'SULLIVAN

## International Rules Series – nobody said it would be easy!

JIM O'SULLIVAN attended school in Coláiste Chríost Rí in Cork and joined the staff of the then *Cork Examiner* in 1962, remaining with the newspaper until his retirement in June 2009. Having reported on general news and a variety of sports, he was appointed Gaelic Games Correspondent in 1971. This coincided with membership of the selection committee of the All Stars scheme from its inception that year.

He was a McNamee (GAA Communications) award winner in 1980, inducted into the Hall of Fame in 1997 and honoured by the Kerry Communications Committee and the Munster GAA Council. Including replays, Jim reported on a total of 81 All-Ireland senior finals in hurling and football and also covered all of the International Rules Series Tests from 1984 until 2008.

Married with three daughters, his interests include cycling and swimming. He maintains his involvement with the newspaper on a freelance basis.

Nobody said it would be easy! The establishment of a hybrid game combining the best features of Gaelic football and Australian Rules football under compromise rules was always going to be a challenge, both for administrators and players, and so it proved.

A total of 15 test series provided some outstanding memories and forged lasting friendships on both sides. And while games were peppered with an unacceptable level of violence, at their best they produced a level of skill, speed and entertainment superior to what 'traditional' Gaelic football often has to offer.

Scenes witnessed in Perth in the first Test played on Australian soil in 1986 almost caused the abandonment of the tour. And, the future of the series was again called into question after the violence witnessed in Croke

Park in 2006 before a fresh approach from the two associations helped to get things back on track in Australia two years later. For that, respective managers Séan Boylan and Mick Malthouse have to be credited for the major roles they played in ensuring a return to what counts as 'normality' - and a very successful tour.

The concept of an international dimension for Gaelic football and Australian Rules grew from a desire on the part of the GAA in the early 1960s to spread its wings and, coincidentally, from what referee and broadcaster Harry Beitzel described as 'the Impossible Dream - the Mount Everest of all football challenges' - to establish a hybrid game.

He had seen a telecast of an All-Ireland final while on a visit to London and, struck by the similarities in both codes, set about organising a visit to Ireland. In 1967 he brought over a team branded at home as 'The Galahs' ("a demeaning term for a bunch of idiots," he explained) and they defeated the then All-Ireland champions Meath.

After that, Meath, Kerry (twice) and Dublin Colleges travelled out to Australia, there were reciprocal tours to Ireland before the first official 'Test' was played in Páirc Uí Chaoimh on 21 October 1984 and under-17 squads were also involved.

Australia won that '84 game because of physical superiority and a mastery of the round ball which didn't seem possible in a warm-up match in Galway a week earlier. However, the game was tarnished by scenes of violence, with Irish coach Liam Sammon branding the tackling by the visiting players as "crude, to say the least and highly dangerous". Kerry player Tom Spillane observed that each team had played to their own set of rules, adding: "physically, they tore into us."

The result was that it sparked greater interest in the second Test in Croke Park the following Sunday and after further 'incidents' the crowd increased from 12,500 to over 32,000 for the decisive third Test.

The next game was played in 1986, in Perth - at the WACA (West Australian Cricket Grounds), under lights - and Australia won a bruising encounter defined by blatant late-tackling by home players and illegal (rugby-style) tackling.

In retaliating - thereby provoking incidents - Irish players made it clear that they were not prepared to be intimidated, on or off the ball! While it was broadly entertaining, five players were dismissed and the GAA leadership was quick to voice concern about the amount of violence.

Then President Mick Loftus said he would have "no hesitation" in recommending that they abandon the series, commenting: "I would be hopeful for the next two games but if the Australians do not change their attitude, the series must be in some doubt. What happened in Perth is foreign to our game at home..."

The reaction of the two managers was starkly contrasting, with Irish boss Kevin Heffernan remarking that the "the hostilities were excessive and would have to be curbed in some way." For his part, Australian manager John Todd complained that Irish players had been "paranoid about the rough stuff" since they arrived.

Fortunately, recognition on the Australian side of the need for greater discipline saved the tour from a premature ending and, more importantly, helped restore GAA faith in the series.

Further tours took place to Ireland the following year and to Australia in 1990. And, while there was a long gap before the next series in 1999, thereafter tours took place annually until the sequence was broken after the violence in Croke Park in 2006 resulting in a two-year hiatus.

Twelve months earlier in the Melbourne Cricket Grounds, the outlandish behaviour of Australian captain Chris Johnson - with his infamous 'clothes-line' tackles on Irish players Matty Forde and Philip Jordan - caused outrage. While he was sent off, the rules allowed a replacement and after Australia triumphed, he was presented with the trophy.

His behaviour was condemned in the Australia media, with one writer saying that Johnson and three other players 'had not only besmirched Australia's reputation for sportsmanship, but continued the tradition of Australian violence' in the series!

To be fair, Johnson publicly apologised following an investigation which banned him for five Tests, effectively ending his involvement. "You don't know how disappointed I am in myself at what happened," he said in a statement. "To Philip Jordan and Matty Forde, I apologise sincerely to you guys. I'd like to say to them that I can't believe it was me doing those things – it's not the way that I play the game."

While that incident focused mainly on his actions, the flare-up at the beginning of the second Test in Dublin in 2006 involved a sizeable number of players from both sides. Tadhg Kennelly who had been so influential in the (exemplary) Galway Test was unable to continue and Graham Geraghty was injured in a very controversial incident.

For the GAA it was now 'make-or-break'.

A wide consultative process was undertaken leading to proposals being put before the AFL and being accepted. Notably, it was decided that any player red-carded could not be replaced, that sanctions would apply in both codes and that an independent video referee would be used. The way was clear for a resumption of the tours and Sean Boylan was again in charge when Ireland visited Australia in 2008.

On his initiative, the two team groups came together for a social gathering in advance of the first Test. Meanwhile, new Australian manager Mick Malthouse impressed everybody with his positive approach.

"If you talk to our captain, he will say what I have been saying with regards to the passion to win, but equally the passion to show sportsmanship," he said at the media conference before the opening Test in Perth. Boylan's view was that the most important thing was to restore people's confidence in the game. Apart from one unwelcome incident in Perth, the series went off without a hitch.

To Malthouse's eternal credit, he was true to his word. And, along with the Irish management, the two squads played their part in bringing the series back from the brink. Happily the 2008 tour in Ireland, starting in the Limerick Gaelic Grounds, under lights, also went off without a hitch.

Nobody can be certain about the future, but there is much to celebrate in the fact that, by and large, the 'experiment' did prove to be a huge success. Nobody said it would be easy!

# SUE RAMSBOTTOM
## In victory or defeat, do not get carried away

**S**UE RAMSBOTTOM played Ladies Gaelic football for Laois and appeared in her first All-Ireland final at the age of 14 in 1988. She received seven All-Star Awards and holds one senior All-Ireland medal, one minor All-Ireland medal, one club All-Ireland medal and eight county medals.

Sue was 2001 Texaco Player of the Year and scored 7 goals and 17 points in that championship against Wexford, Westmeath, Meath, Dublin, Tyrone and, in the final, Mayo.

An officer in the Irish Defence Forces, Sue was aide de camp to President Mary McAleese from 2000 to 2004 and served with the United Nations in the Lebanon with the 84th Infantry Battalion in 1988 and in Kosovo from December 2004 for six months.

When my friends were besotted with Jason Donovan my heroes were Colm O'Rourke and Barney Rock. And so my life in football was influenced by players who never knew how they helped me reach the All-Ireland stage in Croke Park. My best sporting memory, ironically, is not one that jumps to the forefront of my mind when I think of my time in the Laois jersey as an O'Moore County ladies footballer. Neither is it winning my first county medal on an under-12 boys football team with my native Timahoe or winning an All-Ireland club title with the Heath before the late Lulu Carroll, Mary Ramsbottom, also deceased, Nancy Scully, and Marguerite Bergin organised football for girls in our area. My best sporting memory can be described as one of my 'best life lessons'.

I have great memories of scoring goals in Croke Park on All-Ireland day. The goal I got in the 1996 All-Ireland final against Monaghan stands out - but not my best memory - as it was a goal that I had practised and scored in my dreams and also on the local football field with my friends and family. Receiving the ball from a good distance out, soloing it all the way in to the 21-yard line and, without breaking stride, lobbing the goalkeeper, and doing a big loop around as I returned to my playing position on the field was magic to me, as it is to any person who scores in Croke Park.

My best sporting memory is the 1992 All-Ireland final in which Waterford came out victorious, this time by 2-10 to 3-4. The O'Ryan twins were again the instigators of our downfall. It was their second successive win in a run of five All-Ireland victories in eight years between 1991 and 1998. And Laois had to endure seven All-Ireland defeats (1985 to 1996) as well as a drawn final against Monaghan in 1996 before winning our one and only title against Mayo by 2-14 to 3-10 in 2001.

In 1992 I was in my second year of training as a Cadet in the Irish Defence Forces in the Military College, and things were tough. Life as a Cadet was not all plain sailing and ladies football would not have been seen as a focal point. There was more emphasis on drill, route marching, military history, weaponry, infantry manoeuvres, staff management, and research and presentation of projects than on sport: yes, sport was fine but we had to do it mostly in our own time. But in saying that it became a focal point when the 68th Cadet Class got a day pass to go to the ladies football All-Ireland. For my classmates it was a welcome day away from the Cadet School and all its hardships.

I also got a day pass to play in the All-Ireland but I was given until 2359 hrs on the Sunday night to be back in the Cadet School. Being late back was not an option for any Cadet! Anyone coming back late would face a very difficult time in trying to explain away a late arrival at the Dún an Phiarsaigh guardroom where the Orderly Officer might be waiting to interview the offender.

My memory is not about losing or scoring in Croke Park and the real truth is that I can't remember much of that game. I do remember the banquet in the Burlington Hotel and the anxious feeling I had in my stomach as I was afraid I would be late returning to the Curragh. With all my fussing I was back in my bed in the Cadet School by 2330 hrs.

As a 'reward' for our day pass to Croke Park the 68th Cadet Class got a battle PT run added to the early morning programme. At this stage I was feeling sore, tired and, of course, emotionally drained after losing another All-Ireland – our fourth in seven years. I was doing my best to stay in formation as we ran along the the Curragh plains. I am sure some of my class were feeling worse than I was after their day of freedom!

As each member ran in formation and everyone's right foot hit the ground in unison to the orders of "clé, deas, clé, deas..." a voice rang in my ear: "Not so good now, Ramsbottom, are you?" A Donegal NCO had a much more encouraging approach: "You are some player but ye were still not good enough to win."

The Croke Park field suddenly became a distant memory as I did my utmost to stay in formation and to prove I was not hurting at all in the inside. My main aim now was to concentrate on completing the battle PT run.

That early morning as we ran across the lonely plains of the Curragh an old saying came to mind: 'a slap on the back is not far from a kick in the backside'. Of course, life went on with many slaps on the back and countless kicks in the backside but in 2001 Laois eventually won that elusive All-Ireland title, our only one to date.

My best sporting memory had taught me a life lesson: never get carried away in winning or losing.

# TREVOR RINGLAND
## Play together and live together

**T**REVOR RINGLAND made 31 competitive appearances for Ireland in rugby between 1981 and 1988, scoring nine tries in the Five Nations and the 1987 Rugby World Cup. He also represented Ulster and Ballymena and made four appearances on the British and Irish Lions tour of New Zealand in 1983.

Since retirement he has coached at Ballymena and was a member of the Irish Rugby Football Union. He is a full-time solicitor and was Vice Chairman of the Ulster Unionist Party's East Belfast Branch. In 2006 he was appointed to the Northern Ireland Policing Board.

Trevor is also active with Peace Players International, an organisation devoted to promote inter-religious unity in Belfast through sport. For their work he and David Cullen won the 2007 ESPY Arthur Ashe for Courage Award. He was awarded an MBE for services to the community in Northern Ireland in 2009.

I am fortunate that I have many happy memories from my sporting career but there are probably two that stand out above others.

The first was the young Irish rugby side of the 1984/5 season, full of talent and running and under the coaching of the late Mick Doyle. He recognised the team's potential but also the one thing that could stop it from achieving its goals - lack of confidence in its ability, particularly under pressure! So, having developed the style of rugby that we intended to play, in the pre-match talk before we played our first match of the 1985 Five Nations against Scotland in Murrayfield he said these very important words to the enthusiastic bunch that were listening to him:

"I want you to run the ball and if it doesn't work, I still want you to run it."

It took all the pressure off the team, in that he was taking responsibility for how we played thus freeing us up to go out to produce the sort of rugby that we were capable of, and that we did. It was an exciting game with the Scottish team giving as good as they got but from the very outset we played a style of rugby that was fast, entertaining and exciting for anyone to watch. I was fortunate to score two tries, but the second was to me the highlight because it was the culmination of all the hard work that that young team had put in and all our potential coming together in one score. A real team try and a combination of the power, drive and ball-handling skills of our pack of forwards, the deft touches of Paul Dean, Michael Kiernan and Brendan Mullan and the very direct running of Hugo McNeill helped secure a win in that game and set us up for the Triple Crown success that season.

The second was in a different arena but came out of the Troubles of Northern Ireland. Two schools in North Belfast, Holy Cross and Wheatfield, were only some 30 yards apart; yet it might as well have been 1,000 miles such was the damage that we had done to relationships in our society. A small group of committed young people formed an organisation called Peace Players International with whom I was involved. This was a concept of Brendan and Mark Tuohey, two Americans who recognised the potential that sport could play in reconciliation under the slogan,

*"Those who can play together can learn to live together."*

It provided an opportunity for the leadership of the head teachers in both schools, the teachers themselves and the parents of the children to promote a different type of future, one which brought out the best aspects of our society, rather than those that caused so much tragedy in the past. After four months of work in the individual schools the children were brought together at a neutral venue at Queens University PE Centre and to see those kids coming together and starting to mix within ten seconds, shedding the baggage of our island's too often tragic history, was special indeed.

# DAN SHANAHAN

## The club is everything to me

**D**AN SHANAHAN was one of the pillars of Waterford's hurling success from 2002 to 2010 winning four Munster titles and reaching the All-Ireland final of 2008. He was a three-time All Star and was named Player of the Year in 2007.

His tally of three goals and three points in the 2007 Munster final and his goal in extra time of the 2010 Munster final replay marked him out as a player who could deliver on the big occasion. Dan made his championship debut for the Déise in a 1998 Munster quarter-final against Kerry in Tralee where he scored six points.

Forever loyal to his club, Lismore, he won a county senior medal at the age of 16 in 1993. He and Colette have a daughter, Chloe, and live in Dungarvan.

If there were only one place in the world where I could be for the rest of my life, it would have to be Lismore, the place, the community, and the parish where I grew up and got to know what place, community and parish mean to so many people throughout Ireland as expressed through a GAA club. It is the place where I feel most at home, the community in which I learned about life and the club which gave me a special identity as a player representing my parish.

When the Lismore club developed a hurling pitch near my home it brought lads together from all parts on the town and we got to know people whom we would never have known otherwise. The matches we played there as children led on to greater things with the club and Lismore CBS and our 'Munster finals' were always thrilling and well contested, a herald of things to come as adult players wearing the blue and white of Waterford.

The great strength of the GAA is that players are heroes in their own community: they live and work in their own villages and towns and are available and accessible to everyone. Of course, my family meant so much more to me than anything else. I owe them all a huge debt of gratitude for their help and advice, some of which I politely refused to take on board, and for their support in difficult times as well as in good.

I cannot remember a time when I did not have a hurley in my hand when I was outside my house. It seemed as if it was an extension of my arm! The first games I remember playing in were a five-a-side at school and a Dick Ahern league in the local field. I must have made some progress as by the time I was 11 years old I was selected to play in Croke Park in the Cumann na mBunscol mini-games at the 1998 All-Ireland semi-finals between Tipperary and Galway, and Offaly and Antrim.

That was a wonderful occasion: being out on the hallowed turf, looking up at the enormous stands, playing in front of thousands of supporters, our parents cheering us on, and wondering if we would ever play there again.

I made further progress in the next five years, and I know I did, because I was called into the Lismore senior team in 1993 when I was only 16 years old. I came on as a substitute in the county semi-final against Roanmore for whom my Uncle Tom was playing in the forwards. We won that game and defeated Passage in the final, the latest county title in the history of our club.

The club means everything to me: when I think of the men who coached us as children, the mentors who put us right when we were not able to read the flow of a game and the people who ferried us to matches all over the county I cannot but respect them and the effort they made to develop our skills and nurture our love of hurling. They are the people who stood by me when I did not perform well, who encouraged me when all seemed lost and who lifted me up in victory or defeat.

The club is where all players start off and where they end up. If there is one ambition I have it is to win a second county title before I retire: it is a long time since 1993 and it would be a fitting bookend to my career to win another one or two.

The hurling is all bound up inextricably with community and we all look out for each other. When Waterford lost heavily to Kilkenny in the 2008 All-Ireland final we were devastated. But the supporters rallied us and as we travelled through the streets of Dublin after the game we knew by the way they clapped and cheered that they appreciated the effort we had put in over the year; and I am always grateful for that.

It is a wonderful feeling to play in Semple Stadium, Páirc Uí Chaoimh or Croke Park and to represent the Déise in Munster or All-Ireland finals. We are there because of the time, effort and dedication of the legions of volunteers who give unselfishly of their time to help us bring glory to our county, our club, our parish, our community and our family.

I know I represent the community when I pull on the club or county jersey, but I am one of the community as well. I can be seen in the local shops, I might be talking with young people, coaching children to play the game or just being available to give a word of encouragement to anyone who might need a listening ear.

Inter-county players are not removed from their local village or town: they do not live in large mansions out of sight of the public and they do the ordinary things that everybody else does in the community. They have a great pride in and love of their place, their community and their parish as expressed through their club. And they will go to their Maker with dreams of bringing that pride and love with them and, maybe, playing in county, Munster and All-Ireland finals in the next world.

# FIONA SHANNON

## It takes a great loser to become a great winner

FIONA SHANNON from the Naomh Pól Club in Belfast was born on 14 January 1978 and has a unique record of winning three consecutive World Open Singles handball titles. She won the USA Open Singles and, with her sister Sibéal, the USA Open Doubles in June 2011 and the World Open Doubles title in 2009.

She showed her talent at an early age and was selected Young Female Player of the Year in 1994. Fiona has won 11 Irish Nationals titles including six in succession at senior level from 1995 to 2000. She has 17 All-Ireland senior medals, two All-Ireland juvenile titles and a World 17 and under title.

She was USA Junior Nationals champion at 15 and under and 17 and under and Irish Player of the Year on five occasions. Married to Séamus, they have two children and live in Belfast.

From a very young age I have been playing handball. I have vivid memories of running from school in order to get to the St Paul's Club for the start of our weekly weekend training.

Every Friday, Saturday and Sunday was spent with our coach Mary Lindsay at the club where the emphasis was on learning the basics of handball and having fun. The phrase "nose and toes facing the wall, half a circle, and now hit the ball" will always be etched in my mind as it was a saying that Mary used all the time on the court.

I was very competitive even then and hated losing and whether it was in competition or in training I always had determination and wanted to win. The most vivid memory I have at underage is being defeated by Anna Wrynn of Kildare. I found myself losing my temper during the game and as the match slipped away from me I broke down in tears even before leaving the court. I always felt that I had talent; and at training along with the rest of the girls at home, I was the best. It wasn't until the All-Irelands came about that I realised I was still behind most of the other players in Ireland in terms of my skill and mental ability.

Shortly after this defeat Mary Lindsay introduced me to Seán McEntee, another coach in the club whom she felt would be able to make the necessary improvements to my game as she decided she had taken me as far as she could.

This was a significant turning point in my career and I can honestly say that I wouldn't be the player nor the person I am now had it not been for Seán. This is when the serious training started. Shots were broken down and repetitive skill work took place during every session. Every shot e.g. kill shot, back wall serve, overhead, side arm, under arm etc. was broken down into the basic movements and was rehearsed over and over again with both hands until the skills became second nature.

I travelled the length and breadth of Ireland competing and travelled overseas with Seán as my coach. We grew a partnership that was rare in that at times words did not need to be spoken. When I was playing Seán would be saying to himself: "Go for that shot" or "change your serve", and I would automatically do it. He taught me to keep calm on the court and to always stay relaxed as getting angry and uptight only gives silly points away. This did take a while as I was always a little bit short tempered. It comes with the red hair but through time I learned to control this which definitely improved my game.

Every defeat I have had has been followed by a tremendous victory. My first defeat came at the hands of Bernie Hennessey from Limerick who at that time was undefeated at senior level for many years. This defeat shattered my confidence but it made Seán and myself look at aspects of my game and rectify things. Only two weeks later Bernie and I met again in an Irish Nationals final where I got my revenge and I knew that I wanted to go even further in handball.

I remember at the age of 17 watching the two top women players at the time, Lisa Frazer of Canada and Anna Engle from the USA, battle it out for the World Open Singles title at Croke Park in 1994 and thinking to myself: "I want to be playing and winning a senior world title". This is what Seán and I worked towards and I used all of my achievements before then as stepping stones towards my overall goal which was to be world singles champion. I finally got my chance to compete at this level at the age of 19 but my dream was short-lived as I was beaten in the semi-final. I took this defeat badly and really found it hard to bounce back again. This is when Seán was a great influence on my game as he was always looking at the positives in everything, even in defeat. I clearly remember him saying that "It takes a great loser to become a great winner".

For the next three years we worked tremendously hard on all aspects of my game; mental preparation, fitness, and games. We arranged tougher training matches against opponents who would push me to my limits. Before we knew it the World Championships were around again, this time in Dublin in the same venue where I had watched Lisa and Anna play so many years previously and wished that one day it would be me. I pushed my way to the final and in two straight games won my first senior world title. Words cannot explain how it feels to achieve a dream that you have worked so hard for. I specifically remember that the first person I went to after the game was Seán as I knew that he had made it possible. We had done it, and we did it together.

Since then another two titles have followed which makes me the first ever female player to have won three consecutive world singles titles. This is quite an achievement that has come after a lot of hard work and commitment from both Seán and myself.

Nowadays when I am at games and younger players ask me for advice on how to improve their game etc. I tell them to get a great coach, as I believe my coach has been the means to my success and that behind every great player is a great coach.

Handball has not only taken over the majority of my life over the last 20 years but also Seán's. He had many sleepless nights to help me fulfil my handball dreams and he is still there giving me words of encouragement. I could never repay him for what he has done for me: not only did I gain the best coach ever but also a lifelong friend.

It feels like yesterday watching Lisa and Anna battle it out for the 1994 world title but I still find it hard to believe that all of my dreams have come true in my sporting and personal life.

*Johnny Doyle, Kildare, All Star winner in 2010*

*Gearóid Towey, preparing for the start of the Lightweight Four final at the Rowing World Cup, Lucerne 2006*

*Sue Ramsbottom, Laois, in action in the All-Ireland ladies football final, 30 September 2001*

*Ireland's athletic stars, John Treacy, Catherina McKiernan and Eamonn Coghlan with Tracy Piggott promoting the Playing for Life charity*

*Bernard Dunne celebrates his World Super Bantamweight title win on 21 March 2009*

*Tommy Walsh, Kilkenny, grabs the sliotar in the 2011 All-Ireland hurling final*

*Joey Maher from Drogheda, 1967 world handball champion*

*Eddie Harty, jockey, and Highland Wedding being escorted to the winner's enclosure after the 1969 Aintree Grand National*

*Angela Downey, Kilkenny, winner of 12 All-Ireland camogie medals between 1974 and 1994*

*Bernard Jackman who was capped nine times for Ireland*

*All-Ireland handball winner, Eoin Kennedy, Dublin, with Martin Donnelly, sponsor, Tony Hannon, Handball President, Eileen Dunne and GAA President, Christy Cooney*

*Walter O'Connor, Meath, with the All-Ireland senior handball trophy*

*Valerie Mulcahy, Cork, winner of six All-Ireland medals (2005 to 2011)*

*Paddy Cullen, Dublin, saves Liam Sammon's penalty in the 1974 All-Ireland football final v Galway*

*Katie Taylor arrives home after her world boxing title win in September 2010*

*Con Murphy, RTÉ sports presenter*

*Joanne Cantwell, sports presenter with RTÉ*

*Christy O'Connor, author and writer with the Irish Independent and Sunday Times*

*The Meath team which beat Dublin in the 1986 Leinster football final:*
*Back row, Colm O'Rourke, PJ Gillick, Mick Lyons, Gerry McEntee, Michael McQuillan, Liam Harnan,*
*Liam Hayes, David Beggy.*
*Front row, Colm Coyle, Terry Ferguson, Padraig Lyons, Joe Cassells, Bernard Flynn, Finian Murtagh,*
*Brian Stafford*

*The Kerry 1978 All-Ireland winning team:*
*Back row, Jack O'Shea, Eoin Liston, John O'Keeffe, Charlie Nelligan, Tim Kennelly, Sean Walsh,*
*Pat Spillane.*
*Front row, Mikey Sheehy, Paudie O'Shea, Paudie Lynch, Denis Ogie Moran, John Egan, Ger Power,*
*Mick Spillane, Jimmy Deenihan*

*Jamie Heaslip in possession in the Ireland v USA 2011 Rugby World Cup game*

# JACK SHEEDY

## Enjoy yourself and do the best you can

J ACK SHEEDY made his championship debut for Dublin against Meath in the four-game first round of the Leinster senior football championship in 1991 which Dublin lost by a point. He won five Leinster championships in 1984, 1992, 1993, 1994 – when he won an All-Star Award – and in 1995 when injury ruled him out of the All-Ireland final.

He won two All-Ireland junior medals in 1985 and 1987 and two National League titles and he captained Dublin to win the 2004 All-Ireland Masters football championship. Jack also holds South Dublin juvenile league and championship and county intermediate league and championship medals.

He won two league titles as manager of Edenderry in Offaly and then managed Moorefield, Kildare, to win the Kildare senior championship in 2010 and the Leader Cup in 2010 and 2011.

As a young boy growing up in Lucan and playing for Lucan Sarsfields GAA club, my ambitions were modest and very locally based. I was playing in the under-12 team but, like half the team, I was only 11 years old. That's the way it was in a small village in many counties. To get on the team every Saturday was the main ambition of most of the lads my age and to win against the well-known teams from the larger areas on the southside was the main focus every week. In those days, the early '70s, Dublin juvenile football was divided into northside and southside leagues.

We lived on the border of Lucan and Clondalkin parishes, so it was more practical for my brother and I to go to school in Clondalkin. Football played a big part in our lives at that time but coming from a farming background, ponies, hunting, showjumping and all things farming were all part of our daily lives. Round Towers Clondalkin was the club where most of my schoolmates played and they regularly tried to persuade me to join them, but for me the only team I wanted to play for was Sarsfields. My neighbours all played for Lucan from an early age but due to my commitments on the farm, I didn't begin to play with Sarsfields until I was eleven. It was through my neighbours that I started playing with Lucan, one of whom, Tommy Carr, would later be my team mate with Dublin. We had a group of about 20 players and had great spirit and no shortage of talent.

We travelled in two or three cars to games and the message from our mentors, apart from training to win, was always to go out and enjoy playing football and to try to do the best we could. We certainly enjoyed our football and being quite successful at that time, it was all the more enjoyable, as we went two seasons only losing two games.

This was about the time that Dublin football was making a comeback under the guidance of Kevin Heffernan and they went on to win the All-Ireland in 1974 and this gave a huge boost to Gaelic football in Dublin at juvenile level. The Dublin players became household names all over the county. Guys like Paddy Cullen, Brian Mullins, Tony Hanahoe, Jimmy Keaveney and Anton O'Toole were like gods to the young lads around the clubs. We were brought to Croke Park to watch them playing and these games raised awareness of Gaelic football and also gave people throughout the county a huge lift at a time when it was very badly needed.

However, success at club level was not enough to elevate a player from a small club like Lucan onto a county minor or under-21 squad. Each year, trials were attended, and hopes were raised when you got called for second trials, but the end result was always the same; acute disappointment. Having watched the Dubs during the '70s and seeing them bring success and excitement into football, helped to fuel an ambition which, in some ways, became an obsession. Every young lad that put on a pair of boots during the '70s dreamed about emulating his heroes and getting a chance to play for Dublin.

Eventually, after failing to make the cut at minor lever and again at under-21 level, an opportunity came along in the form of the junior team. I was selected on the junior panel in 1984 and was selected to play against Louth in the first round of the Leinster championship, my first time to wear the blue jersey; finally I hade made it! The dream becoming a reality.

The dream becoming a nightmare! We were beaten by three points and I was devastated, one bloody game and my career was over! However, I must have done something right as I was called up to the senior team for a challenge game against Wicklow the following week. I was brought on, with 10 minutes left, as the fifth sub. I just turned and kicked the first ball I got and it ended up in the back of the net – unbelievable. The match was a draw and after the game I got a lift into town from Tommy Drumm, the Dublin captain who had lifted Sam the previous year, and I don't think my feet touched the ground for a few days.

I was told to attend training the following week and I nearly died when I walked into the dressing room in the old shed in Parnell Park. My dad brought me out and I know he was so proud to see me finally getting an opportunity at this level, because he knew how much it meant to me. He never told me how to play football or what to do, but he reminded me of when I was playing under-12 and the advice that he gave me back then, "Go out and enjoy yourself and do the best you can" – great words of encouragement.

I went into the dressing room and tried to find a spot on the bench to get togged out, without getting in the way or sitting in someone else's spot – a cardinal sin in any dressing room, especially one with so many legends in it! There were heroes from the '70s like Brian Mullins, Anton O'Toole and the younger heroes from 1983, Barney Rock, John O'Leary and Ciarán Duff. I felt like a fish out of water. I found a spot in the corner, got togged out, said nothing and just followed the others out to the pitch for a kick around before training.

I was so nervous I just kept running around to stop my knees from shaking. Luckily there were one or two other lads from small clubs that I had played against, so we stuck together in one corner of the pitch, kicking the ball to each other. After a while the legend that is Kevin Heffernan came out and called everyone together and issued a few instructions and said a few words about the match against Wicklow. His presence was so powerful even the senor guys like Mullins and Mickey Holden paid total attention when he spoke.

He introduced the few new faces to the rest of the squad and sent us for a few laps of the pitch to warm up. I never before had to run so fast for so long just to warm up. Senior training was a whole new experience for me and I had thought that I was fit going out there. But no matter how hard the training was, all that summer I enjoyed every minute of it. We got to the All-Ireland final but were beaten by Kerry.

I remember the banquet the day after when the two teams met for dinner and shared a few pints. It was horrible being there as the losing team, even though I was sitting amongst some of the greatest players ever to have played Gaelic football. I remember thinking how great it would be to come back here as the winning team and because I was playing for Dublin, sure we would be back every year. Dreams!

The next 20 years brought some very low points in my career, but some very high points too. But I can honestly say I enjoyed every minute of it, because I always went out and tried to play my best. Some days it wasn't good enough and other days it was, but I enjoyed it all. My dad's advice, "Go out and enjoy yourself and do the best you can" cultivated my attitude to playing and I am truly grateful to him for that.

# LIAM SHEEDY
# Tipp trip to Croke Park 2010

L IAM SHEEDY was born in Portroe, County Tipperary in 1969. The highlight of his club career was captaining Portroe to county intermediate hurling success in 1990. He played with Tipperary at under-16, minor, under-21 and junior levels before making his senior debut in the National League in 1989.

He had to wait until 1997 to play in senior championship, losing to Clare in the All-Ireland final. He holds Munster and All-Ireland under-21 and junior medals as well as a National League medal. Liam managed Tipperary to All-Ireland successes in minor grade in 2006 and at senior level in 2010, and was 2010 Philips Sports Manager of the Year.

He is Head of Sales Capability, Retail Sales and Marketing with Bank of Ireland and lives in Portroe with his wife Margaret and their daughters Aisling and Gemma.

It's a great feeling after 5 o' clock on 15 August 2010 when you have won the All-Ireland semi-final and everyone involved can look forward to the three weeks' build-up to an All-Ireland final. May 30th and the loss to Cork in the Munster championship is a distant memory within the group at this stage and the team has really improved from game to game throughout the qualifiers, got a performance and a slice of luck in the quarter-final and today had some brilliant play that had coach Eamon O' Shea's imprint all over it.

Waterford were always going to be a difficult assignment as they were Munster champions but Larry Corbett got a vital goal in the first half and Eoin Kelly found the net twice in the second half that gave us the breathing space and we saw it through. We also felt that the team and overall panel were challenged throughout the path to the final and they responded in emphatic fashion. This is where we all wanted to be and after being so close to winning the previous year there was a huge hunger to get back to Croker on All-Ireland final day. No matter who won the semi-final they were going to be underdogs, as Kilkenny had absolutely blown away Cork in the first semi-final and were also hugely impressive throughout Leinster so the general opinion was they were going to take some stopping in their drive for five All-Irelands in a row.

We went back training on the Tuesday night and the spirit within the camp was really good. We are blessed with loads of leaders on the pitch and on the training field and they always bring the best out of each other. Eamon O' Shea and Mick Ryan have always brought huge energy and enthusiasm to their roles and this has made a major impression on the players and challenged them to take their training and performances to a new level. We all knew we would need a massive performance to beat what is without question the greatest team ever to play the game but we also knew it was within our squad to deliver that performance. All of the focus was on Kilkenny in their attempt to make history so we were very much under the radar and we escaped most of the media attention. The time actually flew and all of us learned to enjoy the build-up to days like this as a lot of us were involved in 2008 when we lost the semi-final and that's when you appreciate the empty feeling of not being involved. The week before the final we headed to Carton House in Kildare which is a fabulous facility. We had a very enjoyable time there and mixed the fine-tuning of the hurling with a bit of laughter as the following weekend would be a little bit more serious.

Ger Ryan who double-jobs as Tipperary PRO and liaison officer has all of the suits and gear delivered and fitted there - another job done and dusted and we wouldn't need to see them again until we get back to the hotel after the match. How I was blessed with good people around me. The County Board and Supporters Club have ensured that everything that was required was delivered on and it really makes the build-up so much easier. So, before you know it the week of the match has arrived. All of the interviews etc. have been done by the players so it's time to get the final pieces done and dusted. Mick Ryan addresses the players on the Tuesday and his words really hit home. He is the All-Ireland senior medal winner among the management team and I am nearly ready to go and play myself until Eamon tells me to cop on...

Thursday night is when the team is announced and there are always going to be guys disappointed but it's very clear that everyone in this group has one goal and that is to have an All-Ireland medal on Sunday evening. We know that we have the players to start the job and, every bit as important, we have the substitutes to come on and make the difference. As always, there is good banter in the dressing room and everyone is very relaxed. At this stage all you want is Sunday morning to arrive and get on the bus because we are all at ease in each other's company and share buckets of energy with each other.

Sunday comes around quickly and before you know it the alarm is going off and it's time to get up. As always, my wife Margaret and our two girls, Aisling and Gemma, travel to Portlaoise with me in the car and they keep me company. Caroline Currid supplied me with a Tipp CD every year since she came on board so at this stage all of the family know every song and we are in full voice. Apologies Mick, but we always skip your Rolling Stones number! The music provides great relaxation and the journey flies. In Portlaoise my brother John collects the girls – the fact that he looks more stressed out than me sums him up and I would love to have had a hidden camera on him up in the stand. A quick 'cuppa' and a scone and we all hop on board the bus and head for Dublin.

The journey flies and we arrive at the Radisson St Helen's on time. Word filters through that John Hayes Hotpoint will not be allowed on the sideline due to pitch incursions against Waterford which is a huge disappointment. The panel is gutted for him but I knew it would drive them on even further because of the respect they have for him and all he does for them. John Casey, physio and Mick Clohessy, masseur put the final touches to the lads while Peter Murchan and Kevin Delargy, our doctors, check in with everyone. The pre-match meal is eaten as we will all need our energy later on in the day. We then have our team meeting and it's off to Fontenoys GAA club for the warm-up. Cian O'Neill delivers a top class warm-up as always and everyone is in great form. We get on the bus knowing that all the boxes have been ticked and everything has gone to plan. You could sense driving to the ground that the atmosphere was electric around the place and, as always, the Garda escort was spot on and before you know it you are in the dressing room.

Lads get their gear on, jerseys are handed out by Hotpoint and all of the subs give their final words of encouragement to the starters. I just revisit the key messages with the lads knowing that what I'm thinking is instilled in every one of them already and out we go out to a marvellous reception. Eamon and Cian do the final stretches and striking on the pitch, all the formalities are completed and off they go in the parade. I stand there with Mick and Eamon knowing that the preparation has been spot on and these lads are ready to perform. Our aim now is to spot changes as they are required as the game unfolds.

The ball is in and the intensity is frantic. I felt at times the stand was coming in on top of me with the volume of noise. The players from both sides deserve huge credit for the level of commitment and honesty they display when the stakes are highest – and, remember, all of these players and the management are amateurs but of course work in an ultra professional environment. Where else in the world would unpaid players draw the highest television audience for a sporting event in their own country? We get a great start and Lar Corbett's goal puts us 1-3 to 0-1 up after 10 minutes. The lads have settled very well and with five minutes to go to half time we are six points up and in control. Great teams don't go away and a whirlwind finish by Kilkenny leaves just one between the sides at the break: game on in earnest. We get a chance to catch our breath and are delighted to be a point up half way through.

The 15 minutes fly and everyone commits to leaving everything on the pitch for the next 35 minutes. Kilkenny draw level but we manage to get a hold of the game and Noel McGrath's sublime pass sets up Lar for a cracking goal and he then bags one himself to give us some breathing space but Kilkenny just won't go away. Our bench are superb and Conor O'Brien, Séamus Callinan, Benny Dunne, Séamus Hennessy and David Young make telling contributions and we get six clear with three minutes to go. You still cannot relax because Kilkenny have a habit of scoring goals but when Lar finds the net again after Bonnar's pass we are out of sight and I can relax a little for the first time.

The final whistle goes and it's the most amazing feeling. You want to get to everyone at once so you just run around everywhere. The sheer delight on our faces is unbelievable. Finally, I get to Mags, Gemma and Aisling and emotion is flowing out of us all. Eoin goes up the steps and delivers an unbelievable speech that really shows what a leader and captain he is for the group. It was a really nice moment when I got to lift the Liam MacCarthy Cup with my management team and now lifelong friends, Eamon and Mick.

Then it's a chance to meet my brothers Mike and John and the many friends and well-wishers that have stood by me and the team through good times and bad. I think of my dad, Johnny, and brother, Jim who, unfortunately, are looking down from on high but are with me every step of the way. Then it's off to the Burlington and what a difference a year makes! We arrive at the hotel and the place is manic with excitement. Lar Corbett gets the Man of the Match award and, as usual, heaps the praise on all the lads who passed him the ball. On Monday it's off to Our Lady's Hospital for Sick Children in Crumlin and this makes all of us realise just how lucky we are and how much we should treasure what God gave us.

Then it's the 'Trip to Tipp' and the word filters through that there are tailbacks on every approach road into Thurles. Eoin and I head into the new stand to a rapturous reception and it's some feeling after the experience of the previous year where we got a great reception... but we had no cup. All of the players are introduced to the crowd and my mother Bid of 86 years closes proceedings with a rendition of 'Happy are we all together'. An All-Ireland victory means so much to a county and makes such an impact on people of all ages. The Liam MacCarthy Cup has been to nearly every school in the county since September. I think Tim Floyd and Barry O' Brien may need to go to weightwatchers as they got apple tart in every school they visited!

I was extremely lucky to have been given the opportunity to manage this wonderful county team and also to have a superb management team, extraordinary players, a fabulous backroom team, and a family that supported me every step of the way.

# MIKEY SHEEHY

## The training was horrific... but worth it all

**M**IKEY SHEEHY starred with the Kerry senior football team from 1973 to 1984 winning eight All-Ireland titles as well as 11 Munster medals, three National Leagues and seven All-Star Awards. He also captured four Kerry county titles, one Munster and one All-Ireland club medal with the Austin Stacks club.

Playing mainly in the right corner forward position, he scored 29-205 in 49 senior championship games and 22-251 in 74 National League matches. He appeared in nine All-Ireland senior finals including five-in-a-row from 1978 to 1982 and is one of five Kerry players of that era to win eight All-Irelands, one as a substitute.

Mikey won two Munster and two All-Ireland under-21 medals and appeared in seven Railway Cup finals winning in 1976, 1977, 1978 and 1981. A financial consultant, he is married to Grainne and they have two children. His interests include golf and following Manchester United.

Kerry played Meath towards the end of March 1975 in the quarter-final of the National League and were comprehensively beaten. I left Croke Park with my head around my chest and heart somewhere around my feet. I remember condemning myself to the fact that it was going to be a long time before I saw the great stadium from pitch level again and was embarrassed at the possibility that the exhibition of football I gave that day could have been my last there.

Shortly after that hammering a man called Mick O' Dwyer arrived on the scene and took over the role as trainer and manager of the Kerry team. He embarked on a radical overhaul of the squad and initiated a regime of change. New players were added to the panel and ground rules came swiftly after that; 100% dedication to the cause; 100% dedication to training; and 100% on discipline. Anything short of that, and Micko simply didn't want to know. There could be no excuses, no moaning and if you were injured you showed up for training and he alone would decide whether you were fit or not – sure, what did the physios know! He wouldn't stand for anything that would jeopardise his plan to bring glory back to the Kingdom of Kerry.

The training was horrific, that's putting it nicely! I had never been one to embrace the physical fitness side of the game but Micko assured us that we would reap what we sowed; he was a great motivator. Once he had us up to a standard he referred to as adequate he would introduce the ball. We played challenge match after challenge match but the best ones were always in training. The backs and forwards sessions stand out in my mind with fellows going to the edge to put in a performance, and sometimes over the edge. On one occasion we did 28 training nights in a row, something I certainly wasn't used to.

Our first match of the year was against Tipperary in Clonmel. Looking back at it now, I was raw and a small bit green. It was a game that was extremely tight and Tipperary led for a while until Micko pulled a master stroke and switched John Egan from corner forward to centre forward. John contributed two goals after the move and proved to be the difference. Babs Keating played that day and I think most Kerry supporters leaving the ground were talking about that fact rather than holding any hope for glory in the '75 campaign.

Our next port of call was in Killarney against the old enemy, Cork, in a Munster final clash. Cork were red hot favourites after All-Ireland success in 1973 and Munster glory in 1974. They were a great team. A damp day didn't particularly suit us but we were going on adrenalin. The level of excitement amongst us as the final whistle went was incredible and, to be honest, we were shell-shocked. An All-Ireland semi-final against Sligo beckoned; Croke Park was only around the corner now.

The semi-final was a bit of an eye-opener, literally. After ten minutes I 'collided' with a knee and had to be taken off to receive stitches; so much for my first championship game in Croke Park. I was devastated. After we ran out easy winners, the wound seemed to heal that bit quicker as a date with Dublin in the All-Ireland final loomed. The Dubs were an incredible outfit. Too many greats to name, too many bachelors on our team and maybe a few people who said "You'll win nothing with kids"!

The build-up to the game was out of this world for us. We were only a group of young fellows. Hassle of tickets wasn't hassle at all, it was all new and exciting and we embraced it all. The fact that we were inexperienced probably suited us going into the game in some respects. We were travelling into the unknown, we didn't realise what was around the corner and it didn't really matter.

My ambition since I was able to kick a ball was to wear the green and gold, next was to play in Croke Park and it was an honour to be able to do both at such a young age. My parents were very proud. My father was a fanatic and travelled to every corner of the country to watch Kerry play; he was beaming with the thought of going to watch me. My mother was the same. I'm sure it was justification for sending me off with the shiniest boots for every training session.

With the anticipation came frustration. Would the day ever arrive? The realisation finally came as we boarded the train and met Micko. He was a cool nervous, if there can be such a description. We all realised how big a deal it was for ourselves but Micko always made sure we knew how much it meant to the county. His loyalties were with Kerry always.

As we took to the field I knew I was involved in something very special. The atmosphere was electric as we passed by Hill 16 in the pre-match parade. The Dubs are an incredible group of supporters. We started off great that day and the first 15 minutes proved to be action packed. The ball was thrown in, we got an early foothold and our captain was knocked out. Poor Mickey Ned O' Sullivan was the meat in the sandwich between Sean Doherty and Alan Larkin and it was the end of his All-Ireland final captaincy. That proved a vital point for us and it added fuel to Micko's half-time talk. We now had to do it for Kerry, for ourselves and for Mickey Ned. As it turned out, we won pulling up. I mean that with no disrespect to Dublin; it was just our day. They dished out revenge in later years but that particular Sunday belonged to us.

When the final whistle went I think we were all in shock. The National League game against Meath was a distant memory and the brutal training regime worth it all. I can honestly say it was my greatest sporting memory, one I'll always cherish and one for which I will be forever indebted to the greatest manager of them all, the great Micko.

# HENRY SHEFFLIN
## Pub talk matters in Ballyhale

**H**ENRY SHEFFLIN is the most decorated hurler of modern times with eight All-Ireland, 11 Leinster and five National League medals as well as four Kilkenny, three Leinster and two All-Ireland club titles with Ballyhale Shamrocks. He also has Leinster and All-Ireland Colleges medals with St Kieran's and two Fitzgibbon Cup titles with Waterford Institute of Technology.

He was RTÉ Sportsperson of the Year in 2006, has a record ten All-Star awards, inclueduing eight-in-a-row (2002-2009), and was Texaco, GPA and All Star Hurler of the Year in 2002 and 2006. He is the highest scorer in the history of the All-Ireland championship with the highest average score per game.

Henry works with Bank of Ireland Finance as a Sales Manager for their Motor and Agri business. Married to Deirdre O'Sullivan from Callan, they have three children, Sadhbh, Henry and Siun.

You can say what you like about 'pub talk', but it is not always 'pub talk'! I grew up in a family which owned a public house and, naturally, the conversation – often heated and argumentative – revolved around hurling for most of the year. In spring and summer the county and Leinster championships provided the subject matter, the autumn allowed time to reflect on the glories or otherwise of the playing season, and in winter people looked forward to another season of great possibilities for the local club, Ballyhale Shamrocks, founded in 1972, and for Kilkenny. I enjoyed the banter and the crossfire, always attentive to the voices of experience in these matters which often seemed to be of national importance.

Although I have played in 11 senior All-Ireland finals and won eight titles I regard winning my first county medal as my most treasured memory.

Our club had a very successful run from 1978 – the year before I was born – to 1991 winning nine county titles during that time, but never achieving the coveted three-in-a-row. My father always brought me to the games and I never thought the good times would end: in my eyes, the club would always be successful; it could not be otherwise. But the golden era came to an end when the team was beaten in the Leinster club championship in 1991, and Shamrocks were relegated to intermediate status in 1995.

I was now 16 years old and playing for the intermediates. We regained senior status in 1997 but had to wait until 2005 to reach our first county final which we lost by 1-18 to 2-12 to James Stephens, the reigning All-Ireland club champions. I had a particularly poor game, missing about two goals and five points, and I took it very badly: that hurt for a long time.

In 2006 Ballyhale Shamrocks met O'Loughlin Gaels in the county final and won our 10th title, my first, by 1-21 to 2-11. The special feelings and unbounded emotions I experienced at the sound of the final whistle were overpowering and when I think of that victory I remember the joy and satisfaction it brought to the team, the panel, the selectors and management, and to the whole community. To win the title after a 15-year gap was a really significant point in my career.

The ethos of the GAA is firmly built on club first, and always; county is second, always, but still very important in the lives of GAA players and the association as a whole. The pride and passion at county level is a reflection of the spirit of club evdeavour and pride in one's own place.

This was very evident in Ballyhale when Liam Fennelly captained Kilkenny to win the Liam MacCarthy Cup in 1992: every man, woman and child in the parish basked in the glory of the fact that one of our own led the county to victory over Cork. Of course, hurling was the only topic of conversation in the pub at that time and the achievement of a local player was a huge influence on aspiring young players, especially the 12-year-old Henry Shefflin. I had been under the watchful eye and careful guidance of local teacher, Joe Dunphy, just like the Fennellys, James 'Cha' Fitzpatrick, the Reid brothers and many more have been over the years. Joe was a major influence on the growth and development of young hurlers in Ballyhale but success came slowly for my generation.

We played in Division C, and then B, in primary schools competitions and county championships before progressing to A level in both. To win county and All-Ireland club titles by 2006 was a measure of the intense coaching and development programme undertaken by the school and the club. This too was encouraged and nurtured by the excellent Cumann na mBunscol and underage structures in Kilkenny. People like Paul Kinsella, Brendan O'Sullivan, Pat Dunphy and Ned Quinn had the vision and organisational skills to put proper resources into coaching at the basic levels, and success followed.

If I were to select one very special memory – my first county final victory apart – it would have to be captaining Kilkenny to win the 2007 All-Ireland title. And to be followed by 'Cha' in 2008 and Michael Fennelly in 2009 making it three Shamrocks men in a row to captain the county team to victory on the first Sunday in September, something never achieved before by any club in the history of the GAA, was simply fantastic.

When I reflect on the achievements of Ballyhale Shamrocks from 1978 to 2011 I can only marvel at the time, effort and dedication of so many people without whose support and encouragement success would not have been possible. I think of the teachers, the coaches, the parents, the drivers, the mentors, the selectors, the managers, the fundraisers, the people who keep the grounds and clubhouse in shipshape... so many people who keep the club on its feet and to whom we owe a huge debt of gratitude for their loyalty to the green and white especially when trophies were scarce during the leaner years. It wasn't just 'pub talk'.

# CORA STAUNTON
# From local club to the summit of Everest

**C**ORA STAUNTON represents Mayo in Ladies Gaelic football and has won four All-Ireland and three National League medals. Playing for Carnacon club she won 12 Mayo and 11 Connacht senior titles and three All-Ireland medals. She also has numerous county and provincial underage titles.

She has seven All-Star awards, three Ladies Football Golden Boot Awards and was Ladies Footballer of the Year five times. Other awards include Vodafone Ladies Footballer of the Year 2000, *The Star* Ladies Footballer of the Year 2000, *Irish Tatler* Sportswoman of the Year 2003 and she was Irish Sports Council/*Irish Times* Sportswoman of the Month twice.

Cora plays soccer with Ballyglass, winning the Mayo League and Mayo Cup in 2010, and she won the Irish Intermediate Cup with Knock/Kiltimagh in 2008. She is second youngest in a family of eight and likes watching all sports and socialising with friends.

I have been playing football for almost 23 years. I started as a seven year old playing with the Ballintubber boys team and have greatly enjoyed my time in the game. I have won a lot but also lost a lot too and I suppose, like any sportsperson, you have a tendency to remember the big games you have lost.

I have been lucky enough to play on some great teams and win many titles and awards.

There are some that I treasure more than others like my four senior All-Irelands with Mayo and my three All-Ireland club titles with my club, Carnacon.

Club is where your career starts and ends and where you play with people you have grown up with throughout your life. Carnacon is like a big family and for years we have been striving to be one of the best ladies football teams in the country.

In 2002, we won our first club All-Ireland and this was a huge breakthrough for the club. That year had been a very successful one for Mayo ladies football as we had captured our third All-Ireland title in four years with a narrow win over Monaghan. Carnacon had six girls on the panel and this was a great boost going into the club championship.

On 24 November 2002 we played Carrickmore of Tyrone in the All-Ireland club final and this was our first time to get that far. There was a lot of hype in the parish and all the team were really up for the game. I remember the day very well as we headed off to the biggest game of our lives early on the Sunday morning. We travelled by bus to St Loman's pitch in Mullingar and when we arrived there the girls were very quiet and nervous. I was lucky enough to have been chosen as captain for the year and was really looking forward to the game. It was a huge honour to lead my club out in our first All-Ireland final.

We started the game very well and were a few points ahead but half way through the first half we let Carrickmore back into the game. The sides were level just on the stroke of half time and I was awarded a free 20 metres from goal. I thought about going for goal as it would give us a boost going in at the break. I went for the goal and luckily it went in and we were three points up at half time. The girls were very focused at the break and our managers told us we were playing well and that we were just 30 minutes away from making history.

The second half went by very fast and we played some very good football. We dominated the game with players like Claire Egan, Michelle McGing and Maria Staunton playing some excellent football. Everything was going right for us and our young corner forward at the time, Fiona McHale, scored a great goal to put us well on top. In the end we ran out easy winners on a scoreline of 2-14 to 1-6. I got the last score of the game, a point from distance and I remember raising my hands in the air to a loud cheer as I knew the title was ours and that we were going to be crowned All-Ireland club champions for 2002.

When the final whistle blew the Carnacon faithful ran on to the pitch and it was a great feeling. I remember experiencing a huge sense of joy and relief as we had finally done it - you won't get that feeling anywhere else! I had the pleasure of accepting the Dolores Tyrrell Cup on behalf of a wonderful group of girls and a wonderful management team. The celebrations went on for the week. I remember thinking on our journey home that this is what sport is all about and why I love the game so much. We all play sport for days like these.

We had many more memorable days over the next 10 years, culminating in winning the All-Ireland club title in 2007 and 2008... but there is nothing like the satisfaction of reaching the summit for the very first time; relief, exhilaration and sheer happiness at climbing our own Everest and looking down on the rest of the world with immense satisfaction, knowing that all the hard work and patient preparation was well worth the effort. It doesn't get much better than that!

# JOE STACK

## Anyone there for the five-in-a-row T-shirts?

JOE STACK, a native of Listowel in County Kerry, began his broadcasting career as a current affairs producer and presenter with Radio Kerry in 1992, in the midst of what was a particularly barren period for Kerry football. Having finally seen the 11-year famine end in 1997 he departed his native shores before landing in RTÉ two years later.

He's worked in sport there ever since, making a living from talking about things he'd still talk about, even if he wasn't getting paid! A fan of Kerry, Munster and Liverpool, he is dad to three small boys and hopes that while they might inherit their father's love of sport, they'll get actual playing talent from elsewhere.

Memories though often vivid aren't always happy. It would be probably far easier, and certainly more pleasurable to reminisce on Stephen Roche's Tour de France victory in 1987 or on Ray Houghton's goal in Stuttgart the following year but nothing is burned into my consciousness quite like the events of the final moments of the 1982 All-Ireland football championship, when a group of men who were about to be crowned sporting gods had their accolades snatched from them at the death.

Now, I'd love to tell you that I remember every vivid detail of the entire encounter, that I kicked every ball with John Egan or that I recognised the attacking threat of the Connors, but in reality it was nothing like that.

Maybe those from other counties who claim that with success comes arrogance are right, (and in 1982 five-in-a-row t-shirts had been around for weeks by the time of the final), but it seemed that September's third Sunday was an annual day out for green and gold supporters at the time, when Kerry turned up in Croke Park, collected Sam Maguire and then we all went home for the Listowel races. After they'd been welcomed in Killarney and Tralee the squad would eventually arrive in Listowel to huge excitement one night over race week but then the whole palaver would be forgotten about again till the following year's Munster final.

The year 1982 though was different; this was going to be the day when, 'Bomber', Tim, Pat, Jacko and the rest, and by their efforts, my county would finally be regarded once and for all as the greatest football bastion of all. What's more, it would be an accolade that could never be removed, no matter what Dublin or Cork ever did again. Kerry would be number 1 for ever. Five-in-a-row simply ended all debate. Full stop and no arguments.

I remember two things in particular from that afternoon, firstly the performance of Listowel's Sean Wight in the minor final against Dublin. Sean was a naturally gifted sportsman who spent his early years in Glasgow but took to Gaelic football like a duck to water. Such was his display of fielding that day that shortly afterward, he travelled to Australia where he enjoyed a successful AFL career in Melbourne alongside Jim Stynes. Sadly, Sean died at a young age in 2011.

My other vivid memory of that Sunday was the rain; you see, our seats, though perfectly situated from a viewing point of view, were also at the furthest extremes of the roof of the Hogan Stand; in other words the rain flowing from the roof would fall directly on us and, it seemed, down the back of our necks. Not that we minded too much, sure weren't we about to win five-in-a-row.

I can't really remember many details, not even Mikey Sheehy's penalty being saved, but I do remember feeling the contest was over well before full time, particularly after Páidí Ó Sé kicked the so-called insurance point late on to establish a four-point cushion. The Offaly frees that followed didn't make any impression and only blood relatives would have taken any notice of the appearance of Seamus Darby as a late substitute. In the 29 years since, however, what happened in those last minutes has grown in Kingdom football folklore. To my ears it seemed Croke Park went deathly silent for a split second after Darby struck his shot and even now the pictures in my mind are intertwined with the commentary of the day from Micheál O'Hehir...

" ...Here they come, this is Liam Connor, the full back... a high, lobbing, dropping ball in towards the goalmouth... a shot, and a goal, a goal, a goal for Offaly... there was a goal in it!"

I did have a perfect view of the action and like any good Kerryman I'll swear to my dying day that Tommy Doyle was nudged in the small of the back as the ball came over, but if I'm honest, that's an argument that I only took up in later years. I don't remember much talk of it on the day and certainly if you look at replays, Tommy doesn't look like a man who'd just been fouled. I think for the most part we latched onto that view in Kerry as a means to deal with the severe psychological trauma imposed.

The closing moments were agonising as it became clear the sporting gods had decided they wouldn't be creating any immortals that afternoon and the journey to Heuston Station was a trudging retreat in the rain rather than a march of celebration. It was probably worse for those who left early; another peculiarity on All-Ireland day, and one I could never understand, was the early leaver. These were men and women who had the entire day timed to the precise second and for whom one of the highlights was how early they could be back home in Kerry on final night. Throw-in on final day was half past three, full time and presentation, in or around five o'clock, but if you left with 10 minutes to go not only would you avoid the huge crush in getting out of Croke Park, you could also make it back to Heuston Station in time to make the half-five train which would in turn have you back in Listowel around ten that night.

These driven souls were also in action on 1982 final day and it was another peculiarity of this disaster that some, we heard later, had travelled as far as Limerick Junction before the dreadful news finally reached them of Offaly's last-minute thievery of what should have been rightfully ours. As for the t-shirts; well, we heard the entrepreneur took them to Offaly and sold the lot!

# RONAN SWEENEY

## Let's win it for the two Dermots

ONAN 'ROLI' SWEENEY has been playing senior football for Kildare since 2000. He won a Leinster medal that year and has played over 50 championship games since. He has five Kildare senior titles, a 2006 Leinster club title, four Leinster Leader league medals, a 1997 county minor medal and three Kildare under-21 medals with his club, Moorefield.

He is secretary of the Gaelic Players Association and has been on the executive committee of that body for five years. He is an avid Glasgow Celtic supporter and enjoys attending some of their games.

Ronan says he would not be able to give full commitment to training with Moorefield and Kildare but for the support of his wife, Jackie. A graduate of Waterford Institute of Technology, he likes all kinds of music, enjoys reading sports psychology books and autobiographies and attends some concerts during the closed season.

The evening of Saturday 26 June 2010 was one of the most emotional moments ever in the history of Kildare football, and especially for Dermot Earley, Junior who lined out for his county in an All-Ireland football qualifier match against Antrim on the day his father, Dermot, had been laid to rest.

The Roscommon native who lived in Newbridge commanded the respect of everyone with whom he came in contact. Although I did not know him as well as I would have liked, I only realised after his passing how big a man he was in so many respects. He was the same on and off the pitch: modest, unassuming, and authoritative, a man devoid of airs and graces who was at ease with people of all ranks and stations in life.

The news of Dermot's illness broke around the time Dermot Junior won his second All-Star award but, being the ultimate professional, he never let his dad's illness get in the way of training with Kildare and Sarsfields: that was the way his dad wanted it and Dermot applied himself fully to the task, carrying the flag for the family and Kildare.

Shortly after Dermot's passing Anthony Rainbow, Johnny Doyle and I visited the family home and only then did I appreciate some of his achievements and the respect in which he was held when I saw photographs of him with personalities such as the Secretary General of the United Nations, and George Best, and of Mayo players carrying him shoulder high off the field when he played his last match for Roscommon in the 1985 Connacht final at Hyde Park in Roscommon.

Kieran McGeeney, manager of the Kildare football team, organised every member of the panel to come together to pay their respects to the late Dermot and to sympathise with and support his family on the day before his burial. Even then, at such a difficult time, Mary Earley and her family asked every player to win the game against Antrim the following evening as that was what her late husband would have wanted.

It was very moving to see so many public figures including President Mary McAleese and Taoiseach Brian Cowen in attendance at the removal of Dermot's remains. People came from all over Ireland to file past his open coffin where he lay in his army uniform; former players from Roscommon, Galway, Kerry, Dublin, Mayo, and many other counties, and young people wearing the primrose and blue of Roscommon were tearful as they paid their respects to a man who was loved and admired as a wonderful person.

I cannot imagine how Dermot Junior felt on such an emotional day but he had the determination, power, pride and passion to play for Kildare. Being a leader of the team, and the second oldest player, he put his grief aside as the full panel and management team lined up arm-in-arm for the National Anthem in support of their colleague. At half time there was huge emotion in the dressing room: for the first time I had tears in my eyes before the end of a game and it put into perspective what Dermot was doing for us; we were determined to win the match for him and the Earley family. However, we drew that game but the manner of our victory in the replay in Casement Park, Belfast a week later emphasised our will to win.

The emotion of the two games and the events surrounding them were huge motivating factors for us for the rest of the championship, as they were in 2011; and they will be again in 2012 when we will do all in our power to go all the way in the championship for Dermot Junior and his family.

My other memory is of a completely different series of events. I was nine years old in 1990 when my father brought me to see Ireland play in the soccer World Cup – Italia '90. The overland trip with a group of 50 Irish supporters was an adventure in itself and camping at different venues was just as exciting as the games. It was a brilliant trip, though my father, who is not an outdoors man, was no expert at erecting a tent.

The equaliser against Holland was special and even the Dutch supporters celebrated with us in numbers. The penalty shoot-out against Romania was edge of the seat stuff but my dad could not watch the action so I had to tell him what was happening. It was an unbelievable feeling when Packie Bonner saved the last penalty; and that was a huge influence on my supporting Glasgow Celtic since then. The David O'Leary goal was a great moment and the reaction of the players and management team was something to behold, a scene I replayed in my mind over and over again.

When all is said and done, it is the people who work so hard to introduce young players to sport and who give great service to their clubs and communities who should get a large part of the credit for the achievements of their protégés. In my own case, I am grateful for the coaching and encouragement I got from Anne Edghill, now sadly deceased, who looked after Gaelic football in my primary school in Athgarvan. I am also appreciative of the example of so many of my heroes as a young player, especially Seamus 'Sos' Dowling who coached Moorefield to win the Kildare minor title in 1997 and who played for Kildare in the 1998 All-Ireland final. He instilled in me and in our team the will to win as well as to enjoy the social aspect of sport. Only for these and thousands of volunteers in sport, there would not be any great days in the sporting cathedrals of Ireland and the world. They are the true heroes.

# KATIE TAYLOR
# Roll on London 2012

**K**ATIE TAYLOR started boxing, coached by her father Peter, in 1998, aged 12. Her first gold medal came at the 2005 European Championships in Norway and her second at the 2006 European Championships in Poland.

She became Ireland's first women's world champion in New Delhi in 2006 and claimed her second world title in China, the final match being her 100th bout. She won her third successive world title in Barbados in 2010, her 100th career win.

In 2007, Katie won her third European Championship title in Denmark, her fourth in 2009 in Ukraine without conceding a point and her fifth in Rotterdam in October 2011. She took gold at the 2011 EU Championships in Poland, her fourth EU title in four years. A supporter of Leeds United, Katie played with the Ireland Women's u-17, u-19 and senior football teams, scoring in the UEFA 2009 qualifying rounds against Hungary and Italy.

I was only born in 1986, 37 days after the Chernobyl disaster. It's hard to believe that 25 years on people are still suffering from the effects of what happened. I was born into a healthy environment and was given every chance to grow, be healthy and be successful in sport and in other areas of my life. I find it hard to comprehend that so many children born in Chernobyl since the disaster have had very little chance of living a healthy life. I know that many Irish families over the years have taken children for holidays and in so doing have prolonged their lives. For me it's a privilege to be part of this project which I hope will be a great success and will benefit the people of Chernobyl and help make life a bit more bearable for them.

My sporting memories are like a tapestry woven from many different and brightly-coloured threads. I was involved in sport from a very young age and my school years, primary and secondary, were full of great sporting occasions. In primary school I was mainly involved in athletics and won the schools championships 100 metres and 200 metres four years in a row. I loved the buzz of competing and on joining Bray Runners with my brother I won a couple of county medals with them. Sonia O'Sullivan was one of my sporting heroes growing up. I vividly remember watching her winning world championship gold in the 5000 metres in 1995 and her Olympic silver medal at Sydney in 2000. I just watched those races again – what an athlete! She competed at such a high level for over a decade and is someone I still admire today.

I was involved in quite a few different sports in school including basketball and soccer. I played schoolboy soccer up to age 15 with Newtown juniors and won schoolboy player of the year with them, a team that had great success. I also played with the Irish under-17 and senior teams. I won eircom player of the year with the under-19 squad and captained the team in the European Youth Olympics. I'm still friendly with a lot of the girls with whom I played. But because of my commitment to boxing I had to give up playing soccer.

For me, Roy Keane was one of the best players ever to represent Ireland: whatever people may think of him, on the pitch he was a great player and I found his work rate and will to win very inspiring.

A great moment in Irish sport was when Michael Carruth won his Olympic gold medal at Barcelona in 1992. The whole country was at a standstill, and to beat a Cuban in the final was amazing.

In more recent times I was at Dublin airport to welcome home the Irish boxing team from the 2008 Beijing Olympics where we got three medals, Kenneth Egan winning silver and Paddy Barnes and Darren Sutherland winning bronze. When they walked through the arrivals doors of the airport there was a real sense of pride and excitement as they had lifted the spirits of the whole country, as sporting heroes often do. I think every boxing club in the country was overflowing with newcomers all wanting to be like their Olympic heroes.

Being a keen sportsman himself my father was a huge influence on me growing up. He played soccer and also boxed for Bray boxing club winning the All-Ireland light heavyweight division in 1986. From the time I was able to stand he would put a pair of boxing gloves on me and we would pretend to spar and it wasn't too long after that I knew I had a knack for it. I boxed in my first official bout in the National Stadium when I was 15 and won on points against a girl from Northern Ireland. I also got Boxer of the Tournament award on that occasion.

I have come a long way since then winning four European Union titles, in 2008 in England, 2009 in Bulgaria, 2010 in Hungary and 2011 in Poland, five European Championship titles and three World Championship titles. And I was twice World Boxer of the Year. However, it wasn't all plain sailing – I lost in my first European Championship in my first bout. I was devastated, but it was a real learning curve for both me and my father. I also lost in my first World Championships. We say hindsight is a great thing and sometimes you learn more from your losses than you do from winning. It just made me hungrier and more determined to win; there are no short cuts in getting to the top in any sport – it's all about discipline and hard work. I think the key to my success has been the support of my family who stayed with me through the highs and the lows and kept believing in me.

We are a small country with a great legacy in the history of the Olympic Games, especially in boxing. John McNally was our first winner with silver in Helsinki in 1952. Next came Fred Teidt (silver), and Freddie Gilroy, Johnny Caldwell and Tony Byrne with bronze in Melbourne in 1956 when Ronnie Delany won gold in the 1500 metres. At Tokyo in 1964 Jim McCourt took bronze and this was followed by Hugh Russell's bronze in Moscow 16 years later. Michael Carruth and Wayne McCullagh won gold and silver respectively in Barcelona 1992. And in Beijing (2008) Kenneth Egan (silver), Paddy Barnes, Darren Sutherland and Paddy Barnes (bronze) brought our Olympic boxing medal tally to 12 – one gold, four silver and seven bronze. I hope the best is yet to come. Roll on London 2012 – I can't wait!

# GEARÓID TOWEY

# A tough stint in Oz rescued my career

**G**EARÓID TOWEY was born on 26 March 1977 in Fermoy, attended St Colman's College and graduated from Trinity College Dublin with a degree in Natural Science. When introduced to rowing by his siblings in the Fermoy Rowing club, it became his main sport.

In his 12-year international career he competed in three Olympic Games and became world champion in 2001. He is the only Irishman to have World Championship medals in sculling and rowing and one of only a few in the world with gold medals in all three rowing disciplines. He trained as an actor in London before setting up his own company in Ireland organising innovative sports and adventure events.

Gearóid was part of 'Digicel Atlantic Challenge', a two-man attempt to row the Atlantic Ocean in 2005. He has also taken part in several 'Raids', adventure races covering extreme terrain over several days using kayaks, mountain bikes, trekking, climbing, swimming and inline skates.

He is also a journalist for the World Rowing Federation, *Outsider Magazine* and the *Evening Echo*.

The year 2001 was an epic one for me for a number of reasons, a year I will never forget. It is the year that Tony O' Connor and I became world champions in the Lightweight Pair and although that memory is one which will stay with me forever, the lead up to that performance, from a personal point of view, is equally as precious and memorable.

Almost everyone has a year where they just can't put a foot wrong: 2001 was that year for me although it didn't quite start out like that! The previous year at the Sydney Olympics we had a less than stellar performance as part of the Lightweight Four. I departed Sydney completely disillusioned with rowing and spent the entire flight home deciding what sport I was going to change to. Track cycling was prominent in my mind, not only from the point of view of it being suited to my physique but it also meant training indoors – I was done with training in western European winters on the water.

When I got home I took time out. A lot of time. I couldn't motivate myself to train in anything. I was coerced back to rowing by default when I was asked to race in a local time trial in Nottingham where I was living at the time. I was slowly being trapped by rowing again. I started training again with half an eye on the following season. Nottingham is a cold place at the best of times and soon I found myself out there in the waves with icicles forming on my clothes, like in every winter since I started rowing at the age of 12. I was barely involved; I was only training because of something inside me which drove me to do it, not because of any outward enthusiasm or love for it.

I was in the middle of a training effort when suddenly a light bulb went off in my head and I stopped rowing – the light bulb was illuminating a huge sign saying "Get out of here now, go somewhere and train somewhere warm or your rowing career is finished".

That evening, as I watched my neighbour's garden shed roof being lifted off by howling gales, I made my mind up. I made a few phone calls and immediately booked a flight to Sydney to revive my spirits and my rowing career with a three-month stint at University of Technology Sydney (UTS) Rowing Club – home to some of Australia's best rowers.

I landed in Sydney and reality hit home immediately. I was brought from the airport to the north coast of New South Wales where the club was in the middle of a training camp. It was the start of the summer season for them. Whilst we northern hemisphere athletes settle into winter with long, slow sessions with comforting pots of coffee, not even thinking about the following season when we would have to peak again, Australians are in the heat of summer racing their hearts out at World Championship pace. This meant I was in for a rude awakening when I arrived.

They had all heard that an Irish Olympian was coming to train and race with the club so when I arrived they wanted to dust me up and give me hell on the training track. I arrived unfit, jet lagged and white into a pack of hungry wolves – tall, lean, tanned, mean and in superb racing shape. The first session was a joke, 26km of tempo rowing. I lasted a kilometre with the pack and was promptly shelled out the back. I was accompanied only by the coaching boat engine as he looked at me disdainfully as my new-found friends disappeared over the horizon. My resolve was tested for the next 25km as I crawled into a world of pain, trying to stay at least within viewing distance. My lack of training before I arrived meant my whole body was wrapped in barbed wire and my hands were losing all of their skin. The oar handles looked like they belonged in a butcher's shop. I was getting hammered by everyone but I was having an out-of-body experience. I finished the session thinking I was going to catch the next bus out of town and go backpacking around Australia for a while. I went for lunch with the others – who were probably secretly googling me to see if I really had competed in the Olympics only months before. I was even rehearsing my words to the coaches; "Sorry but I don't think this is for me", "thanks but no thanks" etc. Then one of the coaches sat next to me and said in his broad Aussie accent, "Bit of a tough nut are you mate? You can definitely suffer; you just need to warm up a bit." I swore by those words for the remainder of the camp. I just needed to warm up.

The next few days of camp were harsh but I was getting better. I really connected with everyone and quickly found new friends and real support. By the end of the camp I was able to enjoy my rowing again, I was up there with the others and feeling like a not so unfit and white athlete!

After that, I relished my time at University of Technology Sydney. I had so much fun, my rowing was improving immensely. I was enjoying myself again and I was a young man on his own in Australia having the time of his life, doing what challenged him. I also learned how the body works and how it responds to training and learned that the training I had already done in my years in the sport could not be erased by a few months off.

# JOHN TREACY

## Sonia's Olympic silver – an outstanding achievement

**J**OHN TREACY is Chief Executive of the Irish Sports Council. A native of Villierstown, County Waterford, he became known nationally and internationally when winning the World Cross Country Championships in Edinburgh in 1978. He retained the title the following year at Limerick Racecourse.

A highlight of his distinguished athletics career, which included victories in the Los Angeles Marathon (1992) and the Dublin Marathon (1994), was the silver medal he won in the marathon at the 1984 Olympic Games in Los Angeles.

John studied at Providence College, Rhode Island, qualifying with a BS in accountancy and an MBA. He was Executive Chairperson of non-statutory Irish Sports Council from 1997 and was appointed Chief Executive of the statutory Irish Sports Council in 1999. He serves on the board of a number of bodies including Concern and the National Campus Development Authority.

Sport has played major role throughout my life. I can remember from my earliest childhood in Waterford going out to the local playing field trying to swing a hurley and emulate my hurling heroes of the day. At that time, everybody in the whole county had a huge passion for hurling following the All-Ireland senior hurling victory over Kilkenny, our great rivals and neighbours, in 1959. All my peers wanted to be Tom Cheasty or Phil Grimes as we strove to puck the sliotar as far as we could.

In those days, I also had a great 'grá' for greyhound racing as my late father owned a number of greyhounds. I vividly remember walking for miles over the fields with my father with four or five dogs in train. I did not become interested in athletics until I was 12 when I joined St Nicholas AC in Ring.

From that time on, athletics not only became a major part of my life but also a great passion of mine. My own athletics career has not only given me great memories but has also given me lifelong friends from all over the world. I enjoyed my career immensely and, like most people, I have some special memories that I will carry with me to the end of my life. Among these are my first win in Listowel, my first major international success winning the bronze medal at the World Junior Cross Country Championships in Monza, Italy, the successive gold medals in the World Senior Cross Country Championships in Glasgow and Limerick, the silver medal in the Olympic Marathon in Los Angeles are the obvious highlights. Another great memory was winning the 5000m in Crystal Palace pipping Steve Ovett on the finishing line when he was already celebrating victory.

That's enough of my own! I am no different from the majority of my fellow Irish men and women in that I have a great passion for sport. Who can ever forget the great excitement of the 1990 World Cup, particularly the drama of the penalty shoot-out against Romania, the Irish Rugby Grand Slam success of 2009, the six majors won by Harrington, McDowell, McIlroy and Clarke, Stephen Roche's great treble in the Giro D'Italia, the Tour de France and the World Road Championship in 1987, Michael Carruth's Olympic gold medal in 1992 and Eamonn Coghlan's World 5000m win in 1983, to name but a few.

My own successes and those I referred to in the previous paragraph are all great memories. However, for the purpose of this article I propose to write about the wonderful memories my great friend and fellow runner Sonia O'Sullivan has given me over such a long and outstanding career. Sonia, like me, had early success on the cross country circuit. She then took an athletic sport scholarship in Villanova University just as Ronnie Delany and Eamonn Coghlan had done before her. Sonia went on to a wonderfully successful career winning gold and silver medals in World and European Track Championships and making history by becoming the first woman to double World Cross Country gold medal success in Morocco.

All these successes were wonderful achievements and have a rightful place in the annals of Irish sporting history. However, one of Sonia's achievements supersedes all her other great accomplishments and that is her silver medal at the Olympic Games in Sydney in 2000. What made it all the greater is that it came after her agonising fourth place in 1992 behind the three Chinese, and her disappointment in 1996 in Atlanta.

I had the privilege in being in the Olympic Stadium that evening in September 2000. The atmosphere was electric as the darling of Australian athletics, Cathy Freeman, had delivered a gold medal to the enthusiastic crowd less than an hour before Sonia took to the track. Even though I had great belief in Sonia, I had butterflies in my stomach and I felt a lot more nervous than if I was running the race myself. However, once the race began I started to relax.

After a number of laps, I got anxious again as Sonia dropped back a little and appeared to be in trouble. At this stage I thought her dream of a long-deserved Olympic medal was, to say the least, in jeopardy. However, like all great athletes, she did not panic and gradually eased her way through the field and with four laps to go was back in contention. I once again relaxed and waited with great anticipation of what I felt would more than likely be a sprint over the last lap, which would suit Sonia.

There were still about seven athletes in contention at the bell for the final lap including a number of Africans. With 300m to go the Romanian, Gabriela Szabo, whom Sonia had outsprinted to win the European 5000m gold in 1998, went for home. Sonia was the only athlete who could respond. In a memorable finish, she matched her longtime rival stride for stride. It was anybody's race up to the last few metres with the Romanian just holding off Sonia's valiant effort to lift Ireland's first track gold medal since Ronnie Delany in Melbourne in 1956.

It was a fantastic occasion for Irish athletics and indeed Irish sport. One will never forget Sonia doing a much-deserved lap of honour draped in the Irish Tricolour and taking the podium to be presented with her silver medal.

What a memory! What an athlete!

# TOMMY WALSH

## Bonfires blazed for Tullaroan Féile na nGael victory

**T**OMMY WALSH, born 5 May 1983, joined the Kilkenny team during the 2002 championship and became a regular member of the starting 15 the following year. He has won six All-Ireland medals, eight Leinster medals and four National League medals.

He is the only player in hurling history to have won nine consecutive All-Star awards, one for every year of his playing career. In 2009 he took all the top individual accolades, winning the All-Star, Texaco and GPA Hurler of the Year awards and he was chosen on the Leinster team of the 1984-2009 period.

Tommy plays club hurling with Tullaroan, the all-time roll of honour leaders in club hurling in Kilkenny. At international level, he captained Ireland Composite Rules shinty-hurling team, to victory over Scotland in 2009 and in 2010.

You might expect me to say playing in any one of my six winning All-Ireland senior hurling finals is my favourite memory but, without doubt, my choice is winning an All-Ireland Féile na nGael title with my club, Tullaroan, in Walsh Park, Waterford in 1997.

We come from a small rural parish of 600 people and are a very tight-knit community. Hurling is the passion in this area and when we won the All-Ireland title it brought huge pride and honour to my club.

To qualify for the national competition we had to compete with the best clubs in Kilkenny in the county Féile championship. This brought extra pride to our family as the Kilkenny trophy is named after my grandfather, Paddy Grace.

Féile na nGael is a national festival of youth embracing hurling, camogie and handball. It was founded in Thurles in 1971 by the former GAA President, Séamus Ó Riain and was sponsored by Coca-Cola from the beginning until 2010. The Féile philosophy emphasises the importance of participation rather than winning.

It is a weekend odyssey of games, skills, pageantry, parades and above all else the formation of friendships, and fostering respect for the prowess of others. It inspires young boys and girls to love and enjoy the games as a very valuable part of their heritage, culture and tradition.

As well as five graded team competitions, there are special skills competitions which place great importance on the skills of the games. The Division One hurling competition, for which the Christy Ring sterling silver trophy is the prize, is the premier event and our dream was to bring it home to Tullaroan.

We had about four weeks to prepare for the All-Ireland Féile. Most of the team were also playing in the county under-14 and under-16 hurling championships at the same time. Our preparation consisted of playing these games and two training sessions per week. It was easy to get everybody at training during this period as everyone in the parish was so excited. It was the first time most of us would have left home for a few days and the first time we were going to play hurling teams from outside Kilkenny.

Because of the sheer number of teams playing in the Féile we were hosted by the Piltown club in south Kilkenny. I stayed with the Doyles and they couldn't have done more to make me feel at home.

There were four teams – Tullaroan, Kilmallock, Mount Sion and Piltown – in our group with the top team progressing to semi-final stage. Despite the dreadful weather we blazed our way to the final from our first game against Piltown, defeating our hosts by 6-10 to 0-4.

Kilmallock were group favourites and it was likely that whoever won the match between us and them would progress. When we met in the second game it was a thrilling draw, 1-6 to 1-6. There was a small corner forward playing for Kilmallock who was around 10 years of age who scored a goal and a point and we later found out this was Andrew O' Shaughnessy who went on to be a great player for Limerick.

Because of that result, scoring difference would play a huge part in deciding who progressed. Kilmallock played first and won. That meant we had to beat Mount Sion by at least 31 points if we were to top the group. Our star player Shane Hennessy scored 11-4 and we won by more than the 31 points. We could not believe it!

Within an hour news reached us that our opponents in the semi-final next day would be Craughwell from Galway. They were favourites as they had won their three games against Tramore and De La Salle of Waterford and Sixmilebridge from Clare. In all they had scored 7-23 but we had scored 24-23 so were ready to take them on!

The semi-final was played in Roanmore, County Waterford on the Saturday under dark, threatening rain clouds. We were very nervous in the dressing room as the final words of encouragement echoed in our ears. Then the door was opened and we were on the field of battle.

We attacked from the beginning, got a few quick scores and ran out winners by 2-4 to 0-2. We were in the All-Ireland final of the Féile na nGael Division One competition. The enjoyment was unbelievable and our supporters were ecstatic. The Piltown club held a party for us on the Saturday night as we had reached the premier final.

All roads then led to Walsh Park for our first taste of an All-Ireland final. Our opponents were Sarsfields from Cork and their three main players were Kieran Murphy and Michael Cussen (later to play with Cork seniors) and Kevin Goggan.

It was a tight contest with several goals and we won by four points.

The highlight of the game was the battle between Eddie Campion and Kieran Murphy. Shane Hennessy's 100-yard point in the second half was worth the admission price and was talked about for years afterwards. Shane, Podge Kennedy, Eddie Campion, Michael Walsh, Stephen Maher and I went on to play for Kilkenny in various grades since then.

We had gone to Féile more in hope than expectation, so when the final whistle went the joy and happiness I felt has been difficult to match in anything I have achieved since then. We stayed on the pitch with our best friends, our family and our cousins for a long time afterwards.

The GAA President, Joe McDonagh, presented the Christy Ring Cup to our captain, Shane Hennessy, on that historic day, 22 June 1997, and the memory of that victory will live with me forever.

The homecoming to Tullaroan was very exciting. One of the locals put the team on a trailer at the back of his truck and drove us through the village. There were bonfires that night at the crossroads and the whole community celebrated our famous victory.

Playing in Féile meant everything to Tullaroan and that Féile experience is still talked about. Tullaroan is a proud hurling parish and most people's lives revolve around the hurling club. For the occasion itself the locals fundraised to buy us new socks, shorts and shoes for the Féile parade. This was a huge highlight as the whole panel marched through Waterford behind the Tullaroan flag and the Artane Boys Band. The atmosphere was electric with a lot of Tullaroan locals driving down to cheer us on.

The memory of Féile na nGael 1997 lives on to this day as the first experience of winning an All-Ireland medal is always sweet and memorable. I owe a lot to Féile and its organisers.

# TONY WARD
## Alone it stands

ONY WARD, born on 8 October 1954, played rugby for Munster, Leinster, Ireland, the British and Irish Lions and the Barbarians during the 1970s and 1980s. He made his international debut against Scotland on 21 January 1978 aged 23 and won 19 caps for Ireland during a ten-year period.

In the 1978 Five Nations Championship Tony scored 38 points, a record for a debutant and as an Ireland international he scored 113 points. He also played soccer for both Shamrock Rovers and Limerick United. In 1982 he helped the Treaty City team win the FAI Cup.

Since retiring as a sportsman, he has worked as a sports journalist, most notably with the *Irish Independent*, and as a rugby commentator for RTÉ. While playing rugby he had been a geography and PE teacher in St Andrew's College, Dublin.

I guess in a sense we're all subject to the time of our upbringing. To be more specific, happenings in the early or formative years tend to leave the most indelible imprint. In that respect I am no different than any although I would argue that some of the major sporting events it was my good fortune to experience – specifically in the 1960s and 1970s – would stand alongside the best from any era before or since.

As a child of the Sixties I loved most every team activity; soccer, rugby (League or Union), hurling, Gaelic football - take your pick. Whether the destination was Dalyer, Croker or Lansdowne was irrelevant. The GAA 'Ban' on members taking part in 'foreign sporting activities' was still in place, but who gave a damn? Certainly not this sports daft whippersnapper anyway. If there was a pecking order it read soccer, rugby, Gaelic football in that order. Bear in mind it was '74 before Heffo's Army emerged and made visits to D3 and Hill 16 sexy again.

My earliest memory of the Jones's Road ground, aside from the yearly Primary School Sports, was the Galway three-in-a-row between '64 and

'66. That could have been four save for Dublin's last title success over the Tribesmen in '63 prior to the halcyon days of Kerry and the Dubs in the 1970s – arguably Gaelic football's greatest ever period though many, particularly north of the border, would put a very different case in more recent times.

The maroon names still trip off the tongue... Johnny Geraghty, Liam Sammon, Mattie McDonagh, Martin Newell, Seamus Leyden, Bosco McDermott and all led by the most inspirational of leaders, the inimitable Enda Colleran. At that formative age you ingested everything. It was the golden age of Association Football, or soccer to you and me. What with England winning the World Cup, Glasgow Celtic and Man United the European Cup and of course Leeds United my own pride and passion to this very day. Elland Road and Leeds – the home city of my early childhood – will always represent my theatre of dreams.

Then there was Milltown. I am a southside Dub, lifelong Hoop and proud. In the 1960s we were the 'biz'. Waterford might have dominated the League but the cup was our demesne. Glenmalure was our shrine and I am so proud to have stood and played there. To this day the closure of Milltown represents for me (and I know for many others as well) the greatest sporting tragedy of our time.

Sundays were special with the trek from Harold's Cross (my home patch) timed to be in place for Sean Carroll's pre-match announcement over the PA of "Smyth, Keogh, Courtney, Mulligan, Nolan, Fulham, O'Neill..." and on it went. 'Nailer' (Frank O'Neill) was the man as week after week he fleeced whatever unfortunate left full happened to be in his mazy way.

My own glory days may have been with a different shaped ball but to have worn the green and white and played, albeit for two seasons and a bit, with so many of my heroes as a schoolboy growing up made for a very special period in my own sporting career and one of which I am immensely proud. Rovers will always be my team and given that so few come remotely close to fulfilling their childhood ambition I treasure those times dearly. The Leinster Senior Cup was about the height of our success in trophy terms. My time in my adopted home, my favourite city on planet earth, provided the route to more tangible success with Eoin Hand and Limerick United in the early 1980s.

Space prevents me now but my views on Limerick and the passion I feel for the Treaty City are pretty well established at this stage. Nowhere but nowhere compares with Limerick for unqualified love of sport. To truly understand it you must live it and such was my lot for the best part of a decade in the 1970s and 1980s. I wasn't in Croker in '73 when Eamonn Cregan, Eamonn Grimes, Pat Hartigan and the rest reached the holy hurling grail but I was there two years prior to that in 1971 for both the FAI Cup final and midweek replay against Drogheda when Limerick took the Cup for the very first time. And needless to say, it was nice to be on board with Kevin Fitz, Joe O'Mahony, Al Finucane, Johnny Walsh, Pat Nolan and the rest of the lads when we repeated the feat (and so far the only other time) in 1982.

I was there too in '79 soaked to the skin and standing on the roof of the Tote building overlooking the finishing line at the Limerick Racecourse when John Treacy battled through the mud on his way to a second world cross country success. And, whisper it, there was that day too when a certain Munster side did the unexpected against Graham Mourie and the Grand Slam-winning All Blacks. I guess if push comes to shove 31 July 1978 represents, for many obvious reasons, the pinnacle of my sporting career on either side of the fence.

Where it was, when it was, what it was and what it has remained since ensures that 'Alone it Stands'. Far be it for me to argue other than being personally secure in the knowledge that no ticket stub has ever been required to prove I was there.

Other momentous occasions experienced in the flesh that come to mind include Shamrock Rovers All-Ireland XI v Brazil in 1973 and our 1-0 win over Spain in the World Cup qualifier in Dalyer in '65 when Noel Cantwell (from a 'Nailer' free kick) bundled Iribar, the Spanish keeper, into the net at the school end as the late great Phil Greene used to call it. We lost the return match 4-1 before a Louis Suarez goal put us out of the '66 World Cup in the subsequent play-off in Paris.

I was privileged to attend so many of the great Kerry/Dublin jousts in the '70s using my student ID to get into the special concession area in the Nally Stand (remember it?). I was present and correct also for two of the never-to-be-forgotten jousts in the Dublin/Meath marathon four-game epic in 1991.

In rugby the games are far too many to recall ranging from World Cups, Lions tests deciders, Six Nations, Heineken Cups to schools cup games in Donnybrook where for so many aspiring young Irish wanabees the sporting dream began. In retrospect I envy today's rugby generation their lot. Not alone are they living the dream but they are being very well recompensed for doing so. My heart goes out to the young lads who make the Gaelic Athletic Association tick. As a true-blue amateur from a bygone age I can identify with their dilemma. Another argument for another day, I know, but their commitment is extraordinary.

Still, in the final analysis whether full-blown pro or Corinthian romantic, memories are of great games and great occasions extending way beyond the final whistle... pushed to pick one is as unfair as it is unreal. But for the purpose of this wonderful Chernobyl exercise the day the All Blacks came a cropper on the high Thomond Park altar tops the TW lot. Sweet dreams are made of this.

# DERMOT WELD
## The 1993 Melbourne Cup – A Vintage Crop

**D**ERMOT WELD has consistently been one of Ireland's most successful trainers and is acclaimed as one of the best trainers in the world having saddled big race winners on four continents. He is a qualified veterinary surgeon and was also a very accomplished amateur jockey in his younger years.

He began training in 1972 and has been champion trainer on many occasions. He was the first European trainer to have saddled the winner of the prestigious Melbourne Cup in Australia, a feat he achieved twice with Vintage Crop in 1993 and Media Puzzle in 2002.

While Dermot is mainly a flat trainer who has won all five Irish Classics, he has shown his skill in the National Hunt sphere on several occasions, with Ansar in particular winning the Galway Hurdle in 2001 and the Galway Plate in 2004 and 2005.

*"Nowhere in my travels have I encountered a festival of the people that has such a magnetic appeal to a whole nation. The Cup astonishes me".*
Mark Twain (1889)

The bedroom lit up like a Christmas tree; lightning flashed directly overhead. I could hear the roll of thunder in the distance as the sound of rain on the windowpane made my heart beat faster. It was 6 a.m. on Tuesday 2 November 1993. My day had begun.

Out at Sandown Racecourse, Vintage Crop was relaxed and well as he looked out at the gum trees swaying in the breeze. He knew the big day had arrived. David Phillips had everything arranged. The horse box – or float as it is called in Australia – would collect Vintage Crop at 11:30 a.m. and go straight to Flemington. Peter Stafford, one of Australia's premier

226

farriers, was there to do a last-minute inspection of his racing plates. His feet were nice and cool; Peter had taken excellent care of him since his arrival. We were so fortunate to have someone of Peter's expertise available to us.

Back at the Regent Hotel, organised confusion best describes the scene. Everybody seemed to be going to the races, whether by car, riverboat or train. It was a national holiday and people were coming in from all over Australia. Melbourne was a crowded city and movement by car was going to be difficult from about 10 a.m. I really wanted to go by boat up the Maribyrnong River, which runs all along the backstretch of the track and is a great way to go to the races. However, with the first of the nine races due off at 11:50 a.m., I decided to wait and let the crowds get in before I headed off by car.

It had rained heavily overnight and the streets were flooded. But the storm passed and the morning brightened up to give a lovely day. I listened to the radio as I made my way to Sandown and the news was all about the Melbourne Cup. They discussed what effect the rain would have on the result. The track was reported to be in good order but there was some flooding in the Birdcage or saddling area. The track had needed the rain badly and I knew it could only make the ground good or on the slow side of good.

On my way to the track, I went down Russell Street past the Old Melbourne Gaol where the famous outlaw Ned Kelly had spent his final days. I imagined he just might approve of my plan to take the Melbourne Cup to Ireland.

Despite the damp morning, there was a carnival atmosphere everywhere. The dress code ranged dramatically from morning suits to outlandish costumes. I was not just going to a race meeting but to the biggest party of the year in Melbourne. The Cup has become the biggest corporate entertainment day of the year with preparations often starting a year in advance. The party is everywhere – from the car parks to the stands. Few tracks in the world have such magnificent floral arrangements and the roses at Flemington are particularly impressive.

When I got to Flemington, Vintage Crop had already gone for his pre-race dope test and all was fine. He had travelled over from Sandown relaxed and well and was waiting patiently to be saddled for the big occasion. David Phillips had him safely installed in his allotted space in the Birdcage.

The Birdcage is unique to Australian racing; nowhere else in the world had I seen anything like it. It is steeped in Australian racing history and while security is good, I don't think the system could operate in any other major racing country. Each stall has its own little iron seat for the strapper and the horse is tied, if necessary, on each side to rings in the wall.

Huge crowds gathered to get a close look at all the horses as they circled around the parade ring. Under an overcast sky, a chilly breeze had begun to blow. Flower petals covered the ground as the horses paraded and the excitement of the occasion was evident on all the faces.

Drum Taps looked amazing. His coat glistened and with Frankie Dettori aboard, he looked assured of a big run. Subzero, ridden by Greg Hall and trained by Lee Freedman, looked particularly well. He liked a cut in the ground so everything was in his favour. Castletown, who finished third in the previous year's Melbourne Cup, looked eager to win for New Zealand.

Fraar was the most fancied of Sheikh Hamdan Bin Rashid al Maktoum's three runners. He had won the Caulfield Cup and was the mount of Darren Gauci. Next came The Phantom. This tough New Zealander, ridden by Jim Cassidy, had won the Mackinnon Stakes over 2,000 metres the previous Saturday and had thus completed the ideal preparation for the Cup.

Our Pompeii looked ready to run for his life and had become the people's choice. Money flooded in from all over Australia and he replaced Drum Taps as the 5/1 favourite. He was trained by George Hanlon who had trained two previous Cup winners and is one of the all-time great Australian trainers. Our Pompeii was to be ridden by Mike 'The Enforcer' Dittman, Australia's outstanding jockey. This was the combination we had to beat to win the Cup.

Next in the parade came Air Seattle, the mount of Shane Dye. He had finished second in the Caulfield Cup and looked in great form. Silk Ali, the mount of Grant Cooksley, had run in the Dalgety Stakes the previous Saturday and was a tough campaigner. Cooksley, better known as 'The Iceman', was a very good rider who I believe would have done very well if he had come to ride in Europe.

Then there was Cavallieri, one of the outsiders, trained by Laurie Laxon who had won the 1988 Melbourne Cup with Empire Rose, ridden by Kevin Moses. This Perth Cup winner was carrying the hopes of Western Australia.

Bart Cummings had four runners in the Cup and no man had a better record as he had won it nine times previously. Tennessee Jack looked hard and fit. He had won the Dalgety Stakes the previous Saturday and was to be ridden by Damien Oliver, Australia's outstanding young rider. Many shrewd judges considered Damien and Tennessee Jack to be the ideal combination. They would prove very hard to beat.

Frontier Boy came directly behind him. This tough seven-year-old New Zealander was to be ridden by Darren Beadman, a top-class rider. He was a typical Cummings horse – hard and fit and prepared to the minute for the big day. Bart's third runner was Our Tristalight, the mount of Greg Childs. She had been specially set out for the race and had run well in both the Caulfield Cup and the Mackinnon Stakes.

It was Bart's fourth runner, Great Vintage, mounted by Steven King, that I feared most. Lightly weighted at 49.5 kilograms, the bay mare looked the picture of health. She was by the outstanding stallion of the southern hemisphere Sir Tristram and from a good Irish family on the dam side. She had run well in the Caulfield Cup, having previously won over 2,400 metres and was known to like an ease in the ground.

Ultimate Aim, the winner of the Geelong Cup looked exceptionally well and was to be ridden by Patrick Payne. From the corner of my eye, I saw a small, insignificant bay five-year-old. His name was Te Akau Nick and he was born, bred and reared in New Zealand. Such horses are tough and sound and he would prove to be no exception. He was small and light; his current form was not particularly good but he had two factors in his favour. Firstly, he looked fit and well, had a great sheen to his coat and his best form was with ease in the ground. Secondly, he was trained by Gai Waterhouse who would become one of Australia's leading trainers. I had worked for her father on my first visit to Australia many years previously.

Vintage Crop looked magnificent and he stripped fit and well. He was a little bit on edge and jig jogged occasionally but as David patted him on the neck, he settled and relaxed. His impressive frame and huge stride caused awe in the crowd. He was without a doubt the most impressive individual in the race. His chestnut coat shone brightly, even in the cool breeze of the spring afternoon. The dapples were evident on his coat. He looked a trifle lighter than I wanted but overall he looked superb. There was something positive about his walk. His ears were alert; his eyes were focused and eager to behold the amazing scenes before him.

As I looked at my horse, I grew in confidence even though everyone had said it was an impossible dream. There were some really good horses in this race, trained by the leading trainers of Australia and New Zealand and ridden by some of the best riders in the world. This was a very strong renewal of the Cup but I believed in Vintage Crop.

To a neutral observer, what must have been of most interest was which training system would prevail; the Australian or the European. In the Australian system, most of the runners are expected to race three days before the Cup. The races that are used are the Mackinnon Stakes over 2,000 metres or the Dalgety Stakes over 2,500 metres. Bart Cummings had a proven theory that horses must have at least 10,000 metres of lead-up racing, should compete in at least one 2,400 metre race and should run three days before the Cup. This was accepted as the only way to prepare a horse for the Cup.

The European system is very different. Vintage Crop and Drum Taps had not raced for 49 days. No horse in the history of the Melbourne Cup had won on such a preparation. Could we become the first to do so after 132 years?

The 24 jockeys made their way into a packed parade ring. The spring showers were now becoming more frequent. The theory that Melbourne can experience the four seasons in a day was being proved. Michael Kinane and I had discussed in detail the evening before how we would like the race to progress. We had watched numerous videos of previous Cups and had gone through the form of the opposition. We knew our horse's strengths and we also knew what he disliked. We had a framework plan but I always believe that it's the jockey's decision whether to follow that plan or change it as circumstances dictate. I never believe in tying a jockey down with instructions. A trainer should tell the rider everything he knows about a horse but the rider is the person who makes the decisions in the race.

Michael Kinane knew better than anybody what to do and how to do it. He rode with confidence in his ability and he knew that I had full confidence in him too. The Australian trainers commented that he would have problems adapting to the Australian racing format, especially as southern hemisphere jockeys tend to ride much tighter and go the shorter way round but I had no concern. Michael was not only champion jockey of Ireland; he had ridden the winner of the Epsom Derby that year, was currently riding in Hong Kong and was one of the top six riders in the world. We spoke again briefly before my son Mark gave him a leg up on to Vintage Crop. I assured him of how fit the horse was and how confident I was that we could do it. So much of success is based on confidence and belief.

The horses paraded in front of the packed stands. Vintage Crop was number six of the 24 runners. Michael Smurfit's colours were a yellow with royal-blue epaulettes and a blue star on a yellow cap so they were easy to find in the parade.

As the horses cantered down to the start at the 3,200-metre gate, the intensity of the crowd increased. You could feel the build-up, the expectation, the anticipation. Our Pompeii was going to start favourite at 5/1, closely followed by Drum Taps at 6/1 with The Phantom at 8/1. Vintage Crop's starting price was 14/1.

As the horses reached the start, 'Whispering Jack' John Farnham took to the stage and led the crowd in singing 'Waltzing Matilda'. No song stirs the Australians more and the passion and fervour of the occasion was rising to a crescendo. I had once witnessed the singing of 'My Old Kentucky Home' before the start of the Kentucky Derby at Churchill Downs but when it comes to commitment and passion for sport, the Australians have few equals.

The race that stops the nation was about to begin. The final few horses were being loaded into the stalls. Vintage Crop was safely installed in number five. I was happy with the draw but it would be important to break well from the low number. The stands were packed but I managed to get a good position close to the committee rooms. I did not want to talk to anyone or even be recognised. I looked across the track to the boats on the Maribyrnong River with Melbourne's tall buildings in the background. The pressure was intense. In a few seconds, it would be 3.20 p.m., the starting time of the Melbourne Cup. All the things that could go wrong flashed through my mind.

Then in the greatest staying race in the world, the bell sounded and the commentator shouted 'They're off!' A huge roar went up from the stands and the enclosures. Fraar was the early leader with Vintage Crop in about sixth position. Down the river side Te Akau Nick had taken the lead from Frontier Boy and as the field turned away from the Maribyrnong and approached the 1,200-metre mark, Te Adau Nick just led Frontier Boy, Tennessee Jack and Drum Taps with Frankie Dettori going easily. The race was now quickening and as the field turned for home, the same leaders were still at the head of affairs. Our Pomeii, the favourite was under pressure and Drum Taps was one paced. Then Michael produced Vintage Crop with a devastating run, but he still had a lot of ground to make up. Te Akau Nick's stride was beginning to shorten. By the time they reached the furlong pole Vintage Crop had gained the lead and was in full flight. As Michael increased the pressure, the great horse strode majestically towards the winning line. The Melbourne Cup would never be the same again. We had overcome all the odds.

Rod Johnson, the Chief Executive of the Victoria Racing Club stood beside me in the stand and was the first to congratulate me. Later he was quoted in the press as being amazed by how composed I was after winning. What he did not know was that I had gone through every emotion during the race and the end result was nearly impossible to believe. I walked down the steps to the winner's circle, calm and content that what I had planned for so long had actually happened.

The official result was announced over the Tannoy – six, five, ten. Vintage Crop had won by three lengths from Te Akau Nick with Mercator half a length away in third and Great Vintage a further half-length away in fourth. Vintage Crop had won in a time of three minutes 23.4 seconds. He would go into the record books as the first horse trained in the northern hemisphere to win Australia's greatest race.